ENCYCLOPAEDIA OF WOMEN IN SOUTH ASIA
(PAKISTAN)

ENCYCLOPAEDIA OF WOMEN IN SOUTH ASIA

(In 8 Volumes)

Pakistan

(Volume 2)

Editors

Sangh Mittra, Bachchan Kumar

KALPAZ PUBLICATIONS

Delhi-110052

Encyclopaedia of Women in South Asia *(Pakistan)*
(International Studies, Women)

Rs. 7000 (Set)

ISBN: 81-7835-187-0 (Set)
ISBN: 81-7835-189-7 (Vol. 2)

Published in 2004 in India by
Kalpaz Publications,
C-30, Satyawati Nagar, Delhi-110052
E-mail : Kalpaz@hotmail.com

Laser Typesetting at : Shree Vaishnavi Creations, Delhi
Printed at : Mehra Offset Press, Delhi

Contents

1

Historical Background, Geography and People

Location and Area

Pakistan is located in south Asia and extends from the Arabian Sea to the Hindu Kush mountain ranges.

Pakistan shares its total international boundary of 5,847 km (3,631 mi) with four neighbours: Iran (830 km, 516 mi), Afghanistan (2,466 km, 1,532 mi), China (523 km, 325 mi) and India (2,028 km, 1,260 mi). Pakistan's boundary with Iran has been free of serious dispute. The boundary with Afghanistan, the Durand Line, has been the subject of dispute between the two countries since 1947.

Pakistan is divided into three main geographic regions: the northern highlands, the Indus River Plain, and the Baluchistan Plateau. The northern border, including the western border with Afghanistan, is enclosed in the convex arc of the Hindu Kush Mountains. Most of this area is over 2,500 m (8,000 ft), half over 4,500 m (15,000 ft), and there are 50 peaks over 6,700 m (22,000 ft), including the K-2. South of the Khyber Pass are a series of mountain ranges; the Safed Koh Range 4,761 m (15,620 ft), the Toba Kakar Range 2,743 m (9,000 ft), and the Ras Koh Range, west of Quetta. The Baluchistan Plateau is an arid tableland of about 349,650 sq km (135,000 sq mi) with a number of smaller mountain ranges, such as the Central Brahui Range, Kirthar Range, Makran Range, and Sulaiman Range. The Indus River Plain corresponds roughly to the provinces of Punjab and Sind and contains some of the most fertile agricultural regions in the country. West of the Indus River

Plain are the Thal and the Thar Deserts.

The Indus is the principal river system, and it flows through Pakistan for 1,609 km (1,000 mi) of its total length of 2,413 km (1,500 mi). Its major tributaries are the Kabul River, Gumal River, and the Panjnad River which is actually a confluence of five rivers, the Jhelum, the Chenab, the Ravi, the Beas, and the Sutlej. The Indo-Pakistan boundary cuts across four of these rivers.

Weather

Pakistan is basically a dry country, and the general climatic character is one of aridity although differences prevail between north and south. The country has four seasons: a dry cool winter (December to February), a dry hot summer (March to May), the south-west monsoon (June through September) and north-east monsoon (October and November). Average rainfall is less than 25 cm (10 in). Actual rainfall varies from region to region: 152 cm (60 in) or more in the northern highlands to 12.7 cm (5 in) or less in Baluchistan, the Thar and Thal Deserts, and the lower Indus River Plain. The northern mountains and Baluchistan have cool winters and moderate summer temperatures, while the upper and lower Indus River Plains have oppressive summers with temperatures over 37.8° C (100°F) . The highest maximum temperature in the Indian subcontinent was 52.2°C (126°F) recorded at Jacobabad in northern Sind. The heat is made intolerable by the dry wind, called the loo, which blows in summer.

Population

The population of Pakistan was 85,279,000 in 1980 on the basis of the last official census held in 1972 when the population was 64,979,932. Pakistan ranks ninth in the world in size of population.

The annual birthrate is 36 per 1,000, and Pakistan's world rank is 47th in this respect.

The male/female ratio is 113 males to 100 females. In the 1972 census there were 34,417,000 males and 30,475,000 females.

Ethnic Composition

Pakistan is a mosaic of ethnic groups held together only by a common religion. Each group has its own occupation, and even dress, and also its own geographic, linguistic, and social boundaries. The four dominant groups correspond roughly to the four provinces: Punjabis in the Punjab, Sindhis in Sind, Baluchis in Baluchistan, and Pushtuns in NWFP.

Punjabis, who form the numerical majority in Pakistan, comprise three major castes, or endogamous and functional groups : the Rajputs, the Jats, and the Arains. There are a number of other smaller groups, such as the Bilochs, Awans, Gujars, Lohars and Tarkhans. The Sindhis are also divided into scores of ethnic, linguistic, occupational, and caste groupings. Baluchis form an important minority in Baluchistan and Sind; their main divisions are eastern Baluchis with seven tribes and western Baluchis with nine tribes. The Brahuis form 25% of the population of Baluchistan and are believed to be the descendants of the original Dravidian inhabitants of the area. Minor groups in Baluchistan include the Jatts, who are unrelated to the Jats of the Punjab, and the Lassis. Pushtuns or Pathans constitute the dominant ethnic group in NWFP and a sizable minority in Baluchistan. Fiercely independent, the Pathans lack a central organization but each Pathan belongs to a tribe or descent group which determines his home territory and code of conduct. The more important of these tribes in Pakistan are : the Afridis, Yusufzais, Khattaks, Wazirs, Mohmands, Mahsuds and Orakzais.

Ethnic minorities include the Mujahirs or Urdu-speaking refugees from India, the Makranis of Baluchistan, and the Khos and Kafirs of Chitral. The Hindus, Parsis, and some other smaller groups are properly considered as religious rather than ethnic minorities. In 1976 there were 1,970 U.S. citizens resident in Pakistan of whom 1,359 were private residents.

In terms of ethnic and linguistic homogeneity, Pakistan ranks 40th in the world.

Languages

In the 1973 constitution Urdu is declared the official language, though English is to remain official medium of communication for 15 years. Urdu, however, is spoken by only 8% of the population and English by 2%. Over 30 distinct languages are spoken in Pakistan beside a number of dialects. Of these, Punjabi is the most important in terms of the number of speakers estimated at 63% of the population. Some of its dialects are classed as Western, or Lahnda, while others are called Eastern, or Majhi. Punjabi can be written in Urdu, Gurmukhi, or Devanagiri scripts, and it has a large, common vocabulary with Urdu. Sindhi is spoken by only 12% of the population, but it has fewer dialects and has important literary traditions of its own and a separate script.

Religion

Though Pakistan is not a theocratic state it comes very close to being one; Islam is the official religion followed by 98% of the population. In political terms religion forms the basis of national unity for diverse linguistic and ethnic groups, and the temporal Pakistani nation and the religious Muslim community or umma are inseparably one. The constitution invokes Islamic principles and provides for a Council of Islamic ideology to evaluate legislation in terms of its congruence with the Sharia. Both Sunnis and Shias are represented in Pakistan, although Sunnis form the overwhelming majority. A small heretical group, the Ahmadiyas, against whom a number of civil riots have been directed, is now considered as a separate religious sect.

Religious minorities include about 880,000 Christians and about the same number of Hindus, each of whom constituted about 1.5% of the population in the early 1970s. Smaller numbers of Parsis, Sikhs and Buddhists also live in Pakistan.

Historical Background

Pakistan was part of the Indian Empire from 1857 to 1947. The territories that constitute Pakistan were the last to come under British rule. Sind was conquered only in 1842 (15 years before the East India Company transferred its Indian territories to the crown) by Sir Charles Napier who wired the news of his conquest to London with the single cryptic word.

A Review Mission of the World Bank in 1986 suggested that women should be inducted in the mainstream of the developmental and productive processes in order to increase their share in rural labour and income. Women Organisations (WOs) were established in the villages under the umbrella of the VOs. The WOs opened the gateway of independence for many women, enabling them to choose their own skills and occupations for contributing to the social and economic well-being of their own households and those of their community.

In 1983, the AKRSP started its credit programme in partnership with the VOs, which agreed to the following:

(i) cooperate in organising and managing their own affairs on self-help basis;
(ii) generate their own capital through regular savings; and
(iii) upgrade their human skills.

Well trained and highly motivated Social Organisers (SOs) of the AKRSP helped promote the establishment of VOs whose members were required to make regular savings which were deposited with the VOs. To cut the cost of transactions, each VO deposited the total savings of its members in a single bank account, while the accounts of the individual savers were maintained by the VO itself.

Deposits in the bank account could not be withdrawn by the VOs without the prior approval of the AKRSP, which undertook to arrange bank loans. VOs decide on the loan requirements of each member and fund them though a single bank loan for all their members. The AKRSP arranges short-term loans without any collateral but requires cash collateral of 100 per cent for medium-term marketing loans and 30 per cent for other types of medium-term loans.

The AKRSP has been investing the savings of VO members in safe and high yielding investments, like the Khas and other certificates under the Government of Pakistan saving schemes. The credit/banking system of the AKRSP, which is administered by the VOs and WOs, is managed by persons who have not received proper training in banking and accounts. Their maintenance of savings and loans accounts as well as other books and loan documents is, therefore, not up to the mark. The AKRSP has been very successful and has earned international recognition. Such a programme can be successfully replicated only by adopting the following prerequisites:

— Large national/international donations or grants for the development of necessary infrastructure.

- Very careful planning of the project, with expert advice from local / outside consultants and agencies.
- Establishment of suitable social environment conducive to the formation of Village Organisations (VOs) and Women's Organisations (WOs). (This requires well-knit social, religious or cultural structures in villages, which are generally lacking in other provinces.)
- Freedom to the VOs and WOs to decide what they need for their social and economic development, through the 'bottom-up' rather than 'bottom-down' approach.
- Well planned arrangements for training the members of VOs and WOs in skills suitable for their income generating activities, through securing the cooperation of the line agencies for the concerned technology/skill.
- A large number of well motivated and hard working Social Organisers (SOs), who could pay regular field visits to educate the villagers about the advantages of regular savings and joint planning for social and economic activities for which loans need to be raised.
- Constant monitoring and adjustment of strategies by the higher-ups in the project.

UNICEF Credit Programme

Objective of United Nations International Children's Emergency Fund's (UNICEF's) Women in Development Programme is to improve the education, health and decision making status of girls and women between 12 and 25 years of age, to inculcate in them a spirit of cooperation for individual and community development, and to enhance their economic self-reliance. UNICEF efforts were limited to training. The conventional nature and low level of inputs into these efforts produced few results, and consequently led to a policy review.

In 1988, UNICEF decided to step in with credit to help women, having realised that most lending schemes were inappropriate for women in Pakistan because of their low female share in family resources, lack of ownership of property required as security, low mobility, low outreach of information, poor education, training and credit, and exploitation by middlemen. UNICEF's initial credit input for the years 1988-89 of Rs. 200,000 went towards supplementing the capital for loans to women. Besides this grant, Behbud was provided support for a credit and monitoring officer as well as for arranging exchange visits to other projects. Since the idea was to get an entry into Behbud's credit scheme to assess its methodology, no substantive changes were suggested in the terms and conditions for loans to Behbud initially.

In terms of broad categories, the loans which are given are for small agro-based activities, dairy cattle, shops, small business/cottage industries and poultry farming. The loans are interest free and repayable over one to five years depending upon the amount of loans ranging from Rs. 2000 to Rs. 10,000.

The first instalment becomes due two months after the advance, but other details such as the exact amount, repayment rate and payback period are worked out on a case to case basis by the Loan Committee which is composed of the Executive Members of the Behbud Association. Until December of that year, 48 women benefited front the loans, which ranged from Rs. 800 to Rs. 3,000. UNICEF initiated a participatory assessment of its credit scheme through a consultant. This involved small group discussions with loanees and Behbud staff, as well as interviews and house visits covering a randomly selected sample. Based on the consultant's recommendations, the induction of modified guidelines was made a condition for extending support in 1991 and 1992.

In addition to the Behbud programme, UNICEF started its Baluchistan Credit Scheme through two pilot projects in Baluchistan. The starting point of this scheme was UNICEF's visits to women's centres in the area. In UNICEF's view, the effectiveness of such a scheme to generate real and sustainable incomes seemed doubtful, as the level of training provided was low and the machines were distributed at random.

UNICEF suggested that the Zakat Funds with additional funds for loaning to poor women, if the provincial women's cell of the Planning and Development Department, the Social Welfare Departments, Zakat and Cooperatives Department, agreed to its proposed pilot credit scheme.

An Advisory Committee was set up composed of a member each of the Women's Cell, the Social Welfare Department, the Cooperative Department and UNICEF. Their task was to lay down the guidelines and procedural details of the project. An Implementation Committee was also formed, its functions being to screen the applications for loans and to administer and monitor the projects.

The Credit Scheme aims to provide interest free loans to poor women to help them improve their production capacity and therefore their standard of living. It is also aimed at promoting self-help as well as encourage solidarity and cooperation by organising working women in cooperatives.

Initially, a survey form was designed and finalised for collecting information about poor women in Nuski and Pishin and the social welfare department was asked to gather data on 50 deserving women. The Cooperative Department was asked to prepare new bye-laws for Women's Cooperatives, and to undertake registration of the cooperative to be set up. Following this, 15 deserving women were selected initially in Pishin to form a model cooperative. The female social welfare officer is the president of the cooperatives.

An account was opened in United Bank Limited, Pishin in the name of the president of the cooperative and all applications for loans were addressed to her. Fifteen deserving candidates from Pishin were selected and it was decided that a sum of Rs. 5,000 would be loaned to each one. Once this decision was made, UNICEF released an amount of Rs. 80,000 to the Planning and Development Department for payment to the president of the Pishin Cooperative to on-lend to its members as interest free loans. Rs. 5,000 was provided as logistics support.

UNICEF has suggested that a three per cent service charge be paid by loanees. The president of the cooperative disbursed the loans to the deserving women, to be repaid in monthly instalment of Rs. 150 after it grace period of three months. These instalments were to be sent to the President for depositing in the Bank account. The social welfare officer visits the loanees bi-weekly and reports monthly on the progress of the schemes and how it is affecting their lives.

The Implementation Committee members also visit the loanees to review progress. UNICEF Baluchistan Women Credit Scheme is different from its intervention in the case of Behbud, in that it is linked to the government system.

Its focus has been on forming a multipurpose cooperative of 15 women and promoting group loans as well as setting a criteria for loans to the poor according to the concept of Zakat, as the Social Welfare Department had committed itself to granting Rs. 30,000 in cash to each beneficiary of the loan.

Low income women have the capacity to utilise the loans intelligently and they also possess the integrity and discipline to return the principal. The assumptions about what women can or cannot do have been challenged, especially in Baluchistan where they have demonstrated a very keen business sense.

An important outcome in Baluchi-stan is that there is keen interest within the Government on making alternative use of Zakat funds. Rural defaulters are few. The reasons for default are sometimes unavoidable due to family problems or losses. It is also very clear that an effective extension system has a crucial role to play. This underscores the importance of identifying viable support systems for outreach as well as effective supervision of the mainstream lending agency schemes. Such initiatives can best be undertaken as an add-on activity in situations where a focal point for WID activities exists through Government or NGOs. The UNICEF experience is basically limited to interest free or small mark-up related activities. The acceptability of schemes with fairly high interest rates or market rates has not been tested. There was initial resistance to the mark-up, but this was overcome in many cases by presenting it as a service charge rather than as interest or profit.

Orangi Pilot Project (OPP)

In 1980, through a donation by the BCCI foundation, the Orangi Pilot Project (OPP) was established. OPP's work in Orangi attracted other donors who provided grant assistance of Rs. 6.017 million from September 1987 to May 1991. OPP provides small loans without any tangible security after obtaining a promissory note signed by the loanee and two personal guarantees considered acceptable. OPP has developed an effective monitoring system with its field workers keeping a constant liaison with the loanees. Up to the end of December 1991, it had provided loans amounting to Rs. 13 million which were disbursed to 1,071 households. The loan size has ranged between Rs. 7,000 and Rs. 10,000 and the recovery rate has been 97 per cent.

OPP is engaged in a variety of community self-help programmes, covering low cost housing, health and family planning, education, women work centres, etc. In November 1990 Habib Bank began collaborating with OPP, under the project "Banking with the Poor" and decided to work through the Cooperative Society of 54 families of Zari workers.

The Bank approved a credit line of Rs. 0.5 million enabling the society to make joint purchases of raw materials and arrange for marketing its finished products, thereby eliminating the middleman.

Decision regarding this particular activity and the procedures adopted are made by the Cooperative Society itself nor does the Habib Bank restrict, in any way, the use of funds for other related productive activities. Once the society gains experience and confidence, it would be able to attract its members to engage in other income generating activities. The credit line of Rs. 0.5 million has been given by the Bank without collateral from the society but the OPP on its own has provided a security of Rs. 200,000 in the form of term deposit receipts. The Bank charges a mark-up at 16 per cent. The operation appears to have proved cost effective both for the bank and borrowers. Under a collaborative relationship between OPP and Habib Bank, which is the first of its kind between an NGO and a commercial bank in Pakistan, the bank provides a credit line to OPP and the cooperative society in turn provides loan facilities to individual weavers and their families who are its members.

The responsibility of credit delivery to individual borrowers and families therefore rests on the society and the Bank confines itself to dealing directly with the society. Assisted by the OPP, the Cooperative Society oversees the loan operation, carries out close supervision and ensures timely repayment. Over long years of operation in Orangi, OPP has developed an effective monitoring system, keeps a constant liaison with the loanees and maintains strict supervision of loan utilisation and repayments. Each loanee is contacted every week.

OPP considers that this method ensures safety and security of loans rather than the traditional collateral of physical assets which is normally required by the banking institutions. One missing feature in the OPP programme is insufficient stress on social mobilisation of savings to increase self-reliance or as a protection against emergencies. It appears that borrowers are more interested in increasing their assets and improving their quality of life than in the idea of saving with the Bank or creating a common savings fund. Savings take a different form in OPP's programme area, in the shape of more assets owned by individual beneficiaries. Starting with 54 families of Zari workers, about 80 families had joined the Society by February 1992. The most significant development, as seen from the data collected from the field, is the increase in average income per family, which grew from Rs. 1,000 to 1,400, registering a 40 per cent rise. This pilot testing in Orangi has provided an insight to the method of reaching the poor, although it may be difficult to generalise on the strength of this sample because of the limited transactions involved.

Yakki Gate Experience

The Business and Professional Women's Club (BPWC) of Pakistan has the overall objective or making women economically independent. BPWC is an NGO of professional women and was set up primarily to protect and promote the professional interests of its members. The Club has been operating a women's centre inside the Walled City of Lahore providing health and literacy services to local women. Recognising the poverty related problems of the women who came to the centre, BPWC decided to carry out a survey of a neighbourhood (Yakki gate) in the Walled City.

Designed as a two-year experiment project in 1989, and funded by UNICEF the project has already trained about 200 women in skills as diverse its tie and dye, bank, synthetic leather work, block printing, stuffed toys etc. 45 per cent of the women trained are generating regular income. Thirty-two women have taken loans ranging between Rs. 5,000 and Rs. 7000 with excellent repayment record.

Because of good repayment revolving fund is flow operational. The loans are without collateral and through an agreement between the women and the Club. On an average, the women benefiting from the project earn about Rs. 1,000 per month.

Work is procured through direct orders and exhibitions organised by BPWC, which facilitates contacts with outlets run by other NGOs and the social welfare department. The project is run by two trained development activists with experience in community interaction.

Trainers are hired for each training programme and are paid for their inputs by the day. Programmes range from four to six weeks and the average cost of each training programme is about Rs. 10,000 and Rs. 12,000. Constant monitoring and follow-up is carried out to identify problems and arrange advanced training. There is a demand from adjacent neighbourhoods to expand the programme into their areas. All these programmes, though successful within their scope, are too small in scale to serve as a model for an effective national programme.

Women's Access to Financial Institutions

The poor may be unaware of economic opportunities or of markets for products that they are capable of producing. They may also lack skills and the necessary political access to overcome bureaucratic obstacles, or they may not have the capital to apply their skills or capture opportunities. Many interventions by the government, international agencies and voluntary groups have been designed to address one or more of these shortcomings. From the few ongoing efforts, we can identify some impediments in providing women with access to credit and financial institutions. Difficulties faced by formal financial institutions such as banks in dealing with the poor as borrowers are those of perception and certain realities.

Bankers perceive the poor to be bad credit risks. The poor often perceive banks as institutions which exist to serve the needs of their social superiors. This perception results in powerful inhibitions limiting use of banks made by the poor women. Then, there are legal or conventional requirements for the extension of credit by banks. These include the need to offer physical collateral, mostly in the form of property titles, which the poor seldom possess, and completing the formalities of documentation which the poor women find difficult to satisfy.

From the standpoint of the poor women, the bank's network of branches does not appear to be planned with the needs of women in mind. Poor women borrowers require loans which are very small by normal banking standards. But banks find the approval and processing of such loans relatively expensive, since the transaction costs of admini-stering such loans do not vary with size.

It is more profi-table to give bigger loans, with a given probability of repay-ment, than loans to small borrowers who cannot be charged as much as large borrowers. Charging full costs for very small loans would make the costs for borrowers prohibitive.

Banks may be prepared to accept such losses on lending which is thought likely to generate profitable business in other ways, such as providing access to a relatively low-cost source of deposit, but they do not perceive the poor women as offering that opportunity. Formal commercial channels within the financial sectors are limited for the poor.

But the informal economy provides certain alternative channels of finance. However, these informal sources provide a volume of credit which is, taken as a whole, inadequate for the needs of the poor and often very expensive in relation to their means. The presence and penetration of formal financial institutions is limited, especially in the rural areas. Poor women have to compete with the more prosperous members of society for credit from the informal sector. No data are available concerning the proportion of this credit to women in Pakistan.

Delays in credit transactions encourage women to borrow from professional moneylenders, who usually operate outside the legal and regulatory framework which applies to financial institutions. While their interest rates are high, such transactions have some advantages for borrowers as credit is available immediately. Banks can meet the credit needs of the poor by adopting well conceived delivery systems. However, for various reasons, credit to poor women has not been institutionalised. When implementing credit programmes, it is recommended that the following critical features should be taken into consideration:

- Timely availability of credit is a crucial requirement for a successful credit programme aimed at poverty alleviation, and it should be available in amounts that are commensurate with the capacity to repay and the needs of the poor.
- Successful enterprises of the poor require successive increments of loan capital in order to improve their

financial stability and enable them to increase their activity.

- Credit programmes should focus on the process which starts with group formation, awareness creation and establishing the fundamental conditions for initiating sustainable economic and social activities.
- Institution building and social infrastructure should be given prime importance in the early phase of credit programmes.
- Detailed collaboration and exchange of information is necessary between government organisations, banks, academic institutions and the peoples organisations.
- Activities need to be implemented at two levels; one by the NGO acting as an intermediary, and the other by the village level organisation of poor women.
- Implementation should be by the VOs/CBOs/NGOs.
- Village organisations should be made part of the participatory process through which the credit is provided.
- Government should provide additional support to NGOs and have flexible policies which encourage participatory activities and development.
- While NGOs/CBOs/VOs should have independent status, each of these organisations should be transparent and accountable.
- Participatory monitoring should be set up at the community level.
- Continuous dialogue should take place at all levels with access to support services for problem solving, when required.
- Coordination is necessary between economic and social activities. Savings, asset creation, income generation, health, education etc., are all part of a process and cannot be kept apart in credit programmes.
- NGOs should establish a baseline data for participants and a comparable group of non-participants, prior to the commencement of a particular loan programme, in order to measure the impact of these programmes.
- New policy initiative should be taken to link commercial banks to NGOs.
- Credit programmes for women must be based on a grass roots system to prepare poor borrowers for the credit

relationship and in order to have adequate provision for the supervision and follow-up of borrowers once loans have been taken by them.

Any credit programme for women should operate in such a way that all its costs can be recovered and a certain amount of profit can be earned. This requires earning an income, which in credit programmes comes largely from interest charges. This should be large enough to cover salaries, all other operating costs, the cost of funds, and some allowance for bad debt and inflation. Failure to meet these conditions would result in the eventual financial collapse of the programme unless a subsidy is provided.

In theory, it is possible to cover any amount of cost in a credit and savings programme by:

- Increasing the differential between the interest being charged and the cost of funds;
- Increasing the repayment rate or decreasing bad debts;
- Increasing the volume of profitable loans. In practice, these measures often face constraints such as government regulations that impose ceilings on interest charges, unavailability of low-cost funds, demand for loans which, in turn, depends on the availability of opportunities for making profitable investments.

The government focussed on subsidising credit to the loanee rather than easing the collateral requirements with the result that the credit programmes have not been successful in reaching the poor. It needs to be recognised that the banks require a larger spread both because of the higher risk of default and the higher transaction costs in making advances to small businesses.

Banking operations need to be subsidised to ensure that the cost of credit to small producers is not any higher than it is to large producers. However, an NGO may initiate a certain activity for which a bank could provide credit. Linkage between the Bank and NGO is one of the successful approaches that should be given due consideration. The OPP/Habib Bank credit programme has been an innovative approach to poverty alleviation, enabling poor women and men to strengthen their capacity to survive, meet their social needs, enter into income generating activities, increase their savings and utilise these savings along with available credit, both for further improving their socioeconomic conditions and that of their families as well as sustaining the developmental process.

The objectives of using NGOs as intermediaries between banks and borrowers are:

- To provide credit to borrowers at a reasonable cost;
- To demonstrate to commercial banks the credit-worthiness and viability of small borrowers especially women;
- To increase outreach of credit delivery to the lowest income group level of borrowers; and
- To explore ways of reducing the costs incurred by commercial banks in reaching small borrowers and savers.

In the first stage, NGOs will be used as intermediaries between banks and borrowers to increase the level of outreach of commercial banks to small micro entrepreneurs, especially women. In the second stage, NGOs will begin to target poorer clients after increasing their coverage and graduating their present target groups to formal sector financial institutions. The ultimate goal of this strategy is to link small borrowers directly to financial institutions without intermediation and increasing the availability of credit for the poor.

2

Education and Employment

Community Voice in Planning

The Community Voice in Planning initiative, a collaboration between UNICEF, UNDP and CIET to support government planners in their decision-taking, started in 1996. Three topics were chosen, following government priorities in its Social Action Programme: the gender gap in primary education and how to obtain education for all, community responses to water and sanitation risks, and the bond of care between mother and child and its effect on child malnutrition.

It was carried out in three of the country's four provinces: Balochistan, North West Frontier Province (NWFP) and Sindh. Since provincial planning requires one set of facts and solutions and district planning another, "focus districts" were selected within each province to show how these methods apply at both levels. Data were not gathered for Punjab province as a whole, but Rawalpindi district in that province did participate in the initiative.

Fact-finding cycles included views and experiences of around 25,000 households across the country each year on each selected topic. Each topic was also discussed in 200-300 focus groups with men and women, contributing with community-led solutions from around 2000 people per cycle.

Communities and planners were involved in the search for local solutions that work, how they might work better and how planners can collaborate with communities to achieve more for the same or lower cost. The conclusions were used to create district and provincial plans of action. Findings were widely communicated through the media, adding transparency and political incentive for change to the process.

Topic covered/province and districts:

- Balochistan and focus districts
- NWFP and focus districts
- Sindh and focus district
- Rawalpindi district of Punjab province

Gender Gap in Primary Education

The right to education is established in many binding international human rights instruments. It is one of the key development goals since the pledge by the world's governments in 1990. However, progress over the last decade has been slow and patchy. In three of Pakistan's four provinces, less than half of the girls ever enrol in school compared with 50 to 80 per cent of the boys. In contrast, nearly all the children in the district of Rawalpindi go to school. The effort and investment needed to eliminate the gender gap and achieve education for all in these different settings will be quite different.

In the Community Voice in Planning initiative, CIET methods were used to look behind the indicators to identify the gender gap components which could be changed at local, district and provincial levels. This meant systematically collecting and analysing local data on the known causes of the gender gap, and identifying which of these could be acted on in the different settings. Specific, cost- effective actions with high impact were identified and discussed in the communities and by local and provincial planners.

As expected, the link between the mother's education level, her potential influence on the decision surrounding education of her daughters and the number of girls attending school was found in all districts. In the North West Frontier Province alone, where the gender gap is the widest, it was estimated that around 650,000 more girls would go to school if their mothers had received an education. Across the country, girls were also twice as likely to enrol in school if their mother could influence the decision. However, the father is the sole decision-maker in more than 80 per cent of the homes, and with nine out of ten women in rural areas having no education, the real challenge was how to strengthen the voice of women on the subject of education.

Making fathers more aware of the importance of female

literacy was a first step. More than 300 focus groups, 150 with fathers, were held across the country to discuss findings. The results were also used by local NGOs to apply for grants to start adult literacy programmes for women.

Parent-Teacher Associations

Steps at district and provincial level included support for parent-teacher associations. This was designed for the active participation of mothers and should have a positive effect on both increased enrolment and decreased drop out rates and help to create trust and dialogue between teachers and parents. In rural North West Frontier Province, it was found that a child whose parents did not meet the teacher was 14 times more likely to drop out of school than if parents and teachers were in contact.

In Sindh, partnerships with NGOs helped communities form parent-teacher associations where none had existed. Some 3,600 association members were also trained to be able to act as an interface between the local government and the community. Similar actions were undertaken in the other provinces.

Increased satisfaction with teachers could help reduce drop out rates across the country, and in Sindh it was identified as the most important way to keep girls in school. Asking the girls what they thought about the teachers, many girls expressed a concern about the male teachers. Some girls in the Larkana district said they were asked to do favours in their homes or for money for "invisible things." Some said the teachers simply did not show up to teach. As a follow-up action, the local government in Larkana started a programme to recruit and train local female teachers. The need to recruit more female teachers was also identified and acted on in the Balochistan province.

High Fee Charges

Extra charges, such as bribes to teachers, unofficial fees and payment for text books that are supposed to be freely distributed by the government, increase the cost of education quite substantially in Pakistan. Together with inefficient use of public resources and lack of transparency in resource allocation, this remains one of the biggest barriers to achieving universal access to primary education. Detailed information on school costs to households provided the basis for estimating levels of petty corruption and how costs could be reduced. With lower costs, an increase of 20 per cent could be forecast for enrolment rates in Sindh and North West Frontier Province.

Existing policies to reduce costs only rarely benefitted the communities. Many parents and teachers were unaware of the free distribution of text books by the government and the removal of the requirement for girls to wear school uniforms. Communicated more effectively, these policies could increase the number of girls in school. Helping girls with their homework was another way to reduce drop out rates in all areas surveyed. A girl between 9-12 years old was five to six times more likely to stay in school if she received help at home.

In NWFP

Attitudes toward female education among local religious leaders *(Pesh Imam)*, also played an important role. Getting the religious leaders to promote girls' education could be particularly effective in the rural parts of Kalat district in Balochistan and in the Sindh province as a whole. In rural Dera Ismail Khan district of North West Frontier Province, parents said they'd be motivated to send their girls to school if free drinking water was made available. Building latrines in the schools was found to be an effective incentive throughout the province and in Balochistan province.

Even with limited resources for education in Pakistan, Rawalpindi district shows that it is possible to close the gender gap and get more children into school under the current conditions in the country. Nine out of ten children of primary school age go to school there, with nearly no difference in enrolment rates between boys and girls.

Communication strategies in all provinces helped to add transparency to the process and press government officials for change. "The government system needs transparency so that everyone knows the evidence and who's responsible," commented Mr Zia ul Islam, Secretary of Planning and Development in the Sindh provincial government. Journalists were often part of the data-gathering, and facilitated many of the community discussions around the findings. This enabled them to report first hand on facts and community views.

Community Response to Water and Sanitation Risk

Learning to cope positively with one's living environment can be a question of life or death. In Pakistan, around 250,000 children die of diarrhoea each year. For many of those who survive, mounting garbage heaps and other types of unhygienic environment double the risk for repeated infections that drain away the vital protein their bodies need to grow. As a result, they may never reach their full physical or mental potential.

Many of the hardware solutions in the area of water and sanitation, such as dams and pumps, are costly. They also do not guarantee automatic use by or benefit for those who need them most. Solutions that are most likely to have the greatest impact for the lower cost in one area may not be the same in another. In the Community Voice in Planning initiative, CIET methods were used to look behind the indicators to identify the highest impact action points for defence of children against sanitation risk. Information on what works and what people can do to protect the children in their home environment helped mobilise local response. The findings were fed to planners to make best use of limited resources in their investment options.

Most households that participated in the survey said they throw garbage on the streets or in open places. In the Larkana district of Sindh province, this practice increased the risk of acute diarrhoea by 70 per cent. A more hygienic handling of garbage would be the single most effective intervention to reduce the number of diarrhoea cases in the district. However, a mix of interventions is nearly always necessary. In rural Larkana, lowering the cost of safe water proved to be important, while in urban areas treating tap water could have high health benefits in relation to diarrhoea.

Looking at provincial data for both Sindh and Balochistan, unhygienic disposal of garbage was also found to be strongly linked to hampered child growth and intestinal parasites. In urban areas of the Kalat district in Balochistan, garbage in open spaces was found to nearly triple the risk for dysentery and worms. Promotion of hygienic garbage disposal would be the most effective way to reduce this risk.

The link between a child's nutritional status and the level of education of the mother was found in both participating provinces. In both Sindh and Balochistan, where nine out of ten women in rural areas are illiterate, any efforts to safeguard the healthy growth of children would have to include efforts to increase female literacy. Community solutions to this problem were explored and built into the planning process during the first phase of the Community Voice in Planning initiative.

In Baluchistan

In the Loralai district of Balochistan, reducing the time spent on fetching safe water would yield the biggest health benefits in prevention of diarrhoea and worms. This was also the case in the neighbouring Kalat district, while home visits by health workers to promote hygienic practices were found to be the most effective investment in Jhal Magsi, the third focus district in the province.

In Balochistan, nine out of ten rural households do not treat their water before drinking it (83 per cent in urban areas) and only three per cent knew it could be a risk factor for diarrhoea. Some suggested that information on how to treat water should be taught in adult literacy programs and to children at school. Another household action with considerable health gains is the use of soap when washing the hands. The cost of soap can be offset against what it costs to manage the diarrhoea of one child in the course of the average year.

In Sindh province, the cash savings from avoiding only ten cases of diarrhoea would be enough to pay for the installation of a latrine in the home. If those using open field toilets start using safe latrines instead, this would in turn reduce the number of cases of diarrhoea further. The multiplying effects are considerable. For each proposed action point, communities were asked what messages and channels could be used to communicate evidence and solutions to those who need to be informed. Many pointed out the financial savings through cleanliness as a good motivation factor, along with the fact that lives can be saved or improved by adopting simple hygienic practices at the household level.

Preferred channels for communication were key informants, religious leaders, community health workers, NGOs and mass media. In one area, it was suggested to include messages around hygiene in the Friday prayer. In other areas, "cleanliness committees" were formed to deal with garbage disposal. Findings were discussed at provincial and district level workshops open to the press, planners, NGOs and community representatives. For the provinces and each focus district, plans of action were created against which progress will be measured over time.

Bond Care

The care a mother receives during pregnancy and after delivery determines how well she will be able to feed and care for her child. This includes breastfeeding, psycho-social care, food preparation, hygiene and home health care.

When a woman's rights are violated, when she is blocked from getting the information she needs, from going to school, from sharing information with her peers or when she is beaten at home, her child is significantly less likely to get the care s/he needs.

This connection between women's rights and child rights – the bond of care – was explored as a programmatic opportunity to prevent child malnutrition in Pakistan through the Community Voice in Planning initiative.

The CIET survey identified what actionable components of care could translate into improved child survival, protection and development in a way that enables planners to compare alternative interventions in terms of their cost-effectiveness. Although suggestions from mothers, fathers, community leaders and health workers varied from place to place, some common themes emerged during comparison and aggregation of local evidence:

The education level of a woman was linked to the nutrition status of her children. In some areas, lack of education of the mother could be linked to the child's delay in reaching developmental mile-stones, such as sitting. An action plan to increase girls' enrolment in school was established during the first phase of the Community Voice in Planning initiative. It included measures to educate mothers as well as their daughters.

Domestic violence was found to severely damage the bond of care and could be linked to a higher risk for acute or chronic malnutrition (starvation and hampered growth). Despite the difficulties in reporting on violence, one in six women openly said they had a serious quarrel at home during the previous year, often including physical abuse. It is likely that this is only the tip of the iceberg. Men discussed this finding in focus groups to come up with solutions for local action. For an issue that is rarely discussed, opening up the dialogue on domestic violence was in itself a breakthrough in many areas.

Obstacles for Women

Obstacles for women to attend antenatal care included lack of awareness of its importance, money to pay for it, and limited access to the health facilities. As a result, over half of women interviewed did not attend doctor's check-ups during their pregnancies. Yet, a woman who did not get this care was more likely to have poor health practices and to have an acutely or chronically malnourished child.

Although almost all women breastfed their infants, many introduced other liquids and solids before completing the recommended four months of exclusive breastfeeding. There was also a widespread mis-understanding that colostrum should be discarded while, in fact, it allows the child to get natural immunisation.

The findings were presented by local government planners at district level workshops where they, together with community representatives, NGOs and civil society organisations designed action plans. Detailed local evidence allowed for regional adjustments while, aggregated, it was used to guide provincial planning in three out of the country's four provinces.

"Earnest, honest discussion and practical steps suggested for improvement of children's health," proclaimed the headline in Balochistan Times following the bond of care workshop in Quetta in September, 1999. Journalists were involved throughout the Community Voice in Planning initiative to add transparency to the process, to hold decision-takers accountable for implementation of their plans of action and to inform the public.

Evidence-led Communication Tools

CIET is concerned not just with gathering high quality evidence but also with the use of that evidence to change things for the better. With support from the Canadian International Development Agency, results from CIET's earlier work in

Pakistan on maternal and child care are the ingredients for new communication tools designed for, and tested with, lady health workers, to increase the effectiveness of their interaction with households. This pilot project is being done in collaboration with the National Programme for Family Planning and Primary Health Care in the province of Sindh.

Access to Justice for the Women of Karachi

CIET's social audit approach was adapted to evaluate public services as experienced by the public they are intended to serve. The justice system and the concept of justice were reviewed with 1881 women in household surveys, 40 gender stratified focus groups, interviews with 12 key NGO service workers and 38 police officers, and institutional reviews of 19 police stations throughout Karachi.

Community Monitoring of Public Services

As part of Pakistan's devolution process, more than ten thousand households from ten districts across Pakistan were given the opportunity to voice their experience and level of satisfaction with health, education, judiciary and police services. Health and education services providers were also interviewed and the results were discussed in 238 gender-stratified focus groups. This extensive body of information, gathered in partnership with UNDP and UNESCO, is part of a stakeholder system that will provide the National Reconstruction Bureau and the districts a baseline to monitor the progress of the devolution reform process.

As a result of this pilot, a similar system is being established for all 97 districts in Pakistan. Funded by the Canadian International Development Agency, such a system will provide a mechanism for coordination between sectors, contribute to the improvement of service delivery and inform the increasing participation of communities.

Social Audit of Abuse Against Women

This social audit, begun in September 2001, aims to define the extent of abuse against women in Pakistan and to look behind the resulting statistics to identify positive actions to prevent abuse. Additional objectives are to:

- raise awareness among communities and their leaders to issues of abuse against women and options for actions

- promote the creation and implementation of community-based strategies to eliminate abuse against women
- define an action plan for the GoP to support community based strategies to eliminate abuse against women.

Headed by the Federal Steering Committee on Family Protection Programme (FSCFPP) which is chaired by the Ministry of Women's Development and includes the Ministry of Justice and the Ministry of Interior, and in close consultation with government provincial focal points, this project has gone through an extensive design phase involving a review of all available studies and reports on the subject and systematic consultations with stakeholders in civil society, government, academia and the donor community. In mid-2002 a questionnaire to be administered to more than 20,000 households is being intensively piloted, and selection of sample districts and detailed planning of fieldwork are underway.

Results of the household survey, key informant interviews and institutional reviews will lead to discussions at community level of ways of responding to the issues identified and these in turn will be brought to district, provincial and federal levels in order to build up an evidence-based constituency for change. CIET is undertaking this work under a contract with the United Nations Development Programme (UNDP) through its Gender Equality Umbrella Project, with funding provided by DFID (The UK government Department for International Development).

3

Social Status

According to the 1998 Human Development Report, Pakistan ranks 138 on a list of 174 developing countries on the Human Development Index (HDI); 131 on a list of 163 countries on the gender development index (GDI); and 100 on a list of 102 countries on the gender empowerment measure (GEM). There are still far fewer women in the country compared to men. The latest provisional census figures of 1998 show that of a total population of 130.6 million 48 per cent are women and 52 per cent men, a sex ratio of 92.5 women for every 100 men in the country. This indicates just a slight improvement over the census figures of 1981 according to which women comprised 47.5 per cent of the population. In 1998, the Report of the Federal Bureau of Statistics suggests that this marginal increase of 5 per cent in the figures could be due to a decline in the level of mortality and improvement in data collection, while the continuing disparity is mainly because of the excess mortality of young girls and women in child-bearing age. Recent statistics also indicate that life expectancy today is higher among females (64.6) that men (63.9). There is still considerable disparity between the health status of males and females in several areas. The infant mortality rate for girls between the ages of 1-4 years is 66 per cent higher than for boys, suggesting significantly less favourable treatment of girls.

Mortality

Mortality continues to be higher among females till the age of 40. Moderate levels of anaemia are considerably higher among females than males in almost all age groups after the age of 1, and severe levels are also generally higher, particularly in the 15-44 age group. Among poorer households, chronic malnutrition is more prevalent among girls than boys. The maternal mortality rate mostly reported as 340 maternal deaths for every 100,000 live births, is alarmingly high, and even this is considered an underestimation by many. It is estimated that one women in every 38 dies from pregnancy-related causes. As and when calculated for married women, the fertility rate on an average is 8 live births throughout the marital reproductive span, and 5.2 live births when fertility is measured for all women of reproductive age. This is the highest in the 9 selected Muslim and other neighbouring countries including India, Bangladesh, Sri Lanka, Egypt, Turkey, Indonesia, Malaysia and Iran. The contraceptive prevalence rate was estimated at 24 per cent in 1996-97, compared to 41 per cent in India, 49 per cent in Bangladesh and 66 per cent in Sri Lanka.The literacy rate for females is generally stated to be 24 per cent as compared to 49 per cent for males, though one report estimates it at about 27 per cent during 1997-8.

Illiteracy

Of the 60 per cent illiterate population, more than 60 per cent are women. The primary school enrolment rate for girls during 1996-7 was estimated at about 66 per cent of total female population compared to 90 per cent for males. Moreover, dropout rates are much higher among girls. Of those without basic education opportunities, about 70 per cent are girls. Pakistan is at the bottom of the list of the 9 selected countries in terms of girls' literacy rates of 24 per cent compared, for example, with 78 per cent in Indonesia and Malaysia, 72.5 per cent in Turkey, 66 per cent in Iran, 78 per cent in Sri Lanka, 68 per cent in Egypt, 64 per cent in Iran and 38 per cent in India.

The activity rate according to the 1996-7 labour force survey was 9 per cent for females and 47 per cent for males, while the refined activity rate was 13.6 per cent and 70 per cent respectively. Most official data sources are, however, generally known to greatly underestimate female work participation. Largely due to inappropriate definitions, data gathering methods and cultural inhibitions on the part of both enumerators and respondents. A 1995 report, referring to relatively more reliable sources of information, stated that female labour force participation rates in the rural areas ranged between 57-43 per cent while the participation rate for urban women in 1991 was estimated at 17 per cent. The large majority of rural women work in agriculture as unpaid family helpers, amongst the poorest paid group in the rural sector.

Urban Women

The share of urban women in professional and related jobs was stated to be about 20 per cent in 1992, largely in the traditional teaching and medical professions. They constituted 9.4 per cent of production workers, only one-sixth of whom were paid employees, while most were relegated to temporary, casual or contract work outside the regular workforce. It was estimated that 77 per cent of the economically active women in urban areas in 1991-2 were employed in the informal sector, four fifths of whom were home-based workers with average monthly earning of less than one-third of the factory workers, themselves the lowest level employees in the formal sector.

1993 figures, which are not likely to differ significantly from the current statistics, indicate that only 5.4 per cent of federal government employees are women, mostly in social sectors, and their share at higher levels of employment is negligible. There is no detailed or reliable data available about women's ownership of land or property.

In Rural Areas

However, a 1995 survey of 1,000 households in rural areas of the Punjab showed that only 36 women owned land in their own names, only 9 had the power to sell or trade without permission from their male relatives, and that in nearly two-third of the households, daughters did not inherit land. In 1996-7, there were reported to be about 8 per cent female-headed households, but the actual number is likely to be higher. Sociocultural values, gender biases on the part of both enumerators and respondents and the commonly understood definition of headship of a family belonging to a male member, are some of the reasons suggested for the under-reporting. This is borne out by an intensive study conducted in Karachi in 1987, which indicated that 10 per cent of the households were headed by women. Women and girls in poor households bear a disproportionately high share of the burden of poverty due to their lower status, evidenced by lower endowment of land and productive assets, discrimination in the labour market, and more limited access to economic options and social services.

Although there is overall decrease in poverty, a report on human development in South Asia states that female poverty decreased at a much slower pace than male poverty during the 1970-95 period. Women also carry a double burden of work, performing both productive activities and domestic household responsibilities. This is particularly true for poor women in rural households who have far fewer basic services and facilitates available to them. Women's legal status is totally unequal to that of men. While the Constitution guarantees equality under the law, equal protection of the law and nondiscrimination on the basis of sex alone, other provisions create space for issues of women's rights to be constantly reopened.

Sociocultural norms and religious interpretations are frequently used as the basis for challenging and re-deciding women's rights issues, creating insecurity for women and uncertainty about their rights. Thus, there are several issues relating to women's fundamental rights of choice, security of person, dignity, liberty, freedom of movement etc., on which there are conflicting decisions, and which still need to be finally resolved by the superior judiciary. There are also several discriminatory laws in existence, as well as laws which have a disparate impact on women. But in actual practice, several of the laws with relatively positive provisions, are ignored or not implemented. Some examples are briefly provided.

Family Law

In the matter of family law there is no uniformity of rights, each religious community being governed by their personal or customary law, and discriminatory provisions exist in all of them. Under the Muslim family laws, men and women have unequal rights relating to inheritance, termination of marriage, minimum age of marriage and natural guardianship of children. Polygamy has not been banned or even sufficiently restricted by law; and there are grossly inadequate provisions for women's financial security after termination of marriage.Women have unequal rights under the citizenship laws, in which citizenship through descent is guaranteed only through a father. These laws empower a foreign wife of a Pakistani man the right to acquire citizenship, with no corresponding right for the foreign husband of Pakistani woman. The law of evidence limits women's legal capacity by reducing the value of their attestation of evidence to half that of and unacceptable without that of a man, in matter of written financial transactions.

The Qisas and Diyat Act allows for compromise and compensation in matters of bodily harm and murder, which in view of the prevalent sociocultural biases against women, has a particularly negative impact in cases where the victims are women. The Hudood Ordinances, the most damaging of the laws in the context of women, contain provisions which totally oust women's testimony for the imposition of the had or maximum penalty; and since adulthood has been redefined differently for males and females for the purposes of the ordinances, they make young girls liable to harsher adult penalties at a younger age than boys for offences relating to rape, adultery and extramarital sex.

Women in Prison

Vast majority of women in prisons today, including several minor girls, have been charged under this law. The law is often used for false and malicious prosecution of women to curtail their freedom of movement, freedom of choice in marriage, and as revenge or reprisal for their attempt to exercise their legal rights. While women have equal political rights as men under the Constitution, their political participation at the formal levels is still totally inadequate, and their political representation is negligible. During the last election held in 1997, fewer women than men were registered as voters (55.6 per cent men and 44.4 per cent women), and a smaller percentage actually voted. Women face several hurdles in the exercise of their right of franchise in terms of identification requirements, sociocultural norms discouraging their participation, agreements by candidates and parties in several areas that women would not vote, and the lack of action by official agencies against offenders of legal provisions in this respect. Political parties, by and large, tend to view women as a passive vote bank, following the dictates of men within their families or clans. Even within their own parties, they treat them largely as followers to be strategically used for election canvassing and public campaigns. Thus, most parties do not even have lists of female members. Women's representation on decision-making bodies within parties is mostly quite inadequate, and the number of tickets given to women for general elections is negligible.

There were currently only about 3 per cent women in the National Assembly (7 out of 217) and about 2.3 per cent in the Senate (2 out of 87), making their overall parliamentary representation 2.9 per cent (9 out of 304); and they are just per cent overall in the four provincial assemblies (2 out of 483). At the ministerial level, there is currently no woman with the status of a federal minister and only one with the status of a minister of state (1 out of a total of 21). There was no woman minister at the provincial level. In local bodies prior to the Devolution of Power Plan implemented in 2000, about 12.7 per cent seats had been reserved for women in the Punjab, which fell far short of the 33 per cent demanded and 20 per cent claimed by government, while Balochistan had taken the major initiative of reserving 25.8 per cent seats for women. Local body elections in the other provinces had not been held. In the past, the reports on women's participation in local bodies have not been particularly encouraging because of their own inexperience, the modality of bringing them in the future as a result of the relatively recent efforts and initiatives of women's NGOs and women in political parties. Women's participation in trade unions is still minimal, but there are several active women's groups and a number of advocacy organisations working on women's rights issues. However, in view of recent concerted governmental attempts to curtail their political role, their future effectiveness and role is yet uncertain .Violence against women, in several forms and at different levels, is another area of serious concern.

Domestic violence is fairly widespread and takes forms of physical, mental and emotional abuse. Wife abuse is rarely considered a crime socially unless it takes an extreme form, an attitude reflected in the behaviour both of law-enforcement agencies and the judiciary. Of the 1,000 women involved in a relatively recent survey in the Punjab, 35 per cent admitted to being beaten by their husbands. Domestic violence sometimes takes extreme forms of murder or attempted murder, a commonly used method being that of stove burning.

Custodial Violence

During 1998, 282 burn cases of women were reported in the Punjab alone, of whom 65 per cent died of their injuries. The official figures given for murder of women during 1998 were 1, 974 overall, of which 1, 183 were in the Punjab. Of the 885 reported cases in the Punjab, more than 67 per cent were victims of their own relatives - husbands, brothers, fathers and in-laws. Rape remains the commonest form of violence against women, though only a fraction get reported or prosecuted because of the shame attached to the victim. 706 cases in the Punjab were reported in the press during 1998 alone, of which 55 per cent of the victims were minors and more than half of total cases were of gang-rape

Custodial violence is known to be widespread but, for obvious reasons, rarely reported or pursued. Only 41 cases were reported in the Punjab during 1998, reports registered in just 6, and only 1 person held. The official figures for kidnapped women during 1998 were a total of 4, 529 country-wide. Of Lahore cases, more than half the victims were minors. Sexual harassment of women in the public or the workplace is a common phenomenon, and while frequently reported in the media, is rarely reported to the police or taken notice of. An increasing form of violence, used to settle a score, is that of public humiliation of women by stripping them naked in public.

Several inhuman customary practices, including bartering girls to settle disputes, marriage to the Qur'an and murder of women in the name of honour, continue unabated, sanctified by those who commit the crimes as cultural traditions, and condoned both by the law-enforcement agencies and the courts. Women continue to face the grave biases, discriminatory practices and forms of violence prevalent in highly patriarchal society at several levels. From birth, sociocultural norms prescribe a different set of roles, responsibilities and behaviour patterns for women, denying them equal access to several facilities and opportunities at par with men and maintaining their subservience and subordination. This further affects their own self-confidence, limits their access to information and skills, and reinforces in them the social perception of having a lower social status than men. Combined with their unequal economic situation, the discriminatory or gender-insensitive laws and polices, and lack of sufficient political will to seriously address the root causes of the problem, the task of extricating themselves from this situation becomes monumental.

A legal ideology is a statement of the aspirations and values of a social group. . . . The task. . . . was to find texts that would appear authoritative to even the most recalcitrant lord or reactionary prelate.[1]

Whereas it is true that customs and archaic traditions (manifestations of tribal and feudal systems) are chiefly responsible for keeping the women of Pakistan in subservient positions, it is equallytrue that the laws enacted in the country since its creation have all sought to improve and protect women's position. As pointed out earlier the making of a law has not necessarily meant its effective implementation, and women have not benefited by the mere passage of it. At best such laws have reflected the State's position regarding women. But the so-called Islamic regime decided to arrest even this process. It introduced a series of negative laws that in effect formalize women's secondary position in society. Such legislation includes the Hudood Ordinance, the Law of Evidence and the proposed Law of *Qisas* and *Diyat*.[2]

An additional attempt was made to limit women's participation in the political field. The government-appointed Ansari Commission's recommendations on the form of government contained several clauses blatantly discriminating against women by restricting their right to stand or vote in elections. Similarly, the Council of Islamic Ideology.[3]

Fehmida and Allah Bux Vs. the State

It was not until two years later, when the Fehmida and Allah Bux case became the first of its kind under which a man was sentenced to be stoned to death and a woman to 100 lashes, that women were jolted into action. Shirkat Gah's decision to mobilize support for Fehmida and Allah Bux, and in the process bring about the birth of WAF, has already been discussed in Chapter 5. It would be useful here to outline the details of the case to highlight the manner in which the law can be grossly mis-applied.

Fehmida belonged to a lower middle-class family. She fell in love with Allah Bux, a married bus driver who belonged to a different community from her own and a lower social class. She eloped with him and they got married. Fehmida's parents were outraged by her action, tried to persuade her to return, and then offered a bride to Allah Bux to divorce her. When all their attempts failed they filed a first information report (FIR) with the police which stated that their daughter had been abducted. Fehmida was pregnant by the time she was recovered by the police from Allah Bux's home where she had been living with his first wife and children. Fehmida and Allah Bux claimed that they had entered into an oral marriage and that they had delayed registration of their *nikah* until after Fehmida became pregnant. On the basis of this the judge sentenced both of them to *hadd* punishments. Fehmida's 100 lashes were to be executed two months after the delivery of her child.

The important point in this case is not whether Fehmida and Allah Bux were guilty, but that neither confessed to the crime and there were no witnesses, let alone the four male adults of good repute required under the law. Both the accused repeatedly stated that they were married and produced witnesses to that effect. The fact that the statements of these witnesses held some contradictions regarding the amount decided upon to be paid as *mehr* by Allah Bux, did not detract from the lack of any proof that adultery had taken place. The sentence by the Sessions Judge was therefore unjustifiable. It seems that Fehmida and Allah Bux were being punished for the delayed registration of their marriage—an offence punishable under Section 5 of the Family Laws Ordinance by three months imprisonment or a fine of Rs.1,000/- or both, without affecting the legality of the marriage. Besides, as one commentator on the Allah Bux case stated, marriages before 1961 (i.e., before the Family Laws Ordinance) were not registered, and that fact does not invalidate them. 'Where does the *zina* Ordinance place them,' she asks, 'that they are all committing *zina*? For that would certainly render an entire generation illegitimate.[4]

There were other lacunae in the case. For instance, Fehmida's parents had reported a case of abduction, and the police registered one of adultery; the sentence passed by the judge had no justification in Islam nor in the Ordinance itself, which states very clearly that those who even suspect themselves to be married cannot be punished. That the case and the sentence were weak was amply proven when an eminent lawyer, Khalid Ishaq—an authority on Islamic jurisprudence—pleaded the case in the Supreme Court, from where it was returned to Karachi and finally dismissed. From the women's point of view the case was of historical importance as it heralded a completely new era of women's consciousness and struggle. It also manifested the feeling of insecurity, of being threatened, that seems to have crept into the social environment since the coming to power of the military government. Two years later, when the Safia Bibi case was reported in the press, the women were in a much more belligerent frame of mind, and better prepared for protest and action.

Safia Bibi Case

In July 1983 the news item on Safia Bibi prompted WAF Lahore to call an emergency meeting of several women's organizations to condemn the unbelievable sentence given bya lower court of Sahiwal. Safia Bibi, an 18-year old virtually blind girl had been sentenced to public lashing (15 lashes), three years imprisonment and a fine of Rs. 1,000/- on charges of adultery. The details of case were that Safia, daughter of a poor peasant, was employed in the local landlord's house as a domestic help. According to her statement made to the police she was raped first by the landlord's son and subsequently by the landlord himself. As a result she became pregnant, and finally gave birth to an illegitimate child who later died. Her father registered a case of rape after the death of the child. The Sessions Judge acquitted both the son and the father of the crime, as there was not enough evidence to prove rape under the Hudood Ordinance. Safia Bibi's self-confessed pregnancy was used as evidence of adultery by the judge who, in his opinion, was giving Safia a light sentence because of her young age and near blindness.

The sentence shocked the public at large, particularly because Safia was said to be blind. What escaped the public until it was brought to their notice by WAF[5] was the fact that Safia Bibi's father had registered a case of rape, and the judge had taken it upon himself to sentence a rape victim for adultery, on the bsis of her own evidence.

The WAF Lahore Working Committee went to Sahiwal and procured the case record. The trial proceedings were brought to Lahore and various lawyers, including an active member of PWLA, were contacted in preparation for an appeal. WAF publicized the case both within the country and outside. Before a proper appeal could be filed, the Federal *Shariat* Court, using its *suo moto* powers for the first time, asked for the case to be transferred to it for review. It is believed that this haste emanated from the international embarrassment faced by the government of Pakistan. Pakistan's ambassador to England is said to have been questioned by news reporters in that country, and he wired back asking for an answer. It is rumoured that General Zia himself intervened and asked that the case be transferred immediately.

The verdict of the *Shariat* Court is important as much for the enlightened outlook of the presiding judge, Justice Aftab Hussein, as for highlighting the weaknesses of the Ordinance which lends itself remarkably to lopsided interpretation. First of all it was pointed out that the judge had only partially accepted Safia's evidence and her father's statements, ignoring their claim that she was raped. Under the law, the statement of any witness can only be accepted in full and hence the judge was technically at fault. Moreover, according to the Federal *Shariat*, the Court went on to say that in the case of rape, if the man was acquitted due to lack of evidence and given the benefit of the doubt, the woman must also be given the benefit of the doubt, and the mere fact of her pregnancy was insufficient to prove her guilty. In the words of the judgement :

> It is unfortunate that though a victim of rape, the natural phenomenon of her pregnancy and motherhood betrayed her. She had to suffer the humiliation of a trial, conviction and sentence in addition to the disgrace and dishonour suffered by her at the hands of her fellow human beings in the society.

Chief Justice Aftab Hussain went on to say :

> The principle of *Figh* (Muslim School of Jurisprudence) is that she will be asked about the cause of pregnancy, if she says that she was forced to commit adultery or someone had committed zina with her under suspicion about his identity, her statement will be accepted and she will not be convicted.[6]

Among the lawyers for the defence pleading before the Federal *Shariat* Court, Khalid Ishaq appeared once again.

For the women's organizations a very significant aspect of the case was the high level of sophistication achieved in organization and coordination. Not only did WAF Lahore bring together women's organizations to make a combined and concerted effort, by giving joint statements and holding joint meetings, it also coordinated very effectively with the other chapters. Karachi WAF mobilized women's organizations there, contacted lawyers and geared up for a petition against the Hudood Ordinance. Islamabad WAF made contacts and lobbied, providing much needed information about the stages of the appeal in the FSC. Money was raised by the various chapters for placing notices in leading daily newspapers highlighting the in Justice inherent in the Ordinance. The FSC judgement, however, rendered a newspaper campaign redundant.

Ever since the Fehmida and Allah Bux case, WAF chapters had been concerned about the dangers of this law and had wanted to challenge it in the Federal *Shariat* Court. The Safia Bibi case brought home the need for doing so speedily, and in December 1983, the Karachi branch of WAF along with other women's organizations (APWA, Shirkat Gah, All-Pakistan Women Lawyer's Association, Therik-e-Niswan, Anjuman Jamhooriyat Pasand Khawateen) filed a writ in the Federal *Shariat* Court challenging the *Hudood Ordinance (zina)*. The team of lawyers presenting the petition was headed by Rashida Patel, the most prominent female lawyer in the country, president of the All-Pakistan Women Lawyers' Association and an active member of APWA, and Khalid Ishaq. The writ was admitted for hearing in 1983 but was not taken up by the FSC until 1985, when the passage of the Eighth Amendment (discussed later in this chapter) rendered the petition null.

While the two major cases that WAF took up were those of Fehmida and Allah Bux and Safia Bibi, there were many others that came up during 1982 and 1983. In almost all the cases reported in that period, WAF responded with resolutions, press statements and public protes.

The All-Pakistan Women Lawyers' Association has also appealed, in several cases of one-sided punishment of women, to the Federal *Shariat* Court to intervene, exercise *suo moto* jurisdiction and examine the cases to ascertain that Justice is being done.[7] APWLA's stand is that no sentence should be executed until the Federal *Shariat* Court has confirmed it, in the belief that the lower courts are misguided and may sometimes wrongly convict women.[8]

In January 1983 another unfortunate judgement that was taken up by WAF was reported from D.I. Khan. (Usually the press picks up and reports judgements of lower courts in a routine manner. The Fehmida-Allah Bux, Safia Bibi and other cases followed this pattern). This was yet another case under the infamous Hudood Ordinance. A young unmarried woman had been convicted of *zina* and sentenced to flogging and imprisonment. In her case she had been raped by a male cousin living in her house. When the matter was discovered the cousin had promised her father that he would marry her, but later, when she was found to be pregnant, he retracted. The child was born and died, and was buried in the house to hide the dishonour connected with an illegitimate child. The cousin, on being pressurized to marry her, filed with the police a case of homicide against the girl. As a result, not only was she convicted of murder (on the basis of circumstantial evidence) but also of adultery, since she had had a child. The man was acquitted for lack of proof.

On 30 September 1983 Lal Mai became the first woman to be publicly flogged at Lquat Pur, Bahawalpur District. She was convicted under the *zina* Ordinance and given 15 lashes, executed by amn, with 5,000 people watching. Following closely after the Safia Bibi case, it enraged many women.[9] WAF Lahore organized a picket in protest in October outside the Governor's house in Lahore. Placards condemning the unjust law and demanding its withdrawal were displayed, and a resolution passed unanimously by the general body of WAF was distributed to the journalists and passers-by. The Karachi chapter also passed strongly-worded resolution condemning the flogging.

Not all the cases emanating from Hudood, which were taken up by WAF and other women's organizations, were followed through to the end. But the cumulative impact of public protest was quite forceful. The actions of women's organizations created a public awareness of the law and women's second-class position-besides embarrassing the government. It may not be incorrect to presume that one of the reasons for the *suo moto* review of Safia Bibi's case was the women's organizations concerted campaign.

When, on realizing the implications of the Hudood Ordinance, women and women's organizations rallied together, they were not sure what other means the government would adopt to affect their position. Their foremost fear was that the Family Laws Ordinance would be repealed. This was reflected in one of the first actions that WAF took, that of the signature campaign on five points which were considered of immediate importance (Family laws, a separate women's university, compulsory veiling, participation in sports and cultural activities). There were two significant pieces of legislation, the Law of Evidence and the Law of Qisas and Diyat, which were , however, to become the focus of a raging controversy that pitched women's rights groups (particularly WAF) and right-wing obscurantist scholars and *maulvis* against each other.

The Law of Evidence

Proposed after Qisa and Diyat, the Law of Evidence became law on 28 October 1984, while the former is still awaiting promulgation. It was in April 1982 that the Council of Islamic Ideology (CII) proposed a new Law of Evidence to replace the Evidence Act of 1872, supposedly to bring it not conformity with Islam.[10] This draft prescribed that in all cases other than those covered by the Hudood Ordinance and any other 'special law', two male witnesses, and in the absence of two male witnesses, one male and two females, would be required for proving a crime. In specifically 'female' matters, such as menstruation or delivery, 'which do not usually come within the direct knowledge of men', the evidence of two or even one woman would be acceptable. The proposed law, for which no lawyers or legal experts were consulted, was condemned, and WAF was perhaps the first women's organization to do so publicly. CII's only woman member was said to be out of the country and an all-male council made up of rectionary *ulema* prepared the draft law.

Women's Resistance

The government must have been quite surprised at the reaction to the draft law, for the Hudood Ordinance had not elicited any negative response when it was promulgated. Earlier, the proposed Law of *Qisas* and *Diyat* had also been drafted (in December 1980) with hardly any public protest. But in the meantime a great deal had transpired to make women uncertain and nervous, and the Israr controversy had left women feeling offended and belligerent.

When WAF took up the issue its objective was not only to communicate to the government its rejection of the law but also to inform women about its implications. It organized special lectures and discussions on the issue. For instance, in September 1982 WAF Lahore invited a leading male and a female lawyer to address its general body to explain the implications of the law and to expose the fallacy that this and other such laws were Islamic. Other chapters likewise organized meetings and passed resolutions, expressing their refusal to accept measures reducing women to a second-class position in society.

In order to keep the issue in focus a very active and sustained campaign was undertaken, and WAF Lahore's October 1982 first anniversary function, *Jalsa*, made the issue its central theme. Over 1000 women were regaled by the theatrical skits performed to highlight the absurd implications of the law.

The informal language of theatrical pieces, poems and songs, combined with more formal and conventional methods such as resolutions and speeches, got the message across more successfully than expected. The atmosphere in this particular *jalsa* was so intense that when at the end resolutions were read out for approval, the entire hall resounded with sounds of 'yes' (in support) and 'shame-shame' (against the government's policy of diminishing women to half status). Whether the intricacies of the Law were understood or not, it was more than evident that the women had completely comprehended the implications of it.

In the two years between October 1982 and October 1984, when the Law of Evidence was finally promulgated, it remained the primary issue for women's organizations. The mounting campaign against it reached its high point in February 1983 when women's organizations responded enthusiastically to a call from the Punjab Women Lawyers' Association. The call was to march down the Mall Road (main thoroughfare and shopping mall in Lahore to the Punjab High Court, to present a memorandum against the proposed law to the Chief Justice, on behalf of women's organizations. About 300 women from different walks of life—teachers, students and factory workers—gathered in a side street off the Mall. They were quite surprised to see a large number of male and female police in the area (at least 500 of them).

What followed was a most unexpected confrontation between police and women. The women were told that they could not go to the High Court as that would be a violation of the law which prohibited demonstrations. The women's assurances that they would walk in pairs with enough distance between them so as not to violate the law (Section 144) which prohibits the assembly of more than five people in public, was not accepted by the duty magistrate. Initially, the women decided to stage a sit-in right there in the side lane. Meanwhile, the police had surrounded the women from all sides with a three-deep cordon. The mere presence of the police—a much-hated force in Pakistan—was provocation enough, but it was compounded when force was used to remove from the scene Habib Jalib, an anti-government poet. He had arrived while the women were sitting-in and recited poems specially written in suppot of women, amid much cheering and applause. The police could not tolerate this and tried to reove him forcibly. This seems to have been the breaking point. Enraged women broke through the cordon and started running in the direction of the High Court.

A free-for-all followed. Groups of women zigzagged down the 40-ft wide Mall with police brandishing batons, caught some-what by surprise at the women's spirit and endeavour. While some women had move ahead, others were trapped by the police, beaten up, dragged along the road and rounded up into police vans. In the middle of it all tear gas was also ordered, and the Mall Road presented a bizarre sight of a group of all-female demonstrators involved in a street fight with the police. Fifty women were arrested, but many managed to get to the High Court where male lawyers were waiting with garlands to receive them. Several of the women were hurt, some seriously.

The impact of the 12 February demonstration was tremendous. All of a sudden women were being taken seriously by politicians, for having had the courage to defy existing restrictions; by the government, for having the ability to create a law and order situation; and by other women, who were forced to examine the proposed law which had moved women like them to take on the State. There was also a reactionary section (made up of both men and women) which was infuriated by the women demonstrators, and viewed that march as a violation of the role prescribed for women in Islam. For the women who had participated, very few of whom had even seen a demonstration before, the experience was singulary liberating. To have confronted not only police violence but also to have been arrested and taken into custody was unprecedented. Spirits were high, the resolve to continue the struggle stronger, and solidarity at its peak. Later, when occasions for picketing and demonstrating arose, it was found that a number of the participants of the February demonstration showed no hesitation in coming out time and again. It was as if an invisible barrier had been removed.[11]

The momentum of the demonstration continued. Three days later a protest meeting was organized by WAF to condemn the unprovoked police violence and to carry on with the rejection of the draft law. The government, which had already over-reacted on the day of the demonstration, tried to sabotage the meeting.The reservation of the hall hired in a local hotel (for lack of any other public place to hold a meeting) was cancelled at the last minute. WAF was prepared for such an eventuality, however, and had organized an altenative venue in a private house. It was indeed a feat when over 250 women were diverted and transported to the alternative meeting place. The meeting once again was a tremendous success. Even APWA, which has a policy of not coming out in the streets and is not in favour of confrontation, declared that it had supported the demonstration and that its member present at the demonstration was representing them. It was decided at the meeting that lobbying would continue and that there would be no let-up in the pressure.

Not all organizations were in agreement over the idea of lobbying the members of the Majlis-e-Shoora, whose legality was questioned by them. But WAF's position on this was pragmatic. It sent teams each consisting of three or four women from Lahore to Islamabad in relay. Coordinating with WAF Islamabad these teams met members of the Majlis and pesented them with WAF's written position on the Law, based on progressive interpretation of the Quranic injunctions. There were a number of members , including Allama Razi Rizavi, a Shiah religious scholar, who supported the WAF interpretation and spoke in the Majlis, quoting extensively from *ahadith* to prove that women are in no way inferior to men and that they can give evidence, go to war, be *qazis* (judges), and even lead men in prayers.

The government tried various tactics to restrict debate on the issue in the Majlis, where a committee under the chairmanship of the law minister was formed, supposedly to streamline the draft proposal. The final discussion on it was put off till the last session of the last day, when a large number of members had left the Majlis, which had been in session for over three weeks. The compromise draft presented to the house was then bulldozed through with hardly any discussion. Though a watered-down version of the original, it was sitill unacceptable to women. The law, as passed by the Majlis, stated in its Clause 18 that all matters shall be proved by the evidence of two Muslims, and in the absence of two male witnesses, by the eveidence of one male and two female would be acceptable at the discretion of the court.

The agitation against the law was kept up in Lahore , Karachi and Islamabad. It took many forms. Each rumour of the law's promulgation was met with renewed opposition, resulting in its being shelved again and again. It was not until October 1984 that it was finally passed.

Some of the actions taken against the Law of Evidence :-

8 March 1983:

International Women's Day observed by WAF Karachi and Lahore as a day of protest against the law.

September 1983:

WAF Picket in front of Governor's House, Lahore.

October 1983:

WAF picket in front of Governer's House, Lahore.

December 1983:

Picket in front of Governor's House, Lahore, by several women's organizations.

January 1984:

Press Conference of Women's organizations in Lahore to protest against Law of Evidence, Qisas and Diyat and other issues : WAF Karachi holds seminar, "A woman is a whole person", highlighting the discrimination in the law.

12 February 1984:

Pakistan Women's Day-WAF Lahore plasters city with posters "One woman, one testimony, proposed Law of Evidence unacceptable." Meeting called by WAF Lahore to observe the day. Other women's Organizations participated.

Procession of Six Women's Organizations to denounce police brutality and the proposed Law of Evidence (in Lahore).

October 1984:

General Body meeting of WAF Lahore condemns the law.

November 1984:

WAF demonstrations against the Ordinance in Lahore and Islamabad. Joint seminar by women's organizations against the Ordinance in Lahore.

Women's Point of View

By the time the law was promulgated, it had gone through at least four drafts, and differed, especially on the controversial clause, from the one passed in the Majlis-e-Shoora. The new law basically reiterates the one it seeks to replace (Evidence Act of 1872). Yet it is different in two aspects. First, it overturns the rule of precedence. Under the new law each case is to be judged in isolation from all previous cases. Second, with regard to Women it has added Article 17 which provides that:

> In all matters pertaining to financial and future obligations providing these are reduced to writing the eveidence of two men or one man and two women will be required, so that if one should forget, the other may remind her.

Although substantially modified, women's rights groups objected to the law for several reasons. First and foremost, the law stipulates that no financial or future obligations can be put in writing without the presence of a man. Secondly, the term future obligations is an ambiguous one that can cover any number of circumstances not relating to debt or loan as referred to inverse 282 (*Surah-al-Baqra*) of the Qur'an, which has been paraphrsed. Thus it goes beyond the text of the Quranic mandate. *Surah-al-Baqra* reads as follows:

> When ye deal with each other, in loan transactions involving future obligations for a fixed period of time, reduce them to writing... And get two witnesses, out of your men, and if there are not two men then a man and two women, for witnesses, so that if one of them falters (or errs) the other can remind her.

By including *Surah-al-Baqra* as part of the law the attempt has been to create an impression of the law being truly Islamic. In fact the above verse is the only on of the eight verses in the Qur'an relating to evidence where a distinction is made between men and women . Seen in the context of seventh century Arabia the verse is an indication of the inclusion of women in matters of monetary transactions where women may not have been so active. Ironically, the same verse is being used in 20th century Pakistan to exclude them. The Quranic verse refers very explicitly to the evidence of one and not two women, the presence of the second woman being to remind in case the one who is the witness forgets. The testimony of one woman is therefore primary.

The law makes no allowance for the fact that an educated literate woman who can read the documan will be a more reliable witness than an illiterate man who cannot read what the has signed. Women activists argue that if in an oral transaction a woman can be a full witnews it is illogical to reduce her evidence to half when it is reduced to writing.

Women's organizations emphasize the fact that the spirit of the Qur'an is based on Justice, and various Quranic verses (4:135, 24:6-9) clearly show that both men and women are called upon to be witnesses for the sake of Justice. They argue that the essential prerequisite for testimony is intelligence, the ability for retention and faithful reproduction, not necessarily connected with the sex of a witness. They conclude therefore, that the Law of Evidence is just one more attempt to push woman out of all public spheres and to reduce her status to half that of a man's.[12] The women cite the instance of (*l'aan* in which the wife's evidence has the same weight as that of the husband's.

The Law of Qisas and Diyat

This law was drafted in December 1980 by the Council of Islamic Ideology. It was passed by the Majlis-e-Shoore (in August 1984) and still has to be presented to the National Assembly elected in February 1985 for approval. It covers all aspects of intentional and unintentional murders, bodily injuries and abortion. The word *qisas* literally means retribution and covers punishment in the logic of an eye for an eye, while *diyat* is blood money for murder, or financial compensation for physical injury in lieu of retribution.

The draft was circulated to select lawyers, *ulema* and organizations, including APWA, for comment. APWA convened a meeting of 18 other women's welfare and professional organizations and on 11 January 1981 compiled a report recommending changes in the law.[13] While the comments made by APWA and the other organizations are well articulated and substantiated with facts, these did not become public knowledge, as they were sent to the proper quarters, i.e., the CII.

Once again it was WAF which, soon after its formation, raised the issue at national level. In early 1982 it was discussed at various General Body meetings and the drive was to publicize its potentially negative aspects among the widest range of people.

The original draft proposal of the law stated in Section 25(b) that the *diyat* for a female victim of an offence of *qatletkhata* (unintentional murder) would be half that of a male. The law proposed that in case of death, the blood money for a man should be fixed at 30.63 kg of silver (or its equivalent) and only half this for a woman, similarly, in all instances of compensation for bodily injury, an injured or miamed woman would only receive half the compensation due to a man for the same injury. On the other hand, women guilty of murder or causing bodily injury would be liable to the same punishment as men.

Women and women's organizations rejected this provision of the law, not only for its abhorrent attitude of placing a price on human life but also because the Quran does not specify any amount for *diyat*, nor does it mention the question of gender in this regard.

The Qur'an on the matter of *diyat* says:

> It is not for a believer to take a believer's life except by mistake; and he who kills a believer by mistake should free a slave who is a believer and pay blood money to the victim's family unless they forgo it as an act of charity.

The above verse makes no reference to the sex of any of those involved, nor is any mention made of greater or lesser amounts of compensation among the believers.[14] Thus the biggest complaint of women has been that a discriminatory law is being pushed through using the pretext of Islam.

The reason given for reduced *diyat* for women by the protagonists of the law is that man is the breadwinner and supports the family, and therefore with his death the family loses its provider. Such an argument overlooks the contribution of women in the maintenance of their househods (if not always in economic or material terms, most certainly in physical and indirect ways). The vast majority of Pakistani women living in rural areas are the backbone of agricultural production and an argument such as that stated above just reflects the attitude of the males who are unwilling to acknowledge women and their economic contribution.

The reality of there being a large number (not necessarily in terms of percentages) of women who have entered professions at various levels has also been disregarded by the law on *diyat*, and is an additional reason for its rejection by women's rights organizations. By not making a distinction between the non-earning male and an earning female the law denies the fundamental objective of any law, that is, to achieve Justice.

Qisas

The other clause singled out by women as discriminatory was Section 10 (b) in the proposed draft Ordinance. According to this, for proof of murder liable to *qisas*, the testimony of two Muslim male witnesses (fulfilling the requirement of *tazkia-e-shahood*) was necessary. Women as witnesses would be admissable for awarding *tazir*, i.e., lesser punishment. Thus a woman's eye-witness evidence has been reduced to the status of circumstantial evidence in all instances of murder or bodily injury.

On this question the almost unanimous opinion of women's organizations is that under this law, if a murder is committed in the presence of women, the murderers can get away unpunished. The proposed law does not accept the evidence of non-Muslims except in cases where the accused is a non-Muslim. Thus the testimony of any number of women or non-Muslims is being excluded for maximum punishment.

When women agitated about this provision they were told by no less a person than Minister for Information Raja Zafrul Haq himself that in certain circumstances *tazir* could also be death. In other words, if the women feared that their testimony could not get any one sentenced to death, their fears were unfounded. Such a response further infuriated the women who were not trying to gain the right to get people condemned to death. For them the issue was of being accepted as equal human beings capable of giving responsible evidence.

Abortion

Another aspect of the law rejected by women dealt with the issue of abortion. Sections 96 and 97 of the proposed law declared abortion (*Isqat-e-hamal*) illegal in any circumstances, carrying a punishment of seven years. The punishment is for both the person who performs the abortion and for the expectant mother who undergoes it.

Besides being contrary to Quranic injunctions the law reflects total insensitivity to women. Even the existing law, which is quite stringent, allows abortion in the case of physical danger to the mother. The proposed law does not admit this possibility, and it does not even exempt rape victims, who would have to live with not only the trauma of violence but a constant reminder of it in the shape of an unwanted child. Pakistani society has no place for an illegitimate child at the social and legal levels, and therefore to condemn a child to this inhuman situation is immoral at best.

Resistance

APWA raised the issue of abortion for rape victims at its triennial conference in 1982 in Lahore. Subsequently WAF took it up in its campaign against violence against women and in its resistance to the Law of *Qisas* and *Diyat*.

If 1983 could be termed the year of the Law of Evidence, then 1984 was that of *qisas* and *diyat*. Besides press statements, resolutions and press conferences, the campaign against this law included special lectures, talks, seminars and articles in the media. A joint march by women's organizations was held in Lahore in April1984. It was interspersed by five-minute sit-downs when slogans were chanted. During this march people on the roadside sympathised and commended the protesters for their efforts, and expressed condemnation of the law.

The campaign against the proposed law of *Qisas* and *Diyat* followed the same pattern and pursued similar methods adopted for the law of Evidence. Subsequent to the split in WAF in September1983, following which the original WAF called itself WAF National, (see Chapter 9) most of the action in Lahore was through a coordination committee of various women's organizations. While the ramifications of the split were negative in a variety of ways, it is to the credit of WAF(N) that it did not allow it to interfere in the movement for resisting unequal laws or any other campaign relating to women's issues.

The culmination of the protest was in June, just before the draft law was to be discussed in the Majlis, when WAF(N) conducted a survey among women in Lahore. Thousands of questionnaires were distributed among college students, working women and housewives from different sections of society and over two thousand of the leaflets were returned with an over whelming majority rejecting the law. These were then mailed to the members of the Majlis-e-Shoora when the session of *qisas* and *diyat* started.

Impact of the Resistance Campaign

The most significant impact of the agitation against the draft Law of *qisas* and *qiyat* was similar to that of the Law of Evidence. The inherent discrimination became a recognized issue and was publicized widely. It must be kept in mind that women's organizations operating in large urban areas do not have the numerical strength to reach all sections of the population. Therefore they have to rely a great deal on the media. The fact that the press took up the women's issue and covered the women's point of view prominently greatly contributed to the spreading of awareness about the laws.

That the government also became sensitive to women's pressure was reflected in the law being shelved several times and also its being sent to various commitees of the Majlis, reminiscent of the government's tactics vis-a-vis the Law of Evidence. The persistent pressure and lobbying of the women members of the Majlis finally bore fruit by the time *qisas* and *diyat* came up for discussion. When, in the Majlis session of July 1984 the law was literally forced through by Information Minister Zafarul Haq in a House lacking quorum, the women, along with the members of the minority communities and some male lawyers, staged a walkout. During the debate women had heatedly expressed their rejection of it.

The problem with the proposed Law of *qisas* and *diyat* is not only its discriminatory provisions against women, but other measures likely to affect the interest of the public at large. Women have persistently agitated on the aspects concerning them, but it has not been taken note of at a general level. One of the Majlis committees—that of Chaudhry Altaf—pointed out the inherent weaknesses of the law, not least of which is the critical issue of the conflicting interpretations of Islam by the dozen or more sects that exist in Pakistan. The changes and recommendations of this committee were unceremoniously bypassed, however, and yet another committee under the chairmanship of Raja Zafarul Haq was formed. And it was his draft which was finally passed by the Majlis. This draft referred the issue of *diyat* to the *Federal Shariat* Court and the *Shariat* Bench of the Supreme Court. The controversial point of *tazir* punishment—which, according to the proposed law, can even be death—has also been refered to the FSC for its opinion. Thus, the efficiency of the committee is places in doubt; if it cannot feel competent to deal with the above two clauses, then why should it be deemed competent in the case of others?

If taken together, the laws discussed above point to a single demoralizing fact, namely the exclusion of women's evidence over a very wide field, tantamount to cutting women's worth by half. While women's testimony is not admissible for maximum punishment in theft, adultery and rape under the Hudood Ordinance, it is reduced to circumstantial evidence in matters relating to murder or bodily injury in the proposed Law of *Qisas* and *Diyat*. Finally, one woman alone cannot testify in matters implying financial and future obligation, according to the Law of Evidence. Which are the matters left (if any) ask women, where a woman's evidence will be acknowledged as that of a responsible human being?

Qazi Courts

The present government, as had been discussed earlier, claims that it came into power and stayed on to establish an Islamic State in Pakistan. Of the measures taken to do so most have focused on women (the reasons for this were discussed earlier). The legislation discussed above forms part of that scheme. That the government has been inherently contradictory and its approach to Islamization suspect is best highlighted through the judgement of the Federal *Shariat* Court in its reference relating to the *qazi* courts.

The background to the case is that the government passed an order providing for the setting up of Islamic Courts to deal with cases according to Islamic Law and in order to expedite the process of Justice.[15] The Ordinance has provision for both male and female *qazis* (judges/magistrates). Through a petition the appointment of women as *qasis* (judges) was challenged in the Federal Shariat Court in August 1982. In the petitioner's view women discharging their functions of *qazi* without observing *purdah* would be a clear violation of the injunctions of Islam. Besides this, the petitioner pleaded that during the time of the Prophet and his companions women were never entrusted the duties of qazi, and since under Muslim law the evidence of a woman is half of that of a man and her share in inheritance is equal to half of that of her brother, the judgement of two women does not therefore fulfil the qualification of *qazi,* according to the established principles of Muslim jurisprudence.

The respondent in this case was the government of Pakistan, represented by the Attorney General and Khalid Ishaq and Rashida Patel among others. The judgement, which is of historical importance for the lucid and detailed arguments given to prove that women are competent to become *qazis* and that one woman is quite capable of sitting as a judge, dismissed the petition.

Since it is not possible to discuss all the reasons given in the case, suffice to say that the argument used by the counsel for the government was based on Quranic principles and on precedents from the early period of Muslim history. The salient points of the judgement are:

(a) A woman can be appointed *qazi.*

(b) There is no limitation as regards age or *purdah,* or that female judges can only be appointed to decide cases concerning female issues.

(c) It is not correct that the value of the evidence of a women is half that of the evidence of a man.

(d) There is no law, custom or usage regarding *purdah* enforceable by law.

(e) The view that a woman cannot appear as a witness in matters of *hudood* and *qisas* is only a juristic view and is not based on either the Qur'an or *ahadith.*

Also cited in the arguments used against the petitions, was the *fatwa* (edict) given by the *ulema* whereby candidature Mohtarama Fatima Jinnah for the office of head of State was supported in 1964.

It can be said without any doubt that the judgement is the most well-argued and substantiated document in support of women's position. It also reflects the wide scope of interpretation that is possible within the rules set down in the Qur'an. The government's contradictory position is curious. On the one hand it bases its arguments for women's case to be a *qazi* on all those arguments that it negates in the laws that it has promulgated or proposed as Islamic laws.

Women's organizations have repeatedly and persistently referred to the positive judgement of the FSC to bolster their argument against the various discriminatory laws. How the law-makers in Pakistan defend their dual position is difficult to comprehend.

The Crimes Ordinance

Perhaps the most mystifying piece of legislation so far promulgated is the ordinance on crimes against women. Decreed on 3 June 1984, it came in the aftermath of a prolonged campaign by women's organizations following a horrifying incident in Nawabpur, a city in Southern Punjab. A carpenter suspected of having an 'amorous' relationship with the daughter of the local landlord (for whom he happened to be working) was beaten to death by the landlord and his accomplices inside his home. The women in the house-the sole witnesses of the murder—were disrobed, dragged out of their home, molested and forced to march naked down the street. Women in Pakistan, especially in the rural areas, are often made targets of retaliation in disputes between men. In this case innocent women were victims of a vendetta perpetrated by the local landlord, whose 'honour' had been violated by a man from a lower class.

Women's organizations had been concerned with the issue of violence against women and had focused on it through various channels, such as seminars organized by Chapters of WAF, a play performed by Therik-e-Niswan, and resolutions passed by other organizations. But the Nawabpur incident and several others around the same time, reported extensively in the press, seemed to reflect a marked heightening in the barbaric nature of crimes committed against women. A fresh campaign was launched by women's organizations against violence against women.

In May 1984 an action committee of six organizations was formed in Lahore and it announced a plan of action in a joint press conference. The plan included representatives of various organizations visiting the scenes of crimes and meeting women victims in order to expose the inJustice emanating from a patriarchal social system as well as the weaknesses inherent in the existing and proposed laws; and observing 27 May as a Black Day for women. The campaign culminated in a demonstration in Lahore in which families of victims participated.

In Karachi women's organizations made similar efforts, including a silent picket organized by the WAF chapter. The issue became a national one, with people from all sections of society expressing their opinions on it.

Women's organizations were indeed surprised when, barely a week after their campaign, the Ordinance against crimes was passed. It provides for the death penalty or life imprisonment for assaulting or using criminal force against a woman, to strip her naked and in that condition expose her to the public. The Ordinance did not apply if the women were beaten up, stripped naked , raped or killed within the confines of the house: only in public. That it was a response to the nationwide agitation is quite obvious. To make a law on a specific crime is perhaps unprecedented in the history of law-making, and its promulgation was no more than a pacifying gesture to agitating women.

Most women's organizations received the Ordinance with a feeling of elation, for it was seen as being the result of their efforts. Some even hailed it, and members of some organizations, including the breakaway faction of WAF in Lahore, appeared on TV during prime viewing time (the national news) to express their satisfaction with the measures. The original chapter of WAF in Lahore, however, saw it as a ploy by the government to silence women and acquire a fair and sympathetic image for itself.

In a resolution passed on 5 June WAF (National) in Lahore declared that the Ordinance:

> Was a hasty response of the government.. As a reaction it is aimed primarily at pacifying women and women's organizations with what appears to be strong measures. The Ordinance... will only apply to those who parade women naked in public and does not apply to the vast majority of crimes which take place within the *chador* and *chardewari*.. crimes against women are intrinsically linked with their low staus in society.
>
> ....if the government is really concerned ... it should stop proposing laws which legally reduce women to half human beings ...as women are treated as man's property worth half a man's life.

According to WAF (National) the solution lay not in passing ordinances which would however be implemented, but by making the authorities directly accountable for such crimes in the areas under heir jurisdiction, and in promoting women's right and increasing their status in society so that they were no longer used as pawns in disputes between men.

The in effectiveness of the law and the false expectations of deterrence from it was demonstrated by the fact that there was no visible decrease in the incidence or severity of reported crime. Even those involved in the Nawabpur incident were not sentenced to the punishment prescribed in the Ordinance, in spite of the fact that there were innumerable witnesses to the event. It amounted to yet another instance of a measure taken for political exigency.

Ansari Commission's Report

The Ansari Commission was appointed by General Zia on 10 July 1983 and assigned the task of examining the recommendations made by previously-formed committees (Cabinet Sub-Committee, Special Committee of the Majlis-e-Shoora and CII) and to submit viable proposals regarding the system of government. The Commission, composed of 19 members besides the Chairman. Muhammad Zafar Ahmad Ansari, was given three weeks in which to prepare its report. It was a time when agitation in Sind was brewing and Zia, aware of people's restlessness, had promised to announce the framework of the future political set up by 14 August 1983 (Pakistan's Independence Day). Hence the pressure for a quick set of recommendations. Why yet another commission was needed when three committees had already given proposals defied logical explanation.

The Commission finished and submitted its report to the President on 4 August with a dissenting note from Justice (Retd.) Muhammad Gul. It felt that it had succeeded in making proposals in conformity with the injunctions of the Quran and *Sunnah,* and that a truly Islamic state would come into existence if the proposals were adopted as a whole and together. The recommendations covered the entire ambit of political life—the organizational set-up of the State, elections, political parties, judiciary, provincial administration, etc. A number of the recommendations can be faulted, but only the provisions affecting women fall within the scope of this study and will be reviewed here.

The women's organizations' stongest reservation has been about the provision whereby the office of *Amir-e-Mumlakat* (head of state) is closed for women. Chapter II, Clause 5 of the report states that the *amir* should be Muslim and male . Since in the Commission's opinion a female head of state was un-Islamic the protest cited instances from Muslim history and pointed to the spirit of equality and Justice inherent in Islam. The women posited that by excluding women, not only was the commission going against Islamic injunctions, but also being discriminatory. The dissenting opinion of (retd.) Justice Gul says as much.

The second – most-objected-to recommendation is about women's membership in the Majlis-e-Shoora (elected assembly) contained in Chapter III, Clause II. Besides the qualifications prescribed for all Muslim members of the Shoora, additional conditions are suggested for women. These rquire women candidates to be not less than 50 years of age and have the written permission of husbands if they are alive. After fulfilling these qualifications women would be considered eligible to contest election for any general sea.[16]

Restricting women's eligibility to just ten years less than the official retirement age, double that of the age eligibility of men, and making it mandatory to get written permission from husbands, was viewed by women as adding insult to injury. Such a measure would imply token representation of women, besides denying them the right to make decisions about themselves. In other words institutionalizing the dependence relationship between husbands and wives.

The Commission also recommended the establishment of a separate women's university. Women activists, who viewed government measures regarding women as efforts at petrifying their position in society, opposed this suggestion. The Ansari Commission's Report was thus viewed as yet another sinister move to deprive women of their political rights after having reduced their position legally.

Subsequently, when on 13 August 1983 General Zia announced the political framework for the Islamic system to be introduced in Pakistan, several of the recommendations of the Ansari Commission were adopted, e.g., non-party elections, more powers for the Head of State, raising the number of women's reserved seats to 5 per cent of the House, etc. But those restricting women's participation in elections were ignored. Whether this was in recognition of the objective reality of the election having been promised and the political expediency of avoiding alienating almost half the electorate, or a result of women's agitation is not quite certain. In all probability political expediency was the deciding factor. This was amply proved during the referendum for Zia's continuation as President in December 1984. Zia made a special appeal to women for their vote and ordered special arrangements to facilitate the voting process for them. The local T.V. repeatedly showed female polling booths with women lined up to exercise their right of franchise.[17]

1985 Onwards

In December 1985, Zia-ul-Haq officially lifted martial law, reviving political parties. To the dismay of optimists who had hoped for a transfer of power, he clarfied that 'the present democratic system that began this year is not a rival to its predecessor (martial law) but a continuation of it.[18]

In 1985 the political environment had witnessed a change. For one, elections to the national and provincial Assemblies were held in February. The Senate (upper house) had been indirectly elected, having no women members, and nor reserved seats for women. The number of women's seats was raised to 20 in the National Assembly. For the first time 13 women contested the general N.A. seats (though only one—Syeda Abida Hussain of Jhang—was successful and two women were elected to general seats to the Punjab provincial Assembly (for the Sind Assembly, Gulnar Unnar, challenging the local pir, lost by a very narrow margin). This was in stark contrast to the 1977 general elections when Nasim Wali Khan was the only woman to contest and be returned on general seat.[19] Also in 1985, by a remarkable innovation in parliamentary practice a majority of those elected on a non-party basis to the Assemblies declared themselves to be the Official Parliamentary Group. Showing equal ingenuity in 1986, the O.P.G then appropriated one of the Pakistan Muslim League factions (Pagara group) after the lifting of martial law.

The revival of political activities had its impact on the women's movement. Attention shifted away from women's issues, and an apparent respite from the persistent attack on women's rights lulled activists into a false sense of security. Additionally, women who had been under relentless pressure found themselves exhausted, encumbered by petty rivalries (often over-shadowing the real issues) and with slackness seeping through their ranks. As a consequence the Eighth Constitutional Amendment Bill evoked only belated protest resolutions, despite its serious implications.[20] The Bill, passed in October 1985, indemnifies and validates all the ordinances and laws promulgated by the military regime, and has rendered the Hudood Ordinance and the Law of Evidence unchallengeable in any court of law.[21]

The repercussions of this brief lapse of attention reactivated women's organizations, which were then better prepared to counter the Ninth Constitutional Amendment and Shariat Bills. The latter was moved in the Senate in July 1985 by two private members belonging to the Jamaat-e-Islami. Providing for the Qu'an and Sunnah as the main source of Shariat, the Shariat Bill further seeks to establish the supremacy of one Muslim Sunni sect, the Hanafis, and the hegemony of a particular group of 'recognized *ulema*' who would be appointed to the courts. There would be no court of appeal against a judgement of the *shariat* courts which would have jurisdiction over all matters, undermining the powers of the legislature. To preempt the passage of the Shariat Bill the Muslim League Government moved the Ninth Amendment Bill in the Senate, and in July 1986 it was passed by the Senate. The basic difference in the two bills is that the Government-sponsored bill exempts economic and fiscal matters from the purview of the Shariat courts and lays less emphasis on the role and powers of the *ulema*.

For women, both bills are equally detrimental. They endanger the Child Marriage Restraint Act (1929), the Dissolution of Muslim Marriages Act (1939) and the Family Laws Ordinance (1961). The Constitutional protection given to these laws will be removed by the passage of the Ninth Amendment Bill, making each challengeable in the Federal Shariat Court. The negative ramifications of both bills have been raised by women's organizations in their campaign to mobilize support against them since late 1985.

Women have not been alone in rejecting the Shariat Bill. The important Shiah minority, other Muslim groups and all the major political parties except the Jamaat-e-Islami have also opposed it. Apart from the imposition of a particular school of Muslim jurisprudence the main concern has been the danger of sectarian clashes that could be triggered off by the adoption of the bill.[22] The Ninth Amendment has not faced such wide ranging opposition and apart from women's organizations, only the more educated and secular sections of society and the secular political parties have spoken out against it.

To sum up, clearly the government's legal and political measures all have negative implications for women. The enactment of the above discussed legislation in reality gives statutory sanction to the entrenchment of age-old social discrimination and repression of women. Laws influence and shape social attitudes. If the government displays discrimination towards a section of society it strengthens the forces opposed to that section. In Pakistan the obscurantist/male chauvinist has found strength from the laws being promulgated and proposed in the name of Islam.

Women's resistance has, therefore, focused primarily on the un-Islamic content and implications of the laws. While humanitarian arguments as well as those based on the principles of the UN Charter (to which Pakistan is a signatory) have been used, women and women's organizations have felt that justification within the framework of Islam has more weight. Women have found supporters from among the enlightened and educated male scholars and lawyers. In the course of their struggle women have realized that political expediency is at the root of government policies and have therefore tried to expose the hypocrisy of intent in government measures.

When talking of women's resistance the presence of women vocally supportive of government measures should not be ignored. Generally, belonging to the women's faction of Jamaat-e-Islami or its student wing, these women have attacked the progressive women's lobby with venom and have exhibited the kind of demagogy associated with the fanatical Islamicists.

The most recent example of this was in May 1986 when a female MNA of the Jamat-e-Islami, Nisar Fatima, launched a vitriolic attack against a WAF member, Asma Jehangir, from the floor of the Assembly and used this as an excuse to demand a ban of WAF. On the basis of hearsay she accused Asma Jehangir of having cast aspersions on the prophet during a seminar on the proposed Ninth Amendment Bill, organized by WAF Islamabad on 17 May 1986. She further alleged that WAF was a platform for anti-Islamabad on 17 May 1986. She further alleged that WAF was a platform for anti -Islamic activities. Although this did not have the desired effect, it was part of the jamat's campaign for speeding up the passage of the Shariat Bill.[23]

The Facets of the Women of Pakistan

The Pakistani society is one of a kind. Where on one side it places women as the centre of attention and life, it then on the other considers them no more than secondary citizens.

For years the role that a woman played as a citizen, a member of the family, or a homemaker has been highly undermined and today it has turned into a tradition to degrade a woman's ability. However, over the years this scenario has changed, and the awareness of her abilities, her rights and her status has reached almost all parts of Pakistan, which is an underdeveloped third world country. Pakistan was formed on the basis of the Two-Nation theory, which emphasised Islamic teachings and values, and is therefore called the Islamic Republic of Pakistan.

Islam gives the best and the most balanced code of life, but pseudo-fundamentalists converted the teachings of Islam to read in the best interests of men and highly unjust towards women. Despite this the woman of Pakistan has come a long way in proving herself.

There are many faces of the woman of Pakistan. In the rural areas of Frontier of the villages of Sindh, she lives with the identity of either the mother of the future feudal lord, wife, daughter or sister of the feudal. Since the day she is born, she is to live with the individuality of another individual, which has to be a man related to her. In fact, it maybe considered quite uncomely for a woman to live with her own individuality. This then leads to situations where the woman has to kill all her feelings, desires and even her own thoughts to survive, as they put it, 'with honour'.

The rural areas of the country witness instances where feudal lords have numerous wives, incorrectly using the logic of Islam that a man is allowed four marriages. What they tend to ignore is that the marriages are allowed under specific circumstances: to widows, divorcees, etc.

Religion has been exploited at the hands of the men for years now, and the women have learned to submit to their whims and decisions. But the past did see cites like 'Marvi' in the rural Sindh, who fought all feudal laws to get education in a University. The feudals are actually scared of their rights as wives, sisters and above all, as women.

There is no escape for the women still in many parts of the country from this unspoken imprisonment they face, in which all decisions about them and themselves are made by their custodians, who may be their father, brother or their husbands. No one cares to find out what they want in life, or about their ideas or thoughts.

There may be another aspect to this also : that is the protection that the woman enjoys being the one who is never thought of to go out to handle trade or business. It is implied that the men of her house will always be responsible to provide for her, and give her every luxury in life. They are such queens that even imagining work is not allowed. But is this protection that keeps them unaware of their own identities and strength a blessing or is it a curse?

The real women are not these princesses, but the women in the form of the wife of the indigent farmer, or the daughter of the old man who is still working so hard to provide for his huge family. She is born with three sisters and is never expected to study, but just prepared since childhood that she just has to learn to cook and clean to take care of her future husband, who may be the age of her father. It is implied that her parents may not have a choice, as they are in a state of destitution and she is a burden on them who has to be taken in by another man.

It shouldn't matter if she is his third or fourth wife, if she likes him or not, what to talk of love! And like this many girls are born and raised as the fairer sex in Pakistan. The day of a woman in the village of this country may involve raising her kids, cooking food, and in many places where no electricity and gas is still not there she walks miles to cut wood from jungles, fetch water from rivers and wells, submit to the needs of her husband as he wishes, manage the home and be happy in whatever meager amount of money she is given. What she learns is to be happy as what she is and not ever exploring her own wishes.

The Situation Women in Pakistan

"No nation can rise to the height of glory unless your women are side by side with you; we are victims of evil customs. It is a crime against humanity that our women are shut up within the four walls of the houses as prisoners. There is no sanction anywhere for the deplorable condition in which our women have to live."

Mohammad Ali Jinnah, 1994

(taken from the US Library of Congress report "Pakistan-A Country Study")

Men, Women, and the Division of Space

Gender relations in Pakistan rest on two basic perceptions: that women are subordinate to men, and that a man's honour resides in the actions of the women of his family. Thus, as in other orthodox Muslim societies, women are responsible for maintaining the family honour. To ensure that they do not dishonour their families, society limits women's mobility, places restrictions on their behaviour and activities, and permits them only limited contact with the opposite sex. Space is allocated to and used differently by men and women. For their protection and respectability, women have traditionally been expected to live under the constraints of Purdah (purdah is Persian for curtain), most obvious in veiling. By separating women from the activities of men, both physically and symbiotically, purdah creates differentiated male and female spheres. Most women spend the major part of their lives physically within their homes and courtyards and go out only for serious and approved reasons. Outside the home, social life generally revolves around the activities of men. In most parts of the country, except perhaps in Islamabad, Karachi, and wealthier parts of a few other cities, people consider a woman — and her family — to be shameless if no restrictions are places on her mobility.

Purdah is practiced in various ways, depending on family tradition, region, class, and rural or urban residence, but nowhere do unrelated men and women mix freely. The most extreme restraint are found in parts of the North-West Frontier Province and Balochistan, where women almost never leave their homes except when they marry and almost never meet unrelated men. They may not be allowed contact with male cousins on their mother's side, for these men are not classed as relatives in a strongly patrilineal society. Similarly, they have only very formal relations with those men they are allowed to meet, such as the father-in-law, paternal uncles, and brothers-in-law.

Poor rural women, especially in Punjab and Sindh, where gender relations are generally somewhat more relaxed, have greater mobility because they are responsible for transplanting rice seedlings, weeding crops, raising chickens and selling eggs, and stuffing wool or cotton into comforters (razais) . When a family becomes more prosperous and begins to aspire to higher status, it commonly requires stricter purdah among its women as a first social change.

Poor urban women in close-knit communities, such as the old cities of Lahore and Rawalpindi, generally wear either a burqa (fitted body veil) or a *chador* (loosely draped cotton cloth used as a head covering and body veil) when they leave their homes. In these localities, multistory dwellings (*havelis*) were constructed to accommodate large extended families. May *havelis* have now been sectioned off into smaller living units to economize. It is common for one nuclear family (with an average of seven members) to live in one or two rooms on each small floor. In less densely populated areas, where people generally do not know their neighbours, there are fewer restrictions on women's mobility. The shared understanding that women should remain within their homes so neighbours do not gossip about their respectability has important implications for their productive activities. As with public life in general, work appears to be the domain of men. Rural women work for consumption or for exchange at the subsistence level. Others, both rural and urban, do piecework for very low wages in their homes. Their earnings are generally recorded as part of the family income that is credited to men. Census data and other accounts of economic activity in urban areas support such conclusions. For example, the 1981 census reported that 5.6 per cent of all women were employed, as opposed to 72.4 per cent of men; less than 4 per cent of all urban women were engaged in some form of salaried work. By 1988 this figure had increased significantly, but still only 10.2 per cent women were reported as participating in the labour force.

Among wealthier Pakistanis, urban or rural residence is less important than family tradition in influencing whether women observe strict purdah and the type of veil they wear. In some areas, women simply observe 'eye purdah": they tend not to mix with men, but when they do, they avert their eyes when interacting with them. Bazaars in wealthier areas of Punjabi cities differ from those in poorer areas by having a greater proportion unveiled women. In cities throughout the North-West Frontier Province, Balochistan, and the interior of Sindh, bazaars are markedly devoid of women, and when a woman does venture forth, she always wears some sort of veil.

The traditional division of space between the sexes is perpetuated in the broadcast media. Women's subservience is consistently shown on television and in films. And, although popular television dramas raise controversial issues such as women working, seeking divorce, or even having a say in family politics, the programmes often suggest that the woman who strays from traditional norms faces insurmountable problems and becomes alienated from her family.

The Status of Women and the Women's Movement

Four important challenges confronted women in Pakistan in the early 1990s : increasing practical literacy, gaining access to employment opportunities at all levels in the economy, promoting change in the perception of women's roles and status, and gaining a public voice both within and outside of the political process. There have been various attempts at social and legal reform aimed at improving Muslim women's lives in the subcontinent during the twentieth century. These attempts generally have been related to two broader, intertwined movements : the social reform movement in British India and the growing Muslim nationalist movement. Since partition, the changing status of women in Pakistan largely has been linked with discourse about the role of Islam in a modern state. This debate concerns the extent to which civil rights common in most western democracies are appropriate in an Islamic society and the way these rights should be reconciled with Islamic family law.

Muslim reformers in the nineteenth century struggled to introduce female education, to ease some of the restrictions on women's activities, to limit polygyny, and to ensure women's rights under Islamic law. Sir Syed Ahmad Khan convened the Mohammedan Educational conference in the 1870s to promote modern education for Muslims, and he founded the Muhammadan Anglo-Oriental College. Among the predominantly male participants were many of the earliest proponents of education and improved social status for women. They advocated cooking and sewing classes conducted in a religious framework to advance women's knowledge and skills and to reinforce Islamic values. But progress in women's literacy was slow: by 1921 only four out of every 1,000 Muslim females were literate.

Promoting the education of women was a first step in moving beyond the constraints imposed by *purdah.* The nationalist struggle helped fray the threads in that socially imposed curtain. Simultaneously women's roles were questioned, and their empowerment was linked to the larger issues of nationalism and independence. In 1937 the Muslim Personal Law restored rights (such as inheritance of property) that had been lost by women under the Anglicization of certain civil laws. As independence neared, it appeared that the state would give priority to empowering women. Pakistan's founding father, Mohammad Ali Jinnah, said in a speech in 1944:

> No nation can rise to the height of glory unless your women are side by side with you, we are victims of evil customs. It is a crime against humanity that our women are shut up within the four walls of the houses as prisoners. There is no sanction anywhere for the deplorable condition in which our women have to live.

After independence, elite Muslim women in Pakistan continued to advocate women's political empowerment through legal reforms. They mobilized support than led to passage of the Muslim Personal Law of Sharia in 1948 , which recognized a woman's right to inherit all forms of property. They were also behind the futile attempt have the government include a Charter of Women's Rights in the 1956 constitution. The 1961 Muslim Family Laws Ordinance covering marriage and divorce, the most important sociolegal reform that they supported, is still widely regarded as empowering to women.

Two issues—promotion of women's political representation and accommodation between Muslim family law and democratic civil rights—came to dominate discourse about women and socio-legal reform. The second issue gained considerable attention during the regime of Zia ul- Haq (1977-88) . Urban women formed groups to protect their rights against apparent discrimination under Zia's Islamization programme. It was in the highly visible realm of law that women were able to articulate their objections to the Islamization programme initiated by the government in 1979. Protests against the 1979 Enforcement of Hudood Ordinances focused on the failure of Hudood Ordinances to distinguish between adultery (*zina*) and rape (*zina-bil-jabr*). A man could be convicted of *zina* only if he were actually observed committing the offense by other men, but a woman could be convicted simply because she became pregnant. The Women's Action Forum was formed in 1981 to respond to the implementation of the penal code and to strengthen women's position in society generally. The women in the forum most of whom came from elite families, perceived that may of the laws proposed by the Zia government were discriminatory and would compromise their civil status. In Karachi, Lahore, and Islamabad the group agreed on collective leadership and formulated policy statements and engaged in political action to safeguard women's legal position.

The Women's Action Forum has played a central role in exposing the controversy regarding various interpretations of Islamic law and its role in modern state, and in publicizing ways in which women can play a more active role in politics. Its members led public protests in the mid-1980s against the promulgation of the Law of Evidence. Although the final version was substantially modified, the Women's Action Forum objected to the legislation because it gave unequal weight to testimony by men and women in financial cases. Fundamentally, they objected to the assertion that women and men cannot participate as legal equals in economic affairs.

Beginning in August 1986, the Women's Action Forum members and their supporters led a debate over passage of the Shariat Bill, which decreed that all laws in Pakistan should conform to Islamic law. They argued that the law would undermine the principles of Justice, democracy, and fundamental rights of citizens, and they pointed out that Islamic law would become identified solely with the conservative interpretation supported by Zia's government. Most activists felt that the Shariat Bill had the potential to negate many of the rights women had won. In May 1991, a compromise version of the Shariat Bill was adopted, but the debate over whether civil law or Islamic law should prevail in the country continued in the early 1990s.

Discourse about the position of women in Islam and women's roles in a modern Islamic state was sparked by the government's attempts to formalize a specific interpreting of Islamic law. Although the issue of evidence became central to the concern for women's legal status, more mundane matters such as mandatory dress codes for women and whether females could compete in international sports competitions were also being argued.

Another of the challenges faced by Pakistani women concerns their integration into the labour force. Because of economic pressures and the dissolution of extended families in urban areas, many more women are working for wages than in the past. But by 1990 females officially made up only 13 per cent of the labour force. Restrictions on their mobility limit their opportunities, and traditional notions of propriety lead families to conceal the extent of work performed by women.

Usually, only the poorest women engage in work—often as midwives, sweepers, or nannies—for compensation outside the home. More often, poor urban women remain at home and sell manufactured goods to a middleman for compensation. More and more urban women have engaged in such activities during the 1990s, although to avoid being shamed few families willingly admit that women contribute to the family economically. Hence, there is little information about the work women do. On the basis of the predominant fiction that most women do no work other than their domestic chores, the government has been hesitant to adopt overt policies to increase women's employment options and to provide legal support for women's labour force participation.

The United Nations Children's Fund (UNICEF) commissioned a national study in 1992 on women's economic activity to enable policy planners and donor agencies to cut through the existing myths on female labour-force participation. The study addresses the specific reasons that the assessment of women's work in Pakistan is filled with discrepancies and undernumeration and provides a comprehensive discussion of the range of informal-sector work performed by women throughout the country. Information from this study was also incorporated into the Eighth Five-Year Plan (1993-98).

A melding of the traditional social welfare activities of the women's movement and its newly revised political activism appears to have occurred. Diverse groups including the Women's Action Forum, the All-Pakistan Women's Association, the Pakistan women Lawyers' Association, and the Business and Professional Women's Association, are supporting small-scale projects throughout the country that focus on employing women. They have been involved in such activities as instituting legal aid for indigent Women, opposing the gendered segregation of universities, and publicizing and condemning the growing incidents of violence against women. The Pakistan Women Lawyers' Association has released a series of films educating women about their legal rights; the Business and Professional Women's Association is supporting a comprehensive project inside Yakki Gate, a poor area inside the walled city of Lahore; and the Orangi Pilot Project in Karachi has promoted networks among women who work at home so they need not be dependent on middlemen to acquire raw materials and market the clothes they produce.

The women's movement has shifted from reacting to government legislation to focusing on three primary goals: securing women's political representation in the National Assembly; working to raise women's consciousness, particularly about family planning; and countering suppression of women's rights by defining and articulating positions on events as they occur in order to raise public awareness. An as yet unresolved issue concerns the perpetuation of a set number of seats for women in the National Assembly. Many women activists whose expectations were raises during the brief tenure of Benazir Bhutto's first government (December 1988-August 1990) now believe that, with her return to power in October 1993, they can seize the initiative to bring about a shift in women's personal and public access to power. Data as of April 1994.

Feminist Movement and Urdu Literature

Feminist consciousness is emerging as a spirit of the age and has become a global trend. No doubt, in the beginning it was an individual trend, but it has now become a movement or school-of-thought popular among the writers of modern sensibility. By feminist consciousness, we mean an awareness of modern movement in this male-governed society where all values are male-oriented. Howerver, at present, women don't allow the continuation of the male-governed system of values. Women are as free and independent as men, and this new cultural trend is becoming a philosophical standpoint of women.

Feminist thinkers have been divided into two parts; one is the Anglo-American woman thinker who regards women as creative and equal contributors of values. The other thinkers belong to the French tradition and are radical and revolutionary in their approach and style of thinking. According to them, writing is an independent mental activity and male critics cannot discover the reality of the women's world. Gynocriticism is an entirely original and absolutely independent mental activity.

The feminist movement was initiated in the western world and at present, the entire cultural world seems to be in its grip or trend of thought. English novelist, Virginia Woolfe, was not the first writer of the feminist novel. Earlier, Henrick Ibsen, the well-known playwright, wrote *A Doll's House* in which Dora was presented as bewildered, hurt and victimized by the male attitude. Recently, the DHA College for Women staged the play successfully. It was produced by Seema Afridi for the benefit of the students of English literature. It is regarded as the first feminist play written by Henrick Ibsen.

Virginia Woolfe in her well-known writing, *A Room of One's Own*, presented feminist consciousness initally, that is a historical document, French feminist novelist and thinker, Simon de Beauvoir and her philosophical treatise entitled the Second Sex, is regarded as the first great achievement by women writers. It is a philosophical work explaining the situation in which a woman does not enjoy independent status and is thus deprived of the right to think, feel and express independently. Moreover, she explains the complicated phenomenon of ' bad faith' as presented by Jean Paul Sartre in his monumental work, *Being And Nothingness.*

At present, Julia Kristeva, Luce Irigaray and Helene Cixous have appeared on the horizon of feminist consciousness. They have extended the area of feminist thinking in the right direction. Julia Kristeva's work is more philosophical and deals with in-depth feminist problems. She was inspired by Lacan, known as the French

Freud. Kristeva's thesis is a female version of the Lacanian school-of-thought; both are post-Modern thinkers and contributors in feminist philosophical culture.

The essence of the feminist movement is gynocriticism. The term was coined by Ellen Showalter to describe the writings of women that is novel, poetry, drama, essays, letters and journals edited by women. Gynocritical studies deal with female imagination, feminist language and the experience of women expressed in literature. Julia Kristeva, the author of *Language And Desire*; Luce Irigaray, author of *Speculum of the other Woman* and Helene Cixous, author of *The Newly-Born Woman* have discovered new dimensions in the feminist culture. The whole movement of feminism, feminist theory and criticism has been the rediscovery of a hidden tradition of women's writing and the rediscovery and republication of a number of novels and other works by women. In particular, three publishing houses (Virago) Pandora and the Women's Press) have played a vital role in the publication of women's literature, thus popularizing the feminist movement throughout the world.

Like other parts of the world, educated Pakistani women are also fully aware of their rights and the problems faced by them. Urdu literature is becoming richer by women's writings and enjoys a certain amount of freedom of expression in this segregated society. The history of women's writing in Urdu literature is not a recent phenomenon. It started in the poetic compositions of different women—right from Malaya Chanda Bai to recent times.

Prominent and talented women are responsible for establishing the women's style of writing and traditions of the female mode of expression such as Bilquis Jamal, Rabia Pinha, Kaneez Fatima, Safia Shamim Malihabadi and Z.K. Sheen. Recently, Ada Jafri, a prominent poetess, has contributed a lot to women's literature. Qazi Abdul Ghaffar, in his introduction to Ada Jafri's collection of verses, particularly mentioned her name in the field of the feminist way of expression. She is a highly-talented and conscious artist, who has popularized female sensibilities by expressing their sentiments and problems.

Ada was born in a traditional society where women were not allowed to think and express independently, but she was bold enough to express herself without inhibitions. Her individuality is not without social consciousness. She makes herself invisible from the art of poetic construction. Her personality is absent from her poetry. Her early life was spent in jealously-guarded boundaries. Naturally, tradition was ingrained in her personality, but her individual talent could not surrender itself completely and she started taking interest in the rebellious world of modern art. For me, she is genuinely modern sensibility. This unification of modern and traditional sensibility makes her significant for both the schools of thought. Her emotional depth finds expression in her poetry of unified sensibility. The expressive value of her poetic art makes her a prominent figure in contemporary Urdu literature. But Ada Jafri could not resolve the conflict between tradition and modern sensibilities, and both trends weave themselves into her poetic art.

Fehmida Riaz is the Farough Farrukh Zad of Urdu poetry. She enjoys more freedom of expression and strongly believes in it. She is a feminist and an activist. Her relationship with society is deep and inspired by the Marxian theory of gender conflict, class conflict and the Freudian view of men and women struggling against the imposed morality of the bourgeois class. She expresses her female sentiments without inhibitions and unnecessary reservations.

Badan Darida, her collection of verses, is considered a milestone in the development of feminist thought in Urdu poetry . In her other collection of verses, she has gained maturity and a more harmonious mode of expression. The female imagination in Urdu poetry culminates in Fehmida Riyaz. At present, she is the best feminist writer and will be considered a trend setter in feminist literature.

Kishwar Naheed is also a devoted feminist writer. The Second Sex by Simon de Beauvoir is a difficult feminist discourse, but Kishwar Naheed has translated it into Urdu and it has been a source of inspiration for feminist writers. Recently, she has edited an anthology of women's literature, with Khalida Hussain, Asif Furrukhi and Nighat Saleem as co-editors. It was published by the Academy Of Letters headed by Iftikhar Arif. The selection made by them lacks some important names in the history of feminism thought, such as Julia Kristeva and Luce Irigaray who are post-Modern thinkers of the movement.

Kristeva deserves a separate chapter for understanding her philosophical views about womanhood and female language. She is basically a follower of Lacan and his psychoanalytical approach. Mirrorstage and symbolic order are the basic concepts of Kristeva's school-of-thought. Luce Irigaray is also a post-Modern thinker of the movement and this anthology is neither complete nor comprehensive. I think they have not been deliberately ignored, but because of the limitations of the editorial committee. The selection of literature shows the carelessness of the committee.

Perveen Shakir is not a well-known prose poem writer. She was basically a ghazal writer. Her work is extraordinary and should have been selected by the committee to represent Perveen's genuine art. On the contrary, well-known prose poem writers have been ignored by editors such as Azra Abbas, Fatima Hasan, Shaista Habib, Nasreen Anjum Bhatti, Sara Shagufta, Seema Khan Orakzia and others.

However, the selection rightly deserves appreciation and I hope the members of the editorial committee will include the forgotten chapters of feminist thought and the Academy of Letters also will pay due attention while making the selection of feminist literature. The gynocritical studies should have been included in the anthology.

Women Changing Lives : Belquis Ahmadi

(March 7, 2003 Belquis Ahmadi was the tender age of seven when the Soviets invaded her home country of Afghanistan. It was her first encounter with war and as she said in an interview network, "I did not know what war was but I became scared."

Conflict remained in the background for those living in Afghanistan during that time and, of course something positive resulted in this regard which inspired Ahmadi to take the lead.

One of the exercises that made an indelible impression and inspired her to become more involved in trying to make a change was her work at the International Committee of the Red Cross (ICRC) in Kabul in its war wounded surgical hospital. "Through my work at the surgical hospital, I was witness to the most horrifying crimes during war and disrespect for the rights of human beings," Ahmadi noted. "Again, women were the most to suffer from all of the ethnic clashes and men-imposed war and crimes." In addition to the desire to combat the injustice around her, Ahmadi found advocacy work energizing because of the challenge it creates. "I like challenges, and working in the field of human rights, particularly women's rights, is definitely a continued challenge."

Prior to working with IHRLG, Ahmadi was the program manager for the Women's Affairs department at the Agency Coordinating Body for Afghan Relief in Peshawar, Pakistan, which is an umberella organization that facilitates negotiations between the Pakistan and Afghanistan Governments and over 70 Afghan and international NGOs, and the office manager for CARE-International's Afghanistan office.

Making a Dream Reality

But her most challenging work came during the most challenging period of her life. In 1996, after the Taliban took over Kabul, Ahmadi co-founded the Afghan Women's Network in Kabul with one of her female law school professors. The future of the organization became questionable as later in the year, she became a refugee in Pakistan. "As a young woman and a new refugee, I was not welcomed by the Afghan women's groups in Peshawar when I presented idea of re-establishing a network of Afghan women, "reminisced Ahmadi. "Only days after I started working in the refugee community I felt the need for bringing different groups of women together to jointly tackle issues related to women's rights and interests.

Unlike in Kabul, there existed a significant number of women's groups and NGOs in the refugee communities. However, there was less cooperation among them. As soon as I saw this lack of cooperation and coordination among the groups I decided to re-establish the Afghan Women's Network. It took a lot of effort and patience to accomplish my goal and my dreams of seeing women from different backgrounds work together and jointly advocate for women's rights.

"When I left Pakistan in 1999, the Network had around 70 members. Today the Network has more than 500 members and it is consulted in every major decision making process at national, regional and international levels. " As one of ten prominent women's activists, Ahmadi was selected as a delegate in last year's loya jirga in Afghanistan, which was a gathering of over 1000 elected delegates to help determine the new Afghan government.

Ahmadi does not take full credit for the creation of such a dynamic organization and pointed to those who surrounded her as additional driving forces. "There were times that I was ready to quit, but my determination as well as the support I received from my family, friends and members of the network helped me stay focused on my goal and on my dreams."

Women in Pakistan -Victims of the Social and Economic Desecration

The South Asian subcontinent is the least gender sensitive region in the world. It is the only region in the world where men outnumber women. The sex ratio is 105-7 men to every 100 women. In Pakistan, women are not only subjected to financial discrimination, but they are also victims of inhuman customs and laws such as Karo Kari, Hadood ordinance, Qasas and marriage to the Quran and half witnesses according to the state law (whereby in court a female witness is only worth half a male witness).

In the rural areas, women are like slaves subject to drudgery. They are there just to obey their fathers, brothers and husbands. They do not have the right to decide about themselves because women are considered as foolish creatures according to the dominant social and cultural norms. Likewise marriage is also a sort of trade between different families both in the rural and urban areas. They are highly vulnerable to violation of their rights to life.

Woman's right to liberty is restricted in the name of modesty, protection and prevention of immoral activity. In rural areas 90 per cent of women work in the fields. They work for the whole day with their male family members, but they still have to face their wrath. Male family members keep a strict eye on the female family members in the name of "honour". But one must undersand the meaning of henour because in our society honour does not have the meaning of its true sense. Here it really means possession of women as a form of property. Not only are the restrictions of women's liberty maintained in the name of this honour (ghairat) but they also can be part to death if they lose their "honour".

Karo Kari is the form of honour killings. Last year 286 women were murdered in the name of honour by the male family members (and these are only the registered cases). On 11th June 2000, four women and one man were killed in the Dera Jamali village in Sindh. Last year on the same dates a 13 year old girl, Sara, was subjected to this honour killing in Goth Khosa. Two young boys Imtiaz and Arshad were also killed in the same case. The boys had never met the young girl in their lives. But the brother of Sara declared it an honour killing to get less punishment in law. This law also gives some leniency to the killers in such cases. He actually wanted to grab the land of these boys and used this accusation to kill the boys along with his sister.

In the village of Moratha there was a case of Karo Kari (honour killing). The motive of the killing was that the murderer wanted to marry a married woman. He killed the husband of that woman and his own innocent sister and he was released from jail after a few months.

Many of the cases of Karo Kari are related to love marriage. Recently a woman with her little child of five months, husband and four other members of her in-laws, was killed because she had committed the crime of love marriage. Most of the women in Pakistan are not allowed to marry a person of their choice.

There are hundreds of such cases, that are not registered. But if we go to the root cause of these honour killings we see that they are linked to the question of land, water, money and property. But again, only the women of the poor classes are victims of this inhuman custom of Karo Kari. This custom is seldom implemented against rich women.

In the Punjab brothers, fathers and hubands subject 82 per cent of women to domestic violence. The incidence of wife-battering is so common that it is not even recognised as a pernicious form of violence against women. Even in the cases where women receive serious injuries and want to file complaints, they are advised by the police to reconcile with their husbands, as any matrimonial dispute would bring dishonour to them.

This violence against women begins in their childhood. They are not allowed to play games like boys that can help in their speedy mental and physical development. Another practice common in Pakistan, is cutting off a women's nose if she is suspected of having an extra-marital relationship. Sexual assult on women, including rape, remains one of the most common crimes. The Human Rights Commission estimated that rape occurs every three hours. No estimate, however, can be made of the numerous cases that go unreported.

The Islamic Penal Law "Hadood Ordinance" repealed the provisions of the Pakistan Penal Code related to rape cases, in 1979. The Islamic Law of evidence applicable to cases of rape requires the evidence of four adult male Muslims, in order for the penalty of hadood to be imposed upon the accused. Being a half witness by law the raped woman can't even testify against the crime committed against her. According to these laws, testimony of the victim requires strong corroboration for conviction by the court. On the other hand, where sexual intercourse is established but the absence of consent cannot be proved, the presumption that such intercourse occurred with the woman's consent can place her at the risk of prosecution. In both cases, adultery or rape, a woman is kept in jail pending the ruling of the court. 52 per cent of women languishing in the jails of

Pakistan are waiting for their face in these cases. In the case of a woman marrying without the consent of her family, the marriage can be declared invalid and the couple would then be accused of the offence of *zina* (adultery).

If the women victimzed by the offenders contact the law (the police) and the other investigating agencies, the women of the oppressed classes are subject to police brutality and crimes like rape are often carried out while in custody. The incident of sexual assault on women in police custody increased after the implementation of these Islamic laws.

Another Law, "Qasas", is also used to victimize women, because under this law if a person kills somebody and the family of the victim compromises with the killer then they are paid an agreed amount of money, land and of course women by the assassin's family. Marriage to the Holy Quran (the holy book of Islam) is also common in Sindh. Under this law a woman has to live without a husband throughout her life. But this law is only applied among the class of landlords. They use this only to keep and grab the land of their sisters and daughters.

But if we look at the history of Pakistan, we find several women's movements against these criminal laws and customs. But these movements are mostly dominated by the NGOs (Non Government Organisations). And the tragedy of the NGO's is that they believe in this system, its state and its laws. They respect the judiciary as well as the state. They do not have a way out except they simply appeal to the ruling elite and their state to pass such laws that can abolish discrimination against women within society. But the oppression of women is rooted within the system itself. In ancient times the women produced food for the family. In that era women had learned how to cultivate the land. Men used to hunt only. That is why women had a particular recognition in society. And over a period of time she became the head of the family. Even goddesses outnumbered gods in religion dominant in the productive process. Thus matriarchal society, a society where women dominated, withered away. The new forms of property changed the inheritance to men and hence established male domination. After the introduction of this system of private ownership woman gradually became a commodity and hence possessed as private property. These forms developed over time and the exploitation of women continued in different patterns.

It is only with the rapid advancement of technology that want can be abolished and the psychology of dearth and greed can give way to a psychology of possession free consciousness. This will ultimately free women from bondage of domestic labour and the stigma of being inferior human beings.

At the present time capitalism has created a society of want and greed in which human beings have to live a life of cut-throat competition in order to survive. In countries like Pakistan it has also failed to bridge the gap between the rural and urban areas. It has failed to develop different regions evenly and penetrate modernity into rural sections of the population.

Basic needs such as education, health, water supply and transport, etc., are inadequate. On the other hand there is the penetration of all forms of the latest technology, like satellite television, which has distorted the patterns of social and cultural development of these are as. In villages we can see clear forms of combined and uneven development. T.V and satellite is available but tools and methods of farming are thousands of years old. These deformed patterns of development have further aggravated the lives of women in the rural areas. Social life in the countryside and the urban centres has not changed in any spectacular way. It has actually worsened. This intense social crisis manifests itself in the sharp rise in the molestation of women, gang rape and violent crimes against women, both in the rural and urban areas.

The same case applies to the third world countries where capitalism has failed to carry out any of its historical tasks. Outdated customs are still practiced and have not been eradicated. In the cities, outdated customs have much less of an influence, because of the fact that women are playing a major role in the generation of family income. They do not carry out "unpaid labour" like rural women. But they are also facing daunting challenges and problems in the cities.

Even in the advanced countries the exploitation and harassment of women on the basis of gender is rampant.

But the question arises : how long will this continue? Will the women's movements only confine themselves to mere appeals and demonstrations or will all the existent order have to change? In this system of private ownership of the means of production (i.e., capitalism), woman has been reduced to a commodity. The rottenness of the system is evident from the fact that sex has become the third largest industry in the world. The double exploitation of women cannot be understood without analyzing its historical, social and economic basis. Only then can a strategy for its eradication be devised.

The domestic labour of women, looking after the children, cleaning the house, cooking, washing and the many other forms of labour in which women are involved is a full day's work. But this system does not reward this human labour. Hence the cultural, social, moral and ethical roots of society are devised in such a manner that this system gets the labour of women in running society for free and is taken for granted. Hence this condition whereby women do not get back the product of their labour, develops a psychology of alienation. This further weakens and depresses women. Utilizing this situation the rulers of this system create laws, customs and rotten cultural traditions to further oppress women. The brutal military dictator Zia-ul Haq imposed the "Hadood Ordinance" and other anti-women black laws to further facilitate the exploitation of women by capitalism. Even a "democratic" government headed by a woman prime minister, Benazir Bhutto, could not bookish these draconian laws because they were inherent to the system and its state. These pressures upon women further diminished their will, confidence, and determination. These reactionary periods developed a defeatist psychology amongst women. To abide by the ethics of this society, they are lured into behaving as commodities with excessive use of cosmetics and make-up, with a lust for jewellery and a psychology of decoration.

These traits are then further exploited by rich men into further subjugating women and portraying them as "weaknesses" of women. Using this social insecurity, alienation and the pressures on women, the capitalists exacerbate the exploitation of women workers in the factories and mills. It has been seen in general that women work with greater dedication and more meticulously than men. For example, in Pakistan, women are 28 per cent of the total workforce yet they generate 40 per cent of production. At the same time it is a general law of capitalism that women workers are paid less than their male counterparts all around the world. For example, according to the Office of National Statistics in Britain, the average yearly income of male workers in 1999 was £23, 000 (pounds sterling) while at the same time the average wage of a female worker was £16,000 . Hence there was a difference of 42 per cent in their wage earnings. In Pakistan and the rest of the third world this situation is even worse.

At the same time the gender insensitivity is so severe that from the cradle to the grave women are forced to lead a discriminated life. There are more infant deaths among girls than among boys. Every hear 135,000 women die during childbirth in Pakistan. Only 21 per cent of women have access to medical facilities during childbirth.

The tragedy with the women's movements is that women from the upper classes, who mostly dominate them, have never had to suffer the same ordeals as the women of the oppressed classes. The adverse conditions in important sectors such as public hygiene, health and education, have a greater bearing on women of the working classes. Hence the struggle for the rights of women and their liberation have different meanings for women of different classes.

Without the overthrow of the bourgeois state and capitalist exploitation, the emancipation of working class women (who constitute the vast majority in society) is a utopia. Hence the ultimate liberation of women is linked to the class struggle of the workers of all religions, nationalists, races, sexes and colours. The ultimate destiny and victory of this struggle lies in the successs of the Socialist Revolution.

Opression of Women in Pakistan

Women comprise almost half of the population on this planet. A great majority of them are deprived of basic existing facilities of social development. They are struggling for better health care facilities, job opportunities and social Justice, equal rights in different countries all over the world. They are facing discrimination and social exploitation in different societies.

United Nations recent world "Women Conference 1995" held in Beijing last September. Its agenda was:

1. Women oppression
2. Women poverty

This conference arises many questions:

Why women are suffering, in spite of being part and parcel of the society? Why they are not provided with equal opportunities? When they will get rid of their poverty, exploitation and feel free? We think that occasional world conferences are not the solution to the problems women have been facing in the world for centuries. Practical measures are needed to liberate them from their sufferings.

In countries like Pakistan, the lebel of exploitation and suffering is much more higher compared to other countries because of the backwardness of the society, prejudices in the culture and distorted infrastructure. In Pakistan:

Out of 131 million population, 48 per cent are women. Psychologically, people don't feel happy at the birth of baby girl. Women litracy rate is 1.8 per cent. 135,000 women die every year at child birth due to insufficient hospitals and health care facilities. Insecurity at workplace is rife.

Women representation in the Parliament is negligible. They are deprived of basic human rights, facing hikes of exploitation including sexual harassment.

Women in Pakistan need to be organised on class line, because they are facing different social problems, like price hikes, severe unemployoemnt insecurity, looting, poverty.

They are facing discrimination by religious leaders, who always put obstacles in front of them, halting from doing work, getting education and playing any part in the social development of the society.

The poor women are working as domestics, in brick-kiln industry, in construction work, especially building roads, incotton, rice and wheat field, in textile and garments manufacturing industries, working 10 to 12 hours a day getting less than half wages than that of men.

Majority of them are forced to do bonded labour in carpet manufacturing industry. Many are involved in home cottage industry. Apart from that they are chained in different cultural and religious traditions. The previous dictator introduced the discriminatory laws of blasphemy "Hadood Ordinance" against women. Two women witness are considered equal to one man in a court of Justice. We think that under the existing capitalist system of exploitation, there is no way out for the ever increasing miseries of men, women, and children.

Women emancipation lies in the eradication of old, bankrupted ideas with advanced ideology of their liberation from all sorts of oppression which will provide them with equal opportunities of development in the society of modern civilisation.

Women can achieve their rights, get emancipated from terrible exploitation only in a socialist society of peace, Justice and equality.

References

1. M. Tiger and M.R. Levy, *Law and the Rise of Capitalism.*
2. The Law of Qisas and Diyat has been approved by the nominated Majlis-e-Shoora and is now pending discussion and acceptance by the newly-elected National Assembly.
3. The other women's organizations included APWA, *Therik-e-Khawatten,* Punjab Women Lawyers' Association, National Women Lawyers Organization, *Anjuman Jamhooriyat Passnd* Khawateen (DWA), *Anjuman Behbood-e-Khawateen and the YWCA.*
4. Najma Sadeque, 'Zina Ordinance the Unjust Law', *She* , Vol. I, No. 8 April 1984, pp. 75-78.
5. *See Dawn* and *The Muslim,* 6 August 1983.
6. *The Muslim,* 23 December 1983.
7. This was done in the case of a woman convicted in Azad Kashmir and of one Musamat Rabia.
8. Interview with Rashida Patel, *The Herald,* September 1984.
9. Lal Mai's case was taken note of by Amnesty International.
10. The Advisory Council of Islamic Ideology (CII) was provided for both in Ayub's and Bhutto's constitutions. The role of this body was to examine laws for their conformity or repugnance to Islam. It was conceived primarily as an advisory body with the power to make recommendations which the State may or may not accept. Its initiative in the Ayub and Bhutto years was very limited. CII was reconstituted by Zia and has been working with extreme fervour during his regime.
11. One of the authors, with no inkling of possible police presence or action, had taken here 12-year old daughter to the march. The experience of both mother and daughter running down the road hand in hand chased by baton flailing police, with tear-gas shells bursting around them, and finally being arrested and pushed into a police van, is one which will never be forgotten. The politicization that resulted from that 500-yard sprint cannot be matched by any other kind of consciousness- raising experience.
12. For details see WAF's position paper on the Law of Evidence (Appendix).
13. The organizations were: APWA , Federation of Pakistan Business and Professional Women's Club, Pakistan University Women's Federation, Pakistan Nurses' Federation, Sind Girl Guides' Association, Gul-e-Raana Community Centre, Pakistan Women Lawyer's Association, Raana Liaquat Craftsmen's Colony, Anjuman-e-Behbood-e-Samaat Etfal, Kashmiri Women's Association, Pakistan Association of the Blind, Pakistan Soroptomist Club, Pakistan Sociological Association, Pakistan Voluntary Health and Nutrition Association, Family Planning Association of Pakistan, Pakistan Montessori Association, Karachi Ladies' Association, Sind Graduates' Association and Pakistan College Teachers' Association, Sind. To this meeting were also invited Mr

Khalid Ishaque and Mr Waheed Farouqui to give legal advice.

14. Discrimination appears to occur in the case of non-believers but traditional accounts have established that non-Muslims in a Muslim land were entitled to equal *diyat.*
15. In Pakistan it is not unusual for court cases to go on for years, sometimes more than 15 years.
16. The Commission recommended that 5 per cent of the general seats of the House be exclusively reserved as women's seats for the next ten years. A specially constituted council would nominate twice the number of names than there were women's reserved seats available and the *Amir* would then make the final selection.
17. Women's organizations called for a boycott of the referendum and the dual policy of belittling women on the one hand and asking for their support on the other. The Coordination Committee of six women's organizations in Lahore held a meeting in the Lahore High Court and gave the call for a boycott.
18. *Viewpoint*, 2 January 1986, p.13.
19. The circumstances of Nasim Wali Khan's election were quite different. She was a candidate of PNA, the nine -Party Alliance opposing Bhutto, and the wife of a leading politician (Wali Khan). The reason for Nasim's presence in politics was primarily Wali Khan's incarceration. Her display of courage and ability to speak forcefully had added to her image. On the other hand, the women who were elected to the 1985 assemblies were successful on the basis of their performance in their constituencies. The success of these women, Syeda Abida hussain (N.A.), Sajida Nayyar Abidi (P.A.) and Farhat Rafiq (P.A.) has been attributed to their family connections. This is an unfair allegation, for while there is no denying that they belong to the landowner class it is equally true that the majority of the members in the assemblies belong to the same class and are sons, brothers, or sons-in-law of one or other recognized politician.
20. On March 2, 1985, immediately after elections Zia-ul-Haq announced the Revival of the Constitution, 1973, Order 1985. The revived constitution bears such little resemblance to the original document that it is often referred to as the 1985 Constitution by Zia's opponents.
21. The only way to challenge these laws is through raising them in the National Assembly. The NA may use its discretion to refer it to the Federal Shariat Court, thus leading to a possible review.
22. The last two years have witnessed an unprecedented number of sectarian clashes both between varicus *Sunni* sects as well as between *Sunnis* and *Shiahs*. Resulting in injuries and death, these violent clashes have even taken place in mosques.
23. The seminar was presided over by the ex-Chief Justice of the Federal

Shariat Court, Aftab Hussain, who later publicly clarified that nothing derogatory had been said. The so-called controversy focused on the use of the word *'ummi'*, meaning unlettered—a word used in the Quran for the Prophet. Despite there being no evidence to support Nisar Fatima's accusation, the Speaker of the Assembly overstepped his authority. In an unprecedented directive, he advised the Law Minister to institute a case against Asma, although he advised the Law Minsiter to institute a case against Asma, although he disallowed the motion. In a frenetic follow up, the Jamaat-e-Islami demanded Asma's death and a law sanctioning the death sentence for anyone making derogatory statements about the Prophet.

4

Discrimination Against Women

The situation of women in Pakistan depends on geographical location and class. Women fare better in urban areas and middle-and upper-class sections of society, where there are greater opportunities for higher education and for paid and professional work and women's social mobility is somewhat less restricted. Seventy-five percent of Pakistan's female population is, however, rural,and the average Pakistani woman is beset with the "crippling handicaps of illiteracy, constant motherhood and poor health." And, despite the relative privilege of some, all Pakistani women remain structurally disadvantaged and second-class citizens as a result of legal and societal discrimination premised on social and cultural norms and attitudes.

Women's legal and social status has changed throughout the country's turbulent political history, sometimes for the better, lately for the worse. In 1947 British India was partitioned along religious lines to create two independent nations: India, which had a majority Hindu population, and Pakistan, which was predominantly Muslim. Pakistan's relations with its neighbors, above all Afghanistan and India, have also had critical consequences for foreign and domestic politics, particularly with respect to the role of the military and the course of Islamization. The direction of the debate over thecountry's political ideology and the militarization of politics have had a profound impact on the trajectory of women's advancement.

The Partition

The constitutional debates following partition were dominated by protracted arguments over the place of the *shari`a,* or Islamic legal principles, in Pakistani law. While Pakistan's *ulama* argued that the shari`a provided the only legitimate basis for the new state, most politicians fought for a constitution that embodied the principles of modern parliamentary democracy. The debates lasted nine years and ultimately produced a constitution that "demonstrated . . . [an] unwillingness to articulate and implement an Islamic ideology" in that the "relationship of modern constitutional concepts to Islamic principles was asserted but not delineated."

Still, Pakistan's early leaders gave in to the demands of the religious leadership by including in the Constitution the declaration that Pakistan was an Islamic Republic and by granting the *ulama* an advisory role, though it carried little influence. But if there was little confidence in Islam as the basis for building political consensus, there was equally little faith in the country's weak political institutions. As a result there of, the army came to assume a dominant role in Pakistani politics. The intervention of the military in politics eventually led, during the martial law administration of General Zia-ul-Haq, to disastrous consequences for the advancement of women's rights.

Zia's Military Coup

General Zia ul-Haq, then Army chief of staff, overthrew the elected government of Zulfiqar Ali Bhutto in a military coup in July 1977. A beleaguered Bhutto had himself set the stage for his downfall by imposing martial law during a period of widespread civil unrest following a national election held in March of that year. In that election, Bhutto's party, the Pakistan People's Party (PPP), faced a tough challenge from the Pakistan National Alliance, a coalition thatincluded the entire opposition from fundamentalist religious to centrist and liberal parties. In an effort to boost his popularity, Bhutto had made some moves to win over the religious establishment. Although these moves anticipated Zia's later Islamization programs, they failed to win Bhutto much support among religious leaders, who denounced his avowed socialism. Bhutto also alienated the left, which joined the opposition alliance, along with urban middle-class Pakistanis frustrated with Bhutto's increasingly autocratic and repressive rule and failure to implement economic reforms. Although the PPP officially won the election by a large margin, the opposition claimed extensive electoral fraud and immediately began the anti-government agitation that resulted in the imposition of martial law, which led to Bhutto's ouster.

Zia's coup represented the convergence of conservative religious interests with those of the army. In the absence of any clear popular constituency, Zia used appeals to Islamic values to legitimize his regime and cultivated the support of the conservative religious parties. He came to power denouncing Bhutto's administration as un-Islamic, and one of his main rallying cries was the return of Pakistani society to the "moral purity of early Islam." His most vulnerable and strategic targets, along with minorities, were women, whom he promised to return to the sanctity of the *chardivari* (the four walls of the home). Thus the women's status became a lightning rod in Zia's political strategy. Within months of taking power, Zia introduced a series of legal and social changes that reversed many of the legal advances for women of the prior thirty years. This backsliding demonstrated that, despite seeming progress, women's rights ultimately remainedtentative and discretionary. Women's few hard-won legal gains were quickly curtailed.

With the imposition of martial law, Zia suspended all fundamental rights guaranteed in the Constitution that had been adopted in 1973, including the right to be free of discrimination on the basis of sex. He then introduced a series of laws that gave legal sanction to women's subordinate status, including the *Hudood* Ordinances, which changed the law of rape and adultery and made fornication a crime for the first time in the country's history; and the *Qanun-e-Shahadat* Order (Law of Evidence Order), which relegates women to inferior legal status and, in some circumstances, renders the testimony of a woman equal to only half the weight of a man's.

Islamization

Zia also proposed laws regarding *Qisas* and *Diyat*, Islamic penal laws governing compensation and retribution in crimes involving bodily injury. Zia reinforced the legal strictures he imposed on women with a series of informal regulations and unwritten policies designed to curtail women's personal liberty, visibility, and participation in public life.

Zia's Islamization efforts had their greatest impact on Pakistan's criminal justice system. The potential for misuse of power by the police and jail authorities had existed since colonial times, and successive periods of martial law had further increased the powers of law enforcement agencies and eroded safeguards against abuses. Far from providing better protection for people with legitimate grievances, the effect of Islamization was to increase the state's power over the lives and liberties of its citizens, bringing more of them, particularly women, into contact with an already abusive and corrupt criminal justice system.

Zia also undermined the independence of the civilian court system with, among other things, the introduction at the High Court level of *shariat* benches, reorganized and centralized as the Federal Shariat Court (FSC) in 1980, to review all laws to ensure that nonewas repugnant to the Koran or the *Sunnah* (exemplary sayings and directives of the prophet Mohammed) and to hear appeals in certain criminal matters including Hudood cases.

The Zia era produced a decided shift in the uneasy balance between women's rights and religion in Pakistani politics. Until 1977 the constantly changing religious and political alignments worked against both conservative and progressive extremes, and, with the help of a growing number of independent organizations, women were able to secure a steady flow of moderate reforms, although their impact on the majority of women was minimal.

After Zia's coup, the politics of the army and the religious right were so closely aligned that the opportunity for reform disappeared, and women took a step backward. Increased social control of women was an important part of the Zia regime's appropriation of conservative religious values to legitimate state power.

There was no opposition to Zia's policies toward women. In September 1981, women came together in Karachi in an emergency meeting to oppose the adverse effects on women of martial law and the Islamization campaign. They launched what was to become the first full-fledged national women's movement in Pakistan: the Women's Action Forum (WAF). Staging public protests and campaigns against the Hudood

Ordinances, the Law of Evidence, and the Qisas and Diyat laws (temporarily shelved as a result), WAF became one of the main voices of opposition to Zia.

Benazir Bhutto in Power

The coming to power in 1988 of Benazir Bhutto, daughter of Zulfiqar Ali Bhutto, represented an unprecedented alignment of state power with an apparently progressive women's rights policy. However, soon after Bhutto's election, it became clear that, once again, the protection of women's rights had been subordinated to the need to maintain a delicate balance between various political forces, including those representing conservative religious values. Although Bhutto's campaign pledge to repeal the Hudood laws and to remove all other discriminatory statutes had great appeal, her promises on women's rights graduallyproved to be empty.

Nawaz Sharif

During her two incomplete terms in office, she did not repeal a single one of Zia's Islamization laws. The appointment, through elections in 1997, of Prime Minister Nawaz Sharif, appears to have blocked all opportunities for the advancement of women's rights. Sharif, a political protégé of Zia's, had also held office for a truncated term between Ms. Bhutto's two terms. When he first came to power in November 1990, Sharif promised to adopt Islamic law as the supreme law of Pakistan, albeit within a constitutional framework, and in April 1991 he introduced legislation to that effect. Furthermore, in 1997 Sharif and his supporters in parliament enacted the Qisas and Diyat Ordinance-which institutes shari`a-based changes in Pakistan's criminal law-into law, making it a permanent part of the Pakistan Penal Code rather than an ordinance subject to periodic renewal.

Since his party's return to power in 1997, Nawaz Sharif has moved to consolidate his power by undercutting human rights protections and attacking the supremacy of the Constitution. He has proposed a fifteenth amendment to the Constitution that would entirely replace the existing legal system with a comprehensive Islamic one and would override the "constitution and any law or judgment of any court." Introducing his proposal, Sharif told parliament, "Simple changes in laws are not enough. I want to implement complete Islamic laws where the Koran and Sunnat are supreme." The proposal was quickly approved in the National Assembly (lower house), where Sharif's party has a commanding majority, but, as of July 1999, remained stalled in the Senate and continued to face strong opposition from women's groups, human rights activists, and opposition political parties.

Since 1996 courts have admitted cases challenging an adult woman's right to marry of her own free will, ostensibly an established right under family laws. Judges have looked to theKoran to settle the question, in some cases holding that a Muslim woman's marriage is illegal without familial consent. A 1997 ruling by the Lahore High Court, in the highly publicized Saima Waheed case, upheld a woman's right to marry freely but called for amendments to the family laws, on the basis of Islamic norms, to enforce parental authority to discourage "love marriages."

Women, as a daily practical matter, are far outside the mainstream of political life; a coherent program of concrete measures and a deliberate reversal of existing government attitudes and policies are required to change their situation. Women's access to health and education is severely limited, and their levels of economic and political participation are very low. The literacy rate for Pakistani women is only 25 percent; the maternal mortality rate is disturbingly high at 600 per 100,000 births. Prevailing trends in the health and education sectors are not encouraging.

According to one study, "Health and education (especially for women) have been consistently receiving diminishing allocations in the budget (among the lowest in the third world) and much of what is to be distributed disappears through institutionalized corruption. . . Reproductive health services have particularly suffered and are available only where a few major NGOs have outreach, but they cover only a tiny fraction of the population."

Economic Arena

Women's participation in the economic arena is disproportionately low, with women constituting only 28 percent of the country's labor force, and their marginal role in civic and political life is reflected by the fact that there are only seven female members of the federal parliament, five in the National Assembly out of a total of 207 (2.4 percent) and two in the Senate out of of eighty-three (2.4 percent); one woman among 483 male members of the four provincial legislatures (0.2 percent); two women Cabinet ministers; and three women judges in the provincial High Courts. Not surprisingly, in 1997 Pakistan slid back to 120th out of 146 places in the United Nations Development Programme's gender-relateddevelopment index (107 out of 137 in 1996) and occupied the ninety-second of ninety-four places with regard to women's progressive empowerment.

Clear violations of international law on the rights of women occur daily in Pakistan. Laws that discriminate against women remain on the books and are actively enforced, discrimination in access to government resources and services continues unchecked, and discriminatory practices go unpunished. In particular, violence against women remains a serious and widespread problem-to which the government responds with inaction and inertia.

Pakistan's Obligations under International Law

Through its ratification of the U.N. Convention on the Elimination of All Forms of Discrimination against Women (CEDAW) in 1996, Pakistan assumed the obligation to protect women from sexual and other forms of gender-based violence perpetrated by state agents and private actors alike. As a party to CEDAW, Pakistan is obliged "to pursue by all appropriate means and without delay a policy of eliminating discrimination against women" including "any distinction, exclusion or restriction made on the basis of sex which has the purpose of impairing or nullifying the recognition, enjoyment or exercise by women . . . on a basis of equality of men or women, of human rights and fundamental freedoms. . . ."

The U.N. Committee on the Elimination of Discrimination Against Women (CEDAW Comittee), established under CEDAW, has noted that "[g]ender-based violence is a form of discrimination which seriously inhibits women's ability to enjoy rights and freedoms on a basis of equality with men."

As part of its obligation to prevent violence against women as a step toward eliminating sex discrimination, the government is required to ensure that women victims of violence have access to an effective remedy for the violation of their rights. This duty to provide an effective remedy requires the government to show due diligence in investigating and prosecuting instances of violence against women. In such cases, the effective collection of medical evidence is an integral part of a proper investigation, which, in turn, is central to the successful implementation of penal sanctions against perpetrators of violence against women. Similarly, the ability of the police, prosecutors, and judges to evaluate and use medical evidence is critical to ensuring effective prosecutions of perpetrators of violence against women. Hence, pursuant to its legal obligations under CEDAW, the government of Pakistanmust provide an efficient and effective system of collection of medical evidence to facilitate the proper investigation and prosecution of cases of violence against women.

In 1992 the CEDAW Committee adopted a general recommendation and comments on states' obligations under CEDAW that spelled out the facets of any potentially effective remedy to the problem of violence against women. The committee noted that states are obliged under CEDAW to take steps to provide the following:

(a) Effective legal measures, including penal sanctions, civil remedies and compensatory provisions to protect women against all kinds of violence, including *inter alia* violence and abuse in the family, sexual assault and sexual harassment in the workplace;

(b) Preventive measures, including public information and education programmes to change attitudes concerning the roles and status of men and women;

(c) Protective measures, including refuges, counseling, rehabilitation and support services for women who are the victims of violence or who are at risk of violence.

The duties enumerated by the CEDAW Committee extend beyond the criminal justice system and encompass preventive and protective measures, including "refuges, counseling, rehabilitation and support services." The U.N. Declaration of Basic Principles of Justice for Victims of Crime and Abuse of Power similarly provides that "[v]ictims should receive the necessary material, medical, psychological and social assistance through governmental, voluntary, community-based and indigenous means."

In accordance with these recognized standards, the state should take affirmative measures to promote women's access to health care services, including psychological care. The state should alsoestablish immediately quality shelters for battered women that function not as de facto detention facilities but as refuges where women can find safety and shelter without compromising their personal autonomy and freedom of movement.

In its Declaration on the Elimination of Violence Against Women, adopted in December 1993, the United Nations reaffirmed the state's obligation of due diligence, especially as it applies to the protection of women from violence. The declaration denounces violence against women, including violence in the home, as "a violation of the rights and fundamental freedoms of women." It provides that "states should condemn violence against women . . . [and] exercise due diligence to prevent, investigate, and in accordance with national legislation, punish acts of violence against women." The declaration explicitly states that governments' obligation applies regardless of "whether those acts [of violence] are perpetuated by the State or by private persons."

Furthermore, the International Covenant on Civil and Political Rights (ICCPR), which Pakistan has not ratified but is a cornerstone of international human rights law, requires governments to ensure the rights to life and security of the person of all individuals in their jurisdiction, without distinction of any kind, including sex. The ICCPR would require Pakistan to not only refrain from, but also prevent private actors from committing, acts of violence against women.

The Scope of the Problem of Violence Against Women

Women in Pakistan face the threat of multiple forms of violence, including sexual violence by family members, strangers, and state agents; domestic abuse, including spousal murder and being burned, disfigured with acid, beaten, and threatened; ritual honor killings; and custodial abuse and torture. In its annual report for 1997, the nongovernmental Human Rights Commission of Pakistan (HRCP) reported,"The worst victims were women of the poor and middle classes. Their resourcelessness not only made them the primary target of the police and the criminals, it also rendered them more vulnerable to oppressive customs and mores inside homes and outside." Thus the most endemic form of violence faced by women is violence in the home. For 1997, HRCP reported that "[d]omestic violence remained a pervasive phenomenon.

The supremacy of the male and subordination of the female assumed to be part of the culture and even to have sanction of the religion made violence by one against the other in a variety of its forms an accepted and pervasive feature of domestic life." A United Nations report on women echoes this point, explaining the nature of domestic violence generally in terms of the structure of the family:

Comprehensive studies on domestic violence indicate that domestic violence is a structural rather than causal problem. It is the structure of the family that leads to or legitimizes the acts, emotions or phenomenon that are identified as the "causes" of domestic violence under the causal analysis. This family structure is a "structure that is mirrored and confirmed in the structure of society, which condones the oppression of women and tolerates male violence as one of the instruments in the perpetuation of this power balance."

Estimates of the percentage of women who experience domestic violence in Pakistan range from 70 to upwards of 90 percent._According to HRCP, "[T]he extreme forms it took included driving a woman to suicide or engineering an `accident' (frequently the bursting of a kitchen stove) to cause her death . . . usually . . . when the husband, often in collaboration with his side of the family, felt that the dower or other gifts he had expected from his in-laws in consequence of the marriage were not forthcoming, or/and he wanted to marry again, or he expected an inheritance from the death of his wife."

During 1997, the Lahore press reported an average of more than four local cases of women being burnt weekly, three of the four fatally. Police follow-up on these cases was negligible, with only six suspects taken into custody out of the 215 cases reported in Lahore newspapers during the year.

In 1997, there was not a single conviction in a "stove-death" case in the country. The Lahore press also reported 265 homicides against women in the local area resulting from other forms of intrafamily violence. In the majority of cases, husbands and in-laws were responsible for the murders, while in other cases the perpetrators were brothers and fathers.

Honor killings are another recurrent form of familial violence against women, and again the perpetrators continue to find vindication in the eyes of both the law and society. The practice of summary killing of a woman suspected of an illicit liaison, known as *karo kari* in Sindh and Balochistan, is known to occur in all parts of the country. The Sindh government has reported an annual figure of 300 for such killings. HRCP's own findings reveal that in 1997 there wereeighty-six karo kari killings in Larkana, Sindh, alone, with fifty-three of the victims being women.

Sexual assault is also alarmingly common in Pakistan. HRCP estimated that in 1997 at least eight women, more than half of them minors, were raped every twenty-four hours nationwide. The high incidence of sexual assault in the country is partly fostered by the societal subordination of women to men, by the custom of avenging oneself upon one's enemies by raping their women, who are seen as repositories of family honor, and by the impunity with which these crimes are carried out. There is no question that violence against women is an enormous problem in Pakistan that is exacerbated and perpetuated by the government's inadequate response to the problem. In fact, the state's response to domestic violence in Pakistan is so minimal and cases of intrafamily violence are so rarely addressed in any way by the criminal justice system that it was not possible for us to achieve one of our research goals for this report: that is, to track specific domestic violence criminal suits in order to identify larger patterns in the prosecution of domestic violence. We found that despite the staggering levels of intrafamily violence against women, it is widely perceived by the law enforcement system and society at large as a private family matter, not subject to government intervention let alone criminal sanction.

At present there is virtually no prosecution of crimes of assault and battery when perpetrated by male family members against women; even intrafamily murder and attempted murder rarely are prosecuted. Consequently, much of this report deals almost exclusively with identifiable trends in the state response to non-familial sexual assault. It takes a comprehensive look at the way the criminal justice system deals with cases of violence against women, focusing on the interaction between the police and legal establishments and the medicolegal system. Often overlooked, the maintenance of an efficient and responsive medicolegal system is a crucial part of the state's responsibility to ensure that survivors of assault have an effective remedy and that perpetrators of crimes are brought to justice.

The current procedures for obtaining medical evidence in assault cases, particularly in cases of sexual assault of women, are woefully inadequate, neither ensuring that perpetrators are convicted norproviding women with appropriate treatment. Other barriers encountered by women victims of violence who attempt to navigate the criminal justice system include inveterate and widespread bias against them and their cases, official incompetence and corruption at all levels, systemic lack of professionalism and administrative inefficiency.

Domestic Law

Rape. In 1979 Pakistan's rape laws were dramatically changed when General Zia modified strategic aspects of the country's legal system in accordance with Islamic strictures. No longer part of the standard Penal Code, rape was included in the Offence of Zina Ordinance, itself a subcategory of Zia's Enforcement of Hudood Ordinance of 1979. The Zina Ordinance has had a profound effect on the rights of women, as it broadens the category of criminal sexual activity and redefines how such crimes will be handled by the legal system. The prohibited sexual activities, including rape (zina bil jabr), became religious offenses, subject to different standards of evidence and punishment and the appellate jurisdiction of Islamic higher courts.

Pakistan's previous rape laws, repealed by the Zia Ordinance, had defined rape as compulsory sexual intercourse. The new law added to this definition that both a man and a woman may be guilty of rape and narrowed the circumstances in which rape can be said to have occurred. Statutory rape, previously defined as sex with or without the consent of a girl under the age of 14, was no longer a crime.

In addition, the legal possibility of marital rape was eliminated; by definition, rape became an extra-marital offense. The Zina Ordinance defined rape as sexual intercourse without being validly married when it occurs in any of the following circumstances:

(a) against the will of the victim;
(b) without the consent of the victim;
(c) with the consent of the victim, when the consent has been obtained by putting the victim in fear of death or of hurt; or
(d) with the consent of the victim, when the offender knows that the offender is not validly married to the victim and that the consent is given because the victim believes that the offender is another person to whom the victim is or believes herself or himself to be validly married.

Another significant change brought about by the adoption of the Zina laws was that for the first time in Pakistan's history, fornication (non-marital sex) became illegal and, along with adultery, non-compoundable, non-bailable and punishable at maximum by death. Since the crime of statutory rape was eliminatedat the same time that fornication was criminalized, even minor girls can be charged with engaging in illicit sex if they have reached puberty.

The punishment for illicit sex, be it adultery or rape, depends on both the evidence on which the conviction rests and the marital status of the offender. The maximum punishment is known as *Hadd* (literally, "the limit"), the singular of Hudood, and is a mandatory sentence that a judge may not mitigate. Hadd sentences are harsher for people who are married and Muslim *(muhsan)*: if the accused is muhsan and (a) confesses or (b) there are four adult, pious, male Muslim witnesses to the act of penetration, then the accused must be sentenced to death by stoning. If, on the other hand, the accused is non-muhsan and (a) confesses or (b) the crime is witnessed by four adult men, not necessarily Muslims, the accused must be sentenced to a hundred lashes with a whip.

The testimony of four female witnesses, let alone that of the victim alone, is not sufficient for the imposition of the

Hadd punishment. A non-muhsan person convicted of rape may receive, in addition to a hundred lashes, "such other punishment, including the sentence of death, as the Court may deem fit having regard to the circumstances of the case." All Hadd punishments must be confirmed by an appellate court. To date, although Hadd punishments have been imposed, none has been carried out.

On account of their harshness, Hadd sentences require extraordinarily conclusive evidence. If the evidence falls short of the stringent (and discriminatory) threshold required for imposing the draconian Hadd punishments, the accused may be sentenced to a lesser class of punishment known as *Tazir*. It is important to note that insufficient evidence to impose a Hadd punishment doesnot eliminate criminal liability: the Tazir punishment for rape is up to twenty-five years' imprisonment and thirty lashes. For the purposes of Tazir, no distinction is made between a muhsan and non-muhsan offender. Because of the strict evidentiary requirements for Hadd punishments, the overwhelming majority of rape cases are tried at the Tazir level of evidence and punishment.

Evidence for Tazir punishment is governed by the standard evidence code (*Qanun-e-Shahadat*) which was introduced by General Zia in 1984. The evidence code states:

Unless otherwise provided in any law relating to the enforcement of Hudood . . . in matters pertaining to financial or future obligations . . . the instruments shall be attested to by two men or by one man and two women . . . in all other matters, the court *may* accept, or act on, the testimony of one man or one woman.

The only foolproof way to obtain a rape conviction is if the accused confesses or there are four adult male witnesses to the act of penetration. Otherwise, the courts have no consistent standards for proof of rape. For example,according to Section 6(1) of the Zina Ordinance, "Penetration is sufficient to constitute the sexual intercourse necessary to the offence of zina-bil-jabr," and the case law is clear that penetration must be by a penis and not other foreign objects; however, the courts are divided over the extent of penetration required to constitute rape under the ordinance.

Similarly, there is no clarity in the case law as to the

related question of what constitutes proof of penetration, although some corroborative evidence is required. Some cases indicate that even the slightest penetration is sufficient; numerous others discuss issues related to proof of penetration in terms of the presence of semen inside the vagina or a torn hymen, suggesting that evidence supporting full penetration is required. Adding to the murkiness of the issue of proof of penetration, several cases have held that the presence of semen in the victim's vagina is an insufficient indication.

Courts have also ruled inconsistently on what, if any, corroboration as to the non-consensual nature of the intercourse is required. In general, courts are very reluctant to hand down rape convictions in cases where there are no "marks of violence" on the victim's body and the evidence consists solely of the victim's word against the defendant's. Supporting physical evidence from the victim's body has been required to convict even in rape cases where consent has been obtained through the threat of violence, for example at gunpoint, thus limiting thepossibility of struggle. On the basis of a presumption of female consent and a belief that women tend to lie in rape cases, judges ascribe undue significance to bodily evidence of the use of physical force by the defendant and physical, as opposed to verbal, resistance by the woman.

Federal Shariat Court

For example, the Federal Shariat Court overturned a lower court's conviction of rape on the grounds that medical examiners "did not observe any injury on the thigns, legs, elbows, arms, knees, face, back and buttocks of the victim," and held that "she was bound to sustain injuries . . . as she was supposed to put up resistance." Although some victims may have no chance of fending off an attacker, judges seem to require that they resist and also suffer visible physical injury if they wish to see their attackers punished.

In many rape cases where there is no supporting bodily evidence from the victim or defendant, courts have arbitrarily opted to convict the defendant of the lesser charge of adultery or fornication. It appears that judges are reluctant, out of bias, to impose the significant penalties that attach to a conviction for rape but, in the face of the evidence, cannot let a defendant off entirely either.

For example, a court in a 1997 rape case declared that in the absence of marks of violence on the victim's body and her failure on cross-examination to prove adequately that she resisted the defendant's advances, "[the] offence of zina-bil-jabr, thus having not been made out against the accused his conviction under S. 10(3) [the section of the Zina Ordinance establishing the crime of zina-bil-jabr or rape] was altered to S. 10(2) [the section of the Ordinance codifying the crime of zina or adultery/fornication]."

Similarly, the Federal Shariat Court converted a rape conviction to one of fornication on the grounds that "[s]ince no violence was found on her body, it could be reasonable to infer that she was a willing party to sexual intercourse." These cases demonstrate that, based on prejudiced evidentiary requirements and interpretation stemming from a disinclination to credit female testimony about rape, courts at times spontaneously and unilaterally alter the nature of the charges leveled by the prosecution and convict the defendant of the lesser crime of illegal consensual sex instead of rape. In such instances, a correspondingprosecution is not necessarily initiated against the complainant, but the potential for it is created.

An even worse scenario resulting from judges' reluctance to convict in rape cases is that courts sometimes view a woman's charge of rape as an admission of illegal sex unless she can prove, by their standards, that the intercourse was non-consensual and therefore not fornication or adultery. Thus the structure of the Zina Ordinance, and its interpretation by courts, leaves rape victims constantly susceptible to prosecution for illicit consensual sex. As Dr. Justice Javid Iqbal has written, "[T]he court considers the aggrieved party or prosecutrix guilty until she proves herself innocent. . .Thus, when a woman files such a complaint [of rape], instead of seeking justice she places herself at the mercy of the court."

In the early years of the Zina ordinance especially, it was not uncommon for the female victim in rape cases to be prosecuted for adultery or fornication unless she provided extraordinarily conclusive proof that her "participation" in impermissible intercourse was forced; the accused rapist, on the other hand, was usually acquitted of all charges. Such cases revealed that the standard of proof beyond a reasonable doubt was not applied equally, or, put another way, the benefit of the doubt that was rightfully accorded to men accused of rape was often not equally extended to women whose rape charges had been converted into charges against them of illegal consensual sex. While the courts generally required rape charges to be proven beyond a reasonable doubt, they would often accept a woman's rape allegation-once disproved-as *prima facie* evidence that sheengaged in consensual extramarital sex, despite the fact that a failure to demonstrate rape (coerced sex) beyond a reasonable doubt does not automatically prove beyond a reasonable doubt that consensual sex occurred. Such cases are far less frequent in the late 1990s than they were in the 1980s, and some courts have explicitly ruled that a woman's failure to prove an allegation of rape does not constitute *prima facie* evidence of her participation in illicit consensual sex.

Domestic Violence

Pakistani law is even more inadequate in protecting women victims of domestic violence and penalizing batterers. Not explicitly prohibited by a specific, targeted, and distinct set of laws, most acts of domestic violence are encompassed by the Qisas and Diyat Ordinance of 1990, a body of Islamic criminal laws dealing with murder, attempted murder, and the crime of causing bodily "hurt" (both intentional and unintentional). In the absence of explicit criminalization of domestic violence, police and judges have tended to treat it as a non-justiciable, private or family matter or, at best, an issue for civil, rather than criminal, courts.

If a domestic violence case does come before a criminal court, it may be punished either by qisas (retribution) or diyat (compensation) for the benefit of the victim or his or her legal heirs. In qisas and diyat crimes, the victim or heir has the right to determine whether to exact retribution or compensation or to pardon the accused. If the victim or heir chooses to waive qisas, or qisas is judicially held to be inapplicable, an offender is subject to tazir or discretionary punishment in the form of imprisonment. In these instances, judges not only have the power to determine the extent of punishment but also to decide whether to punish the offender at all.

Commentators have noted that the qisas and diyat laws

have, in many respects, converted serious crimes, including murder and aggravated assault, into crimes against the individual rather than the state. One Pakistani researcher has written, "By vesting the primary right of forgiveness in the individual for such a serious crime as murder, the state has exposed the most susceptible sections of society to pressure from the powerful."

The "privatization" of crimes by the qisas and diyat laws has particularly damaging consequences in cases of intrafamily violence, the majority of which involve domestic abuse or spousal murder. As a result of the law, not only are women victims of domestic violence and their heirs susceptible to pressure and intimidation to waive qisas, but the concept of monetary compensation can be meaningless in a situation where payments flow from one member of the nuclear family to another.

Furthermore, murder (*Qatl-e-Amd*) is not liable to qisas "when any *wali* [heir] of the victim is a direct descendant, how low-so-ever, of the offender." Thus, cases in which a woman has been murdered by her husband would be exempt from the qisas or maximum (i.e., capital) punishment for the murder if the couple in question have children, since in that case, a child or heir of the victim would also be a direct descendant of the offender. Diyat in such cases, entailing compensation flowing from a father to his (motherless) children, would be a mockery. Although courts can impose tazir punishment in a spousal murder case of this kind, the maximum they can award is fourteen years' imprisonment. Moreover, courts are directed to weigh the decision to impose tazir punishment "having regard to the facts and circumstances of the case," which grants them a large measure of discretion.

In light of the biased attitudes of the courts with respect to domestic violence, the fact that punishment in such cases of spousal murder has been left entirely to the discretion of judges may well spell total impunity for the most extreme form of domestic violence. In the words of one commentator, "Although it is still unclear how the law will be applied in practice, it may be a means by which the state abdicates its responsibility to control violence in the most common type of intrafamily murder-the killing of a female member by the male head of the family."

The large degree of judical discretion embodied in the qisas and diyat law has been widely criticized in light of the endemic societal and judical discrimination against women in Pakistan. Among the dangers that arise fromdecodification and an increase in judicial discretion is the opportunity for discrimination and corruption.

Since traditional interpretations of Islamic law contemplate the diyat for a woman victim to be half of that for a man, the gender neutral language of the current codified law on diyat is practically meaningless. And the invitation to exercise discretion with regard to the testimony of women in effect encourages judges to manifest their own prejudices and biases against women. The law of inheritance, which governs the distribution of diyat among heirs, is also discriminatory to women, as the shares of female heirs are typically smaller than those of their male counterparts. In addition, the Human Rights Commission of Pakistan noted, "[H]eirs entitled to . . . diyat, were mostly assumed by the law to be male. It was observed that where the blood money [diyat] had to go to a female, the courts, which were responsible for fixing the amount, tended to be less liberal."

Honor killings are another form of intrafamily violence with victims who are mostly women, who are seen as the repositories of family honor. Such killings are also encompassed by the murder provisions of the qisas and diyat laws. However, courts minimize the severity of these crimes by applying to them, in effect, the English common law principle of "grave and sudden provocation." In so doing, courts simply deem that qisas is not applicable to honor killings, and punish these crimes under Section 302(c) of the Pakistan Penal Code (as amended by the qisas and diyat ordinance), which allows for punishment of murder with imprisonment up to twenty-five years where qisas is not applicable.

Importance of Forensic Evidence in Cases of Sexual Assault and Domestic Violence

Medical evidence is central to the successful prosecution of both sexual and other bodily assault cases. The fact that in rape cases Pakistani courts generally require "positive proof of penetration" as well as physical evidence, such as genital injuries, to corroborate the victim's testimony as to the nonconsenual nature of the intercourse renders utterly indispensable a timely and meticulous medicolegal examination of victims as well as a sophisticated understanding of its merits and limitations on the part of courts.

In many casesof sexual assault, medical evidence may provide the only corroboration of the complainant's case, confirming not only the fact that sexual contact or intercourse took place-and with a particular individual-but also that such contact took place without the complainant's consent. Although medical evidence cannot in and of itself prove a lack of consent, it can be strongly suggestive that sexual contact or intercourse was the result of assault and not agreement. Barriers to securing vital medical evidence not only prevent victims of sexual assault from mounting successful prosecutions and obtaining justice, but also heighten the potential for rape victims to be wrongfully prosecuted for adultery or fornication. Medical evidence also plays a critical role in domestic violence cases: a medicolegal doctor's evaluation of the nature and extent of injuries determines the legal classification of incidents of domestic abuse and, consequently, the seriousness of the charges. However, concerns about the medicolegal system in the context of domestic violence remain largely theoretical because in the overwhelming majority of cases, the police simply do not conceive of domestic violence as a criminal matter, nor do they refer victims for medicolegal evaluations. Nor do the police appear to be aware that a charge of criminal "assault" does not always require the victim to have sustained physical injury. Since Human Rights Watch was unable to locate any domestic violence victims who were examined by medicolegal doctors, the remainder of this section will focus on the experience of victims of non-domestic sexual assault.

Despite the fact that criminal charges in cases of various forms of bodily attack depend on a medical determination of the nature and extent of injuries; despite the importance of medical evidence to securing convictions in rape cases; and despite the potential exculpatory role of medical evidence in adultery and fornication cases, Pakistan does not have an efficient and reliable medicolegal system. In general, medicolegal examinations are performed by poorly trained doctors using inadequate facilities and equipment. As bad as the system is for any victim of a violent crime, it has a disproportionately detrimental impact on victimsof rape and sexual assault. As a result, the government's maintenance and toleration of a deeply flawed medicolegal system is *de facto* discriminatory to women, who constitute the majority of rape victims.

Rape victims must get authorization from the police and a magistrate's order before they can be examined by a government medicolegal doctor. In addition, in most urban areas, rape victims can only be examined by a woman doctor at specialized state medicolegal centers. In contrast, most other types of cases requiring medicolegal services can be handled by the medicolegal units attached to most large government hospitals. This also becomes a problem in practice because of the shortage of female medicolegal doctors in government service and their limited hours of availability at a restricted number of state medicolegal centers.

Victims of violence face problems not only in the collection of medical evidence but also in its use in the courtroom. Doctors present it in court without elaboration or explanation; prosecutors rarely question the doctors in order to elucidate its meaning; and judges treat the presentation of forensic evidence as a formalistic part of trials, do not subject the evidence to rigorous analytic scrutiny, and frequently misconstrue its significance. Sexual assault victims are entirely dependent on the police for information about and access to the medicolegal system. Most victims are unaware of the urgency, critical importance, or even existence of medicolegal exams, much less how to go about getting one. A victim cannot usually obtain a medicolegal exam on her own initiative. The medicolegal examination must, in practice, be done at a government facility for which an official police referral, police escort, and a magistrate's order are required.

It is generally advisable that forensic evidence be gathered and documented as soon as possible before time and intervening circumstances alter or destroy the signs and traces that constitute it. In cases of sexual assault in particular, it is critical that forensic evidence be obtained quickly because traces of semen not only disappear with time but can be lost through washing or passing urine.

Other indications of sexual assault, such as internal bruising or swelling, are also often extremely transient. Rather than promptly referring complainants for medicolegal examinations, the police appear to be unaware and unmindful of the urgency of medicolegal evaluations. They frequently delay or block women's access to this vital evidentiary evaluation, thereby compromising the chance of a successful prosecution from the start. The most common problem is, generally pay no attention to complainants until after an FIR is registered, and the considerable time and trouble entailed in filing an FIR automatically delays victims' medicolegal evaluations. Even after an FIR is filed, the police routinely neglect to secure prompt medicolegal evaluations for sexual assault victims.

In some cases, the police have deliberately refused to provide referrals even to victims who affirmatively seek them. Often delays are caused because the police are ignorant as to the procedures to obtain an examination in sexual assault cases. In addition, the police undermine the preservation of forensic evidence by failing to inform victims of the need to refrain from washing themselves or their clothes prior to the examination.

In Rural Areas

Women in Pakistan's rural areas have virtually no chance of getting a timely or professional medicolegal exam. In most rural areas there are no specialized medicolegal doctors, and victims of violence must obtain medicolegal reports from the nearest government clinic or hospital, which often requires traveling considerable distances at substantial expense.

Victims of domestic violence potentially confront fewer barriers to securing a medicolegal examination if their injuries do not entail sexual assault. First, if a vaginal exam is not necessary, victims of domestic violence may be examined by male medicolegal doctors. Furthermore, these victims can be examined at any government hospital that has a medicolegal unit; there are several such hospitals in Karachi and Lahore. The medicolegal units at government hospitals are supposed to have at least one medicolegal doctor on duty twenty-four hours a day. Yet the theoretically greater ability of domestic violence victims to secure a medicolegal examination translates into little: they rarely get to this stage of the criminal justice system given the obstacles discussed above.

Although a post-graduate diploma course in "medical jurisprudence" is offered in Pakistan, the majority of medicolegal officers in the country, including those with supervisory responsibility, have no specialized training in the field of forensic medicine, either academic or practical, before assuming their medicolegal posts. To enter government service as a medical doctor, one must have a degree from an accredited medical college and a diploma in public health. Once inducted into government service, doctors are transferred from posting to posting over the course of their careers, which usually entails a corresponding change in the substantive nature of their duties. Hence, doctors find it difficult to build up specialized expertise in any particular field.

There was little incentive to develop expertise in medicolegal work when they knew they could be transferred at any time. The doctors gave examples of colleagues who had been transferred to different positions shortly after acheiving a high level of skill in medicolegal work and who were replaced by total novices in the field. The doctors also emphasized the fact that medicolegal postings were highly coveted and the appointments process very politicized because the field was perceived as having great potential for corruption, graft, and personal gain.

Dr. Lubna, one of two female doctors on the staff of the Office of Surgeon Medicolegal in Lahore, and two of the three female doctors on the staff of the Office of the Police Surgeon in Karachi told us that apart from a course in medical jurisprudence in medical college, the only training in medicolegal work they received was on the job. "I have training in gynecology and on-the-job training for this work," said Dr. Lubna.

Doctors were also confused about the length of time during which semen may be detected in a woman's vaginal area. Dr. Lubna said, "For twenty-one days semen shows positive in the vagina, so there is no rush." She does not take swabs if twenty-one days have passed since the assault because then, she said, the presence of semen cannot be detected by laboratory analysis. Dr. Shaheen, on the other hand, said that while in a dead body sperm may be detected for up to three weeks for sure, and sometimes even for three months, in a live person the possibility of detecting semen depends upon a number of factors, including whether the woman in question is menstruating, has urinated, or bathed and washed herself. He said, although it was conceivable that sperm may be detected for up to seventeen days in the folds of the vagina, in general, motile sperm could be detected only within three to four hours of the assault. He felt that if a victim was examined more than seventeen days after the assault, there was no point in sending vaginal swabs for laboratory analysis for the purpose of detecting semen.

Staff at the Office of the Chemical Examiner in both Karachi and Lahore disagreed with both Dr. Lubna and Dr. Shaheen. According to a senior chemist at the Karachi laboratory, "Sperm can be found in the vagina for up to seventy-two hours [after the assault]. However, semen on clothing if properly dried and preserved may be detected for years." The head of the semen section at the Lahore laboratory explained that "semen can be detected within three days [of the sexual assault].

However, in its non-motile form, semen may be detected for up to three months." As for the process of semen grouping, which the doctors referred to several times though none knew of an instance when it had been successfully performed, Dr. Lubna said, "[It] can be done for twenty-one days afterthe assault without any problem," while Captain Memon asserted, "For semen grouping to be done, the girl has to come [for an exam] within twenty-four hours. After twenty-four hours sperms dissolve, although the presence of semen can be detected."

Doctor's Role

The medicolegal doctors we interviewed said that in addition to a lack of training in medicolegal techniques and methodology, they receive no training in legal and testimonial procedures. Doctors have no experience as to how to contextualize and interpret medicolegal evidence in a legal framework and testify with respect to it in a court of law. As a result, far from having a significant impact in cases requiring their testimony, medicolegal doctors perform perfunctory, formalistic, and superficial roles in the courtroom with their time on the witness stand reduced to a matter of minutes.

The doctor's role is limited to reading out verbatim the medicolegal report they prepared and submitted to the court hearing the case. Doctors do not provide any meaningful explanation as to the limitations of the report or the range of implications of specific findings or lack thereof. They are present, in effect, merely to admit the medicolegal report into evidence rather than to provide the court with a comprehensive expert opinion as to the significance of the findings recorded in the report.

Furthermore, several medicolegal doctors told us that usually cases take so long to come to trial, often up to a year or more, that by the time they are called upon to testify in a particular case, they have completely forgotten about it and just parrot their report, which is all they are expected to do in any case.

Several doctors specified that basic training in understanding a central element of Pakistan's criminal law, the Qisas and Diyat Ordinance, would be very useful. The Qisas and Diyat Ordinance aims to codify Islamic criminal law, and governs all crimes involving bodily injury including murder and assault but excluding sex crimes. It defines crimes and mandates punishments according tothe nature and extent of injuries inflicted. The ordinance, which establishes fine distinctions between different categories of crimes and incorporates arcane Arabic terminology, has been consistently criticized in Pakistani legal circles and in the press for being extremely confusing.

Because of the ordinance's focus on the type and extent of injuries actually sustained by victims, the role of medicolegal doctors in identifying and documenting the injuries assumes great significance for the framing of criminal charges. In implementing their duties under the ordinance, medicolegal doctors not only need training in properly identifying and classifying victims' injuries, but also a thorough understanding of the scope of the ordinance and the numerous categories of crimes it establishes. While some medicolegal doctors we interviewed termed the ordinance's provisions confusing and difficult to comprehend and apply, others said that they had no problem precisely classifying victims' injuries with reference to the ordinance's crime categories.

In order to be reliable and useful, forensic evidence must be collected, stored, and analyzed under sterile conditions. Ideally, tissue and fluid samples should help the police and prosecutors determine when and if sexual contact took place, whether there was a struggle, and with whom. The facilities at the medicolegal offices we visited did not meet these requirements and thus compromised the quality of the evidence. Based on repeated visits over a four-week period to the premises of the Office of Surgeon Medicolegal in Lahore and the Office of the Police Surgeon in Karachi and on interviews with their staff, we found the physical facilities so inadequate that the performance of professional and thorough medicolegal evaluations was virtually impossible.

Not only does the lack of equipment and amenities hinder the collection of forensic evidence, but it can lead to abusive treatment of the examinees, including exposing them to health risks. Some doctors also complained of feeling frustrated at their inability to perform their duties professionally and responsibly on account of the abysmal condition of their offices and the lack of proper equipment.

The examination room is also very badly lit, with only one ceiling light and a small, unreliable lamp poised above the makeshift examination table. This is very troubling because the goal of the examinations undertaken in the room often is to discern minute lacerations, fine cuts, bruises and discoloration on a woman's body, including her vaginal area, which requires strong lighting, particularly in the absence of specialized examination tools and equipment.

Health Risk's

Doctors performing medicolegal examinations on victims of sexual assault at the Office of Surgeon Medicolegal in Lahore and the Office of the Police Surgeon in Karachi are provided with virtually no instruments, or even supplies, to facilitate the identification and collection of forensic evidence. For example, doctors use wooden rulers to measure the dimensions of wounds on the examinees' bodies. While it is possible that a wooden ruler would suffice to approximate the surface dimensions of a wound, it cannot be used to measure its depth.

In both the Lahore and Karachi offices, there is even a chronic shortage of disposable gloves, which are indispensable to a hygienic and thorough examination. This lack of basic supplies leads directly to abusive treatment of examinees, who are either examined with used gloves or required to purchase gloves for their own examinations.

Health risks for both examinees and doctors are compounded by the fact that, according to a WMLO, female doctors have no access to proper washroomfacilities, let alone bathroom access for examinees. Hence, the doctor added, it was difficult for doctors even to wash their hands. This is a particularly serious lapse given the intimate nature of the examinations performed by the doctors and the shortage of disposable gloves at the office.

The lack of resources devoted to medicolegal services for women can also extend the delays that women experience in trying to obtain examinations. A WMLO told us that the fact that there was only one examination room means long waits for examinees, even if two WMLOs were present. Examinations are also delayed by the periodic power outages that are common throughout Pakistan. A WMLO said,"Often the electricity goes. This room, already dark, becomes pitch black. Since there is no generator here, we have to wait for the electricity to come back on [to continue work]. Sometimes it is gone for hours." The doctor elaborated that at times, if the power outage is prolonged or if the doctor's shift is coming to an end, examinees are sent back and told to return the following day.

Purpose of Medicolegal Examination

The purpose of medicolegal examinations of sexual assault victims, in theory at least, is to collect physical evidence related to the assault so as to help establish its occurence and the identity of the perpetrator. Moreover, medical evidence can be decisive as corroboration of a woman's allegation that intercourse took place without her consent, which, as discussed above, is particularly crucial in view of Pakistani laws that criminalize adultery and fornication. The inadequacy of examinations in Pakistan contributes to the impunity with which violence against women occurs by making it extremely difficult to bring successfulcases against those who commit sexual assault. It also further abuses women victims by subjecting them to sometimes dangerous and often humiliating examinations as well as making them vulnerable to criminal charges of illicit sex.

Though there is no single internationally recognized standard procedure for conducting medicolegal exams in sexual assault cases, many of the protocols that have been developed share most or all of the following elements:

- after obtaining the consent of the victim, the examiner takes a detailed history of the assault, including when and where the assault took place, whether the rape was anal or vaginal, whether and at what point during the assault the attacker ejaculated, and whether the attacker used a condom in the course of the assault;
- a thorough examination of the victim's body for visible injuries, including redness and swelling in the genital area and photograph each injury;
- collection of clothing that was torn or soiled during the assault and lab specimens, including saliva, sperm, blood, and any foreign object that could be used to identify the perpetrator (such as fibers, hair, dried semen) or the location of the assault (such as sand, fibers, and twigs).

Furthermore, as recommended by the American College of Emergency Physicians, a thorough sexual assault exam must address the medical, psychological, safety, and legal needs of sexually assaulted patients and should include counseling about possible pregnancy and testing and treatment of sexually transmitted diseases. Aside from physical findings and collection of laboratory samples linked directly to the assault, only gynecological information relevant to the the interpretation of the findings or laboratory data should be recorded. Such evidence includes the date of the last menstrual period, any recent gynecological surgery, the number of pregnancies and deliveries, and any consensual sexual intercourse within seventy-two hours of the assault.

Pakistan has not formulated any official standard procedures for conducting forensic examinations of sexual assault victims. However, rather than centering on the collection of relevant evidence to establish the nature and extent of victims' injuries, the de facto focus of the examination is to determine whether she is a virgin. The exam is the same for both victims of sexual assault and women charged with illicit sex and involves the taking of vaginal swabs, a quick check of the external genitalia for signs of redness and bruising, and a "finger test" and visual scrutiny of the hymen to determine its condition and the examinee's virginity status. In certain cases women are referred to laboratories where a urine test and ultrasound exam are performed to determine whether they are pregnant and, if so, the stage of the pregnancy. Some doctors may also take the initiative to elicit a history of events from the victim, but they are neither required nor advised to do so, and there is no standard protocol or list of questions for recording a victim's story.

Inappropriate Focus on Virginity Status

There are several problems with the medicolegal doctors' focus on the condition-that is, whether it is torn or intact-of the hymen. This focus on the hymen has no legal or medical basis and instead reflects a misplaced preoccupation with the victim's ostensible virginity status and popular misconceptions about the medical verifiability of virginity. Modern medical standards hold that the use of visual scrutiny of the hymen or the "finger test"-another technique employed by medicolegal doctors in Pakistan-to make a determination of virginity status ishighly suspect. Nonetheless, these tests remain standard procedure in medicolegal examinations of sexual assault victims in Pakistan.

Furthermore, doctors do not simply record the virginity status of examinees on their reports; based on the finger test, they freqently make notations, such as "She is well used to sexual intercourse" or "She is habituated to sexual intercourse," that have no bearing on the issue of whether the defendant raped the victim on the particular instance in question. Such remarks about the sexual history of victims are then used by defense lawyers to discredit and attack their character at trial and potentially expose the women to prosecution for illicit sex. Thus, the medicolegal report becomes a tool for defense lawyers by providing the basis for vilifying, retraumatizing, and stigmatizing the victim, which then serves to discourage other victims from pressing charges.

Finally, with their misguided focus on the examinee's putative virginity status, doctors virtually ignore other important aspects of evidence collection in sexual assault cases that could potentially corroborate elements of a victim's story, most significantly the non-consensual nature of the intercourse. For example, examinees are not required to undress fully for purposes of the examination, and doctors do not take adequate care in checking all parts of an examinee's body for bruises, scratches, bites, teeth marks, or other indicia of struggle or violence. In addition, doctors do not collect stray fibers or debris adhering to the victim's body that could be traced to perpetrators or the location of the assault.

Similarly, Hadd punishments for the crimes of adultery and fornication differ for muhsan and non-muhsan offenders. There is no sound legal justification for performing the finger test on women suspected of adultery or fornication, despite the distinction in sentences for muhsan and non-muhsan offenders, because the test cannot ascertain whether the examinee has previously had *legal* sexual intercourse, which determines her muhsan or non-muhsan status. Even if the test were legally relevant, it should be abandoned given its inaccuracy and inadequacy as a medical technique for its stated purpose of determining a woman's virginity and level of sexual activity.

The focus on the state of the hymen greatly reduces the value of the exam for all victims of sexual assault. Moreover, the uniform focus of and standard procedures applied in every examination renders it virtually useless for sexually active women for whom the patterns of injuries emanating from sexual assault can be considerably different from those of women who are not sexually active and hence require adapted examination techniques that take into consideration an examinee's age, whether she is sexually active, and the number of children to whom she has given birth.

Dr. Lubna from the Office of the Surgeon Medicolegal in Lahore said that in cases in which the victim was a virgin before the rape, the condition of the hymen is a useful indicator of recent sexual intercourse when the examination occurs in a timely fashion because it is possible to discern "a freshly torn hymen" and distinguish between "a freshly torn hymen and an old torn hymen." "We can tell if the hymen is freshly torn with the eye, since it will have abrasions and lacerations around the edges. The edges of a hymen with an old tear are smooth," she said. She added, "For a married woman, one cannot tell if she has been raped or not from the hymen. Also, no injury shows, especially in older women, so generally not much evidence is collected from married women. . . . It helps in thecase of unmarried women that the vagina is tight, to show that it could have been rape."

The police do not expect medicolegal exams of married women to be useful in terms of securing evidence because of the focus on the condition of the hymen. For married women, no internal wounds are possible. Only external bodily injuries can be found." Judge Javed Qaiser also asserted that medicolegal exams of married women were not effective. "The [condition of the] hymen is the only way to determine [for virgin victims] what occurred, though hymens can also be broken by activities like cycling. But for married women, how can medical exams help?" he asked.

A WMLO at the police surgeon's office in Karachi had an answer. She said,"If a woman has been married for a while, there will still be congestion [redness], though only for a day or two. We can find vaginal injuries, but time is of the essence. Also, if the woman has struggled, we can find signs of struggle on other parts of the body such as the breasts, thighs, swollen lips." The fact that doctors do not even consistently ask victims for details about the assault also undermines an exam's value because, in order to be comprehensive and elucidative, the exam should reflect and be informed by the victim's experience. In part because of the mistrust and skepticism discussed earlier, medicolegal doctors examining victims of sexual assault in Pakistan as a rule conduct exams and seek evidence strictly in accordance with written police requests and as ordered by a magistrate.

As Doctor Lubna's derisive and incredulous attitude towards examinees described above indicates, victims arriving at the Office of Surgeon Medicolegal in Lahore are often treated harshly and insensitively by medicolegal staff. Reflecting a similar situation, doctors at Karachi's main medicolegal center spoke to Human Rights Watch of outright harrassment of female examinees by the chief police surgeon for Karachi, Capt. Nizamuddin Memon. Captain Memon broached inappropriate topics related to prostitution and various sexual practices that were not relevant to the purposes of the interview. His unprofessional conduct during the interview coincided with his colleague's descriptions of his behavior in the course of fulfilling his duties, which include examining women to determine their ages based on an assessment of signs of puberty.

Since September 1996 [when he assumed the post of chief police surgeon] there have been only two cases of genuine rape. Others come in the hundreds, but they lie. Those are zina [adultery/fornication] cases. Rape victims do not report attacks based on social factors." Although Capt. Memon's behavior might be an extreme example of abuse of authority, there is no doubt that the criminalization of adultery and fornication serves to create an environment in which all examinees are routinely humiliated and mistreated.

Finally, it should be noted that apart from referrals for pregnancy tests provided by the Karachi medicolegal center, medicolegal doctors fail to provide victims of sexual assault with even minimal treatment for the health consequences of the attack. In the words of Dr. Lubna of the Office of Surgeon Medicolegal in Lahore, "Treatment is not our concern." Although in cases of serious injury, doctors do refer women to government hospitals where they can obtain treatment, in most cases the medicolegal doctor is the only doctor a victim of assault will see. Hence, the failure to provide basic counseling and treatment is particularly troubling.

In Pakistan, the same doctors perform examinations on both victims of sexual assault and women accused of adultery or fornication. The doctors examine many more women in the latter category than in the former. As difficult as the exam may be for a victim of sexual assault, women accused of adultery confront doctors who are even less sympathetic. The doctors' skepticism towards their examinees is sometimes colored by the misguided perception that they are criminals and "wayward" women.

This perception not only violates the professional objectivity expected from a doctor but also denies women their right to the presumption of innocence, since women charged with adultery or fornication are taken for medicolegal examinations prior to trial and many women are wrongly accused of these crimes.

According to doctors, lawyers, and judges, the test results and analysis reports from both the Karachi and Lahore laboratories were not always reliable, largely as a result of corruption and incompetence in the ranks of the laboratory staff. Dr. Akmal Shaheen asserted that he had occasionally questioned personnel at the chemical examiner's office in Lahore when he received unexpected results for certain tests and was told, "Our petri dishes are contaminated." Though these problems affect all cases that involve forensic evidence, they are particularly devastating to the prosecution of sexual assault cases, in which corroborating forensic evidence is crucial.

Laboratory staff explained that their ability to obtain accurate results was often limited by the condition of the samples that they received. They complained that sometimes samples are improperly or inadequately labeled, contaminated, decomposed, or otherwise damaged. But the quality of test results also suffers from incompetence and corruption at the laboratories themselves. Like the medicolegal doctors, the staff at the Office of the Chemical Examiner are insufficiently trained for their responsibilities.

According to a senior chemist at the Chemical Examiner's Office in Karachi, the laboratory takes one-and-a-half months at a minimum to generate a semen analysis report. "It can take three months or more," she said. As for the work load at the laboratory's semen section, she said. "Per month about twenty to twenty-five cases come to the semen section." Additional Sessions Judge Javed Qaiser complained that delays at the chemical examiner's office routinely held up cases and pointed to corruption as the cause of the problem. "Usually the chemical examiner's report is so delayed that even the witnesses and parties have given up on the case. So even if the report is favorable, it is no use . . . The police surgeon's reports arrive relatively on time.

In sexual assault cases, the report of the medicolegal doctor, which is generally prepared within twenty-four hours of the examination of a victim, is admitted into evidence, and the doctor is required to testify in court regarding the examination and her findings.

The doctor's testimony is usually based directly on the report. In Karachi, the chief chemical examiner also testifies in court as to the findings in the analysis reports prepared by his staff, while in Lahore, thefindings of the Office of the Chemical Examiner are simply incorporated into the doctor's medicolegal report, and none of the laboratory staff testifies.

Even more disturbing is the fact that medical evidence, as it is currently collected, presented, and interpreted, often provides little assistance to the prosecutor and may instead serve to humiliate and even incriminate the victim. Referring to the unhelpful substantive format of medicolegal reports in rape cases, Karachi prosecutor Islamuddin Ayubi noted, "[t]he chemical report that records the presence of semen is more important for the prosecution than the medicolegal report." This is a problematic conclusion in its own right since penetration, without ejaculation, is sufficient to constitute rape under Pakistani law.

Doctors' poor presentation in court, lack of training, and the present focus of the medicolegal report on the virginity status of the victim turn these exams into an effective tool for the defense case. Defense lawyers aggressively use the medicolegal doctor's stated findings to their advantage. Any notations in the medicolegal report, such as "She is used to sexual intercourse" or "She is habitual," are seized upon by defense counsel to smear the character of the victim. As a result, it is not uncommon to find the phrase, "a woman of easy virtue," with reference to the victim in judicial opinions in sexual assault cases.

Under the Universal Declaration of Human Rights, its implementing covenants and the United Nations Convention Against Torture, the right not to be subjected to such abuse ranks as one of the most fundamental, guaranteed to all persons without distinction of any kind, including discrimination on the basis of gender. Yet, until recently, torture and ill-treatment of women in custody – as a phenomenon distinct from the mistreatment of men – had received scant attention from those concerned with human rights in the international community. This failure adequately to address women's rights is rooted partly in the human rights community's past emphasis on politically motivated abuses by governments. However, even as human rights monitors worldwide have expanded their focus to include the nature of abuses regardless of their motivation, the international community has barely begun to concern itself with violations of human rights that are gender-specific in character.

A study reports that, more than 70 percent of women in police custody experience physical or sexual abuse at the hands of their jailers. Reported abuses include beating and slapping; suspension in mid-air by hands tied behind the victim's back; the insertion of foreign objects, including police batons and chili peppers, into the vagina and rectum; and gang rape. Yet despite these alarming reports, to our knowledge not a single officer has suffered criminal penalties for such abuse, even in cases in which incontrovertible evidence of custodial rape exists.

In one case in 1988, three women were detained for alleged sexual offenses under the *Hudood* laws and were held in police custody for 48 hours before being produced before a magistrate and ultimately released for lack of evidence. While in police lock-up, all three women were raped and sexually abused by several officers; one of the women, who was 60 years old, had police batons inserted forcibly and repeatedly into her vagina and rectum. Although a judicial inquiry into the incident initiated by local human rights attorneys supported the rape and abuse charges, the police were never prosecuted.

Given the likelihood that women will experience abuse in police custody, we were particularly disturbed to find that many of the women detainees in Pakistan did not deserve to be in custody in the first place. In pointing this out, of course, we do not suggest that such abuse would be justified even if they were deservedly incarcerated. We found that between 50 and 80 percent of all female detainees in Pakistan were imprisoned under the *Hudood* Ordinances, Islamic penal laws introduced in 1979, which in law and in practice discriminate against them.

Hudood Ordinances

Prior to the passage of the *Hudood* Ordinances, women

were not directly involved with the criminal justice system in any significant number; only 70 women were incarcerated in the entire country. By 1991, over 2,000 women were imprisoned under these laws alone. The steep rise in the number of female prisoners in turn increased the opportunity for police misconduct towards women.

The *Hudood* Ordinances criminalize, among other things, adultery, fornication and rape, and prescribe punishments for these offenses that include stoning to death, public flogging and amputation. Human Rights Watch has no opposition to Islamic law *per se* and does not object to laws founded on religion, provided that human rights are respected and the principle of equality before the law is upheld. However, the *Hudood* laws, as written and applied, clearly conflict with these rights and principles. Not only do they prescribe punishments that are cruel and inhuman under international law, but they clearly discriminate on the basis of gender. The laws also conflict with the Pakistani Constitution, which guarantees the right to equality and non-discrimination on the basis of gender.

Under the *Hudood* laws, proof of rape for the maximum (*Hadd*) punishments of stoning to death or 100 lashes in a public place requires the testimony of four male Muslim witnesses to the act of penetration. The testimony of women – not only the victim but *any* woman – carries no legal weight. This requirement means that women who have been sentenced to the maximum punishments, deemed cruel and inhuman under international law, have been so sentenced under a law that prevents them from testifying on their own behalf.

Men have also been cruelly sentenced under these laws, although in general men accused of rape are effectively exempted from the maximum *Hadd* punishments because women can neither testify nor is any person likely to be able to produce four male Muslim witnesses to the act of penetration. We recognize that no *Hadd* sentences have been carried out to date, but nothing impedes the state from doing so in the future.

The majority of rape and adultery or fornication cases attract the lesser (*Tazir*) punishments which entail public flogging, rigorous imprisonment and fines. While the testimony of women is admissible at this level, Pakistani courts still exhibited a bias against women. The courts tend to see women as complicit in sexual offenses, despite a lack of evidence, or evidence to the contrary, and required from female rape victims extraordinarily conclusive proof that the alleged intercourse was forced.

Moreover, many women who alleged but were unable to prove rape have themselves been charged with adultery or fornication for consensual sex, although a failure to prove rape does not prove that consexual occurred. The courts effectively have set a lesser burden of proof for the prosecution in cases involving female defendants.

In some cases, when medical evidence has been introduced in support of a rape charge in which forcible intercourse cannot be proved, the male has also been charged with adultery or fornication. However, medical evidence implicating accused males often cannot be obtained, so they are frequently released for lack of evidence while their women victims are imprisoned pending trial based on their own allegations of forcible intercourse.

The discriminatory provisions of the *Hudood* laws are exacerbated by their discriminatory application by the police and judiciary. According to several Pakistani legal aid attorneys who represent indigent women charged with *Hudood* offenses, the vast majority of *Hudood* cases (most of which are registered by the woman's husband or father) are not supported by the evidence and should not have been prosecuted. In part, judges hear ill-founded *Hudood* cases because they, like the police, are eager to show that they are tough on crime. However, wrongful prosecution of women also reflects a tendency on the part of the police and judiciary to see women as guilty until proven innocent.

In effect, the *Hudood* laws have given legal sanction to biased social attitudes towards women, thus not only legitimating the oppression of women in the eyes of the state but also intensifying it: women who seek to deviate from prescribed social norms now may not only be subject to societal censure, but also to criminal penalties. It is this enforcement of religion and its use as a tool to legitimate abusive state power, rather than religion itself, that is at issue here. Although acquittal rates for women in *Hudood* cases are estimated at over 30 percent, by the time a woman has been vindicated she will have spent months, and in many cases years, in prison and, in all likelihood, been subjected to police abuse while in custody.

Punishment

Even in cases in which no formal charge is brought against a woman, judges often suspect that if she was abducted or raped she must have been behaving inappropriately to begin with and was in some way complicit in the offense. Filing a formal charge against the women in such cases, judges frequently remand female rape and abduction victims to private detention facilities for indefinite periods to await the outcome of the cases lodged against their alleged abusers.

Thirty-nine women had been remanded there against their will by local courts - including one who had been forced to spend more than two-and-a-half years in custody. The facility's administrators justified such prolonged detention as a form of "protective custody" for the women, but in effect it amounted to the punitive detention of innocent women for the crime of being an alleged victim. Then, a local human rights organization filed *habeas corpus* petitions on the women's behalf and fifteen were freed. However, the cases had no effect on the underlying problem of private detention of women accused of no offense.

The possibility of obtaining equal justice in Pakistan has been further reduced over the past decade by the steady erosion of judicial independence, mainly through the government's retention of undue influence over the judiciary and through the establishment of parallel religious and speedy-trial courts. While Human Rights Watch does not oppose religious courts or speedy-trial rules *per se*, both the religious and speedy trial courts in Pakistan have been shown to weaken the independence and jurisdiction of the civil courts and to violate many aspects of due process.

This trend culminated in the adoption of the 1991 *Shariat* Act, which subjects the Constitution and the law-making authority of the legislature to the revisional authority of Islamic religious leaders, many of whom, according to local human rights activists, "have been known to take positions against women."

The discriminatory treatment encountered by women

who enter the criminal justice system reflects the treatment of women as second class citizens by Pakistani society at large. From birth, the life of the average Pakistani woman is characterized by her economic, social, cultural and political subordination. She will receive less food, medical care, and education, be paid and inherit less, have fewer opportunities to participate in civil society, and live a shorter lifespan than her male counterparts.

Even in comparison with women in many other parts of the world, she will on average marry earlier, bear more children, suffer higher rates of maternal mortality and work more hours without compensation. Like women everywhere, she will be subjected to violence in the home and, in some areas of Pakistan, by the community, particularly when she engages in behavior seen to deviate from prescribed social norms.

Eighty percent of all female prisoners in Pakistan are illiterate and nearly 90 percent live on a monthly family income of less than 40 dollars. According to a survey conducted in 1988, over 90 percent of the 90 women prisoners interviewed in two prisons in Punjab were unaware of the law under which they had been imprisoned. Over 60 percent had received no legal assistance whatsoever.

These deplorable conditions are not the exclusive lot of Pakistani women in Pakistani jails. Women from Bangladesh, many of whom have been forcibly taken to Pakistan, often via India, for the purpose of domestic or sexual servitude, are arrested by the Pakistani police, often for *Hudood* offenses, and subjected to the same abusive and discriminatory treatment as that suffered by their Pakistani counterparts.

National Survey

According to a 1991 national survey by a nongovernmental social welfare organization in Pakistan, between 100 and 150 Bangladeshi women are illicitly taken to Pakistan each month. The majority are lured by promises of better jobs, but often end up in brothels where they are compelled to provide sexual services, or in private homes where they are forced to work as domestic servants or, in some cases, to become wives. The average age of the women and girls victimized by this trafficking is 15. At current prices, and depending on the virginity, beauty and health of the girls and women, a sale can bring the equivalent of from U.S. $800 to U.S. $2,000.

Rather than protecting these women and girls by arresting those engaged in their illegal sale and abuse, the government of Pakistan imprisons them while letting the pimps go free. According to the survey mentioned above, 1,400 Bangladeshi women and girls are currently in prison in Pakistan, ostensibly for entering the country illegally or for offenses under the *Hudood* Ordinances. While pimps involved in the sale of Bangladeshi women have occasionally been arrested by the police, we are unaware of a single one who has been prosecuted or punished for trafficking in women or for abuses commonly associated with the practice.

This official inaction exists despite Pakistan's obligations under the Convention for the Suppression of the Traffic in Persons, to which it is a party, to punish such abuses. Rather, as one local observer commented, the government seems bent on "victimizing the victims" rather than prosecuting the victimizers.

Human rights and women's rights advocates have been actively campaigning for over 10 years for the repeal of discriminatory laws, including the *Hudood* Ordinances, good faith prosecution of abusive police, greater adherence to the fundamental principles of due process and equality before the law, and increased legal services for women. Some members of Pakistan's judiciary, particularly at the High Court level, have recognized the epidemic proportions of violence against women in custody and have initiated investigations into instances of the problem that the police themselves have refused to examine. On September 21, 1991, Pakistan's Prime Minister promulgated regulations prohibiting police from keeping women overnight in custody, although they have not been observed in practice, and the Cabinet reportedly is considering legislation that would require women to be detained in judicial rather than police facilities. Despite these welcome measures, the government's response remains woefully inadequate.

Pakistan is obliged under international law and its own Constitution to refrain from torture and ill-treatment of prisoners in custody and to provide female victims of such abuse with equal protection of the law.

But the government has failed to eliminate the overtly discriminatory laws and practices that promote the wrongful prosecution of women and result in their prolonged imprisonment. And rather than remove procedural obstacles to justice for the victims of police abuse, the government has adopted policies that perpetuate police impunity and erode judicial independence.

Finally, the government's response to the fate of the hundreds of Bangladeshi women in Pakistani jails, and the thousands more who have been forced into prostitution and domestic servitude in Pakistan, has aptly been characterized by the local press as one of "bottomless indifference."

As a member of the United Nations, Pakistan has an obligation to uphold the rights and principles enshrined in the Universal Declaration of Human Rights, including the right not to be tortured or to be subjected to cruel or inhuman punishment or degrading treatment, and the right to be free of discrimination on the basis of gender. Moreover, despite the government's stated intention to eliminate custodial violence and gender-discrimination, it has yet to adopt most of the relevant international human rights instruments, including the International Covenant on Civil and Political Rights and the Convention on the Elimination of All Forms of Discrimination Against Women. Although Pakistan is a signatory to the Convention for the Suppression of the Traffic in Persons, it has largely failed to meet its obligations under this agreement. As Pakistan bids to be a significant regional power and reassert its past international standing, the government must take immediate steps to adopt and adhere to international human rights standards and to end all forms of violence against women and gender-discrimination.

National Movement

The first Constituent Assembly of Pakistan included two female members who had been active in the independence struggle. Both pushed for the inclusion of 10 reserved seats for women in the provincial and national legislatures. When the Constitution was finally adopted in 1956, it included women's suffrage for seats reserved for women, which were to be filled on the basis of special women's territorial constituencies, but which amounted to only 3 percent of the provincial and central assemblies. Thus, the Constitution granted women a dual franchise: for the three percent of the seats which were reserved for women and for the general seats as well.

The main victory for women in this period was brought about by the creation of the first national women's movement of Pakistan – the All-Pakistan Women's Association (APWA) – and its activism on behalf of women's rights. The organization was founded by the prime minister's wife, Begum Rana Liaquat Ali Khan, and was seen as an indication of the new government's commitment to improving the status of women. APWA was the moving force in Pakistan's early years behind improvements in women's access to education and health care, and it founded one of the first legal aid services for women.

One of APWA's lasting contributions was its campaign against gender discrimination in the family. The campaign was sparked by the prime minister's decision to take a second wife, which led the government to establish a Commission on Marriage and Family Laws to review and reform existing laws on polygamy and divorce. The Commission recommended improving women's legal rights of marriage, divorce and child custody. But these recommendations became enmeshed in the controversies over Pakistan's national identity that re-emerged in the constitutional debates of the mid-1950s.

Era of Ayub Khan

Pakistan's first government was under increasing attack by both conservative Muslims, for its failure to create a truly Islamic state, and by dissenters within its own party, for failure to stabilize the independent government. These pressures, coupled with mounting social and economic problems, created a crisis of confidence in state power. The government delayed adopting the Commission's recommendations for fear of further weakening its already tenuous hold on power. The government's decision about what to do was pre-empted by General Ayub Khan's military coup of 1958, which established the military as the central governing authority of independent Pakistan. Ayub Khan viewed Pakistan's religious elites along with other dissident voices as obstacles to the country's progress. Although his reign instituted a period of martial law that contributed to the collapse of Pakistan's fledgling democratic structures, the effect on women was mixed: while Ayub Khan undercut some recent gains his regime also encompassed a period of remarkable development for women.

In 1961, after considerable lobbying by APWA and several other women's groups, Ayub Khan's government promulgated the Muslim Family Laws Ordinance, which drew heavily on the Commission's earlier recommendations. Moreover, during his administration from 1956 to 1969, Ayub Khan adopted social and economic polices that led to women's increased participation in the labor market and their improved access to education.

However, these seemingly progressive policies toward women were undercut by Ayub Khan's unwillingness to advance beyond a certain point for fear of compromising his political power base. The adoption of the Muslim Family Laws Ordinance was a major advance, but the limitations of Ayub's policies toward women were exposed by his vehement opposition to the popular candidacy of Fatima Jinnah, the sister of Pakistan's founder, for the office of president in the 1965 elections. Ayub opposed Jinnah on the grounds that no woman could be the head of state of a Muslim country, and he had several *ulama*, whom he had previously denounced, issue religious edicts to the effect that a woman head of state was un-Islamic.

By contrast, driven by their own political calculations, the conservative religious parties, including the Jama'at-e Islami, which had steadfastly opposed every advance in women's rights since the creation of Pakistan, supported Fatima Jinnah's candidacy on the grounds that in "extraordinary circumstances" a woman could hold such an office. In this case, the "extraordinary circumstances" were that her candidacy, which was very popular, might result in the return to power of a government more sympathetic to their views than Ayub Khan's. As noted by Farida Shaheed, the Fatima Jinnah controversy "underscored the manner in which religion has been constantly used by political forces in Pakistan to further their own purposes and justify contradictory positions."

Among the most serious setbacks of this period were the elimination of reserved seats for women (included in the 1956

Constitution) from the 1962 Constitution adopted during Ayub Khan's leadership, and the government's failure to implement the Muslim Family Laws Ordinance. In the absence of a concerted government effort, the law's effect was limited, and pre-existing cultural and religious norms continued to hold great sway.

In 1969, Ayub Khan's government was replaced by one under General Yahya Khan, who again imposed martial law. Yahya Khan's rule was short-lived, lasting only long enough to preside over the bloody civil war that ended with the partition of Pakistan and the creation of Bangladesh. In 1972, General Khan handed over power to Zulfiquar Ali Bhutto, whose Pakistan People's Party (PPP) had won a majority of National Assembly seats in West Pakistan in the election held just before the war. Women played a key role in mobilizing on the PPP's behalf, and the PPP political platform promised equality for women. Bhutto's tenure, while characterized by political oppression similar to that of his predecessors, brought about additional advances for women.

1973 Constitution

Most notable was the adoption of the 1973 Constitution which, for the first time in Pakistan's history, guaranteed women equality under the law and established their rights to full participation in all spheres of national life. That women still had a long way to go to exercise these rights had been underscored by the limited success of women candidates in the 1970 elections. The 1973 Constitution reserved 10 seats in the assembly for women, who would be nominated by the assembly members themselves. This provision was not meant to undercut women's right to stand in general elections, but it made clear that women were still disadvantaged politically and lacked a strong popular constituency.

During Bhutto's administration, reforms opened up the Civil Service, the Foreign Service and other government agencies to women, and women's participation in government increased dramatically. With government support, an independent Commission on Women's Rights was established in 1975 to examine the status of women in Pakistan and propose legal reforms to improve their social, legal, political and economic conditions. In this period, the number of independent women's organizations engaged in social welfare and grassroots political activism increased.

The general failure of Bhutto's economic reforms alienated a wide spectrum of political groups, most importantly those from the urban middle class and the left, that had previously supported him. Bhutto's promotion of women's rights, while failing to address the vast social and economic inequities suffered by the majority of women in Pakistan, also added to a conservative backlash from religious parties who drew their support from the middle class Pakistanis who had been hit hardest by Bhutto's economic reforms.

Finally, the military, which became increasingly disturbed over the deterioration of law and order, blamed the persisting problems on Bhutto's "populist" policies and overthrew him in a coup led by General Zia ul-Haq in 1977. Zia's coup represented the convergence of conservative religious interests with those of the army. In the absence of any clear popular constituency, Zia cultivated the conservative religious parties to bolster his legitimacy. In return, he provided those parties, which had never had strong support from the electorate, with access to national political power.

Zia came to power denouncing Bhutto's regime as un-Islamic, and one of his main rallying cries was the return of Pakistani society "to the moral purity of early Islam." His most vulnerable and strategic targets were women, whom he promised to return to "the sanctity of the *chardivari* [the four walls of the home]," thus resuscitating the family and women's role in it, as the cornerstone of a Muslim way of life. Within months he had introduced a series of legal and social changes that reversed many of the legal advances for women of the prior thirty years. This backsliding demonstrated that, despite seeming progress, the status of the majority of Pakistan's women had not changed substantially since independence. Women's few hard-won legal gains were easily curtailed.

Martial Law

With the imposition of martial law, Zia suspended all fundamental rights guaranteed in the Constitution, including the right to be free of discrimination on the basis of gender. He then introduced a series of laws that gave legal sanction to women's subordinate status, including the *Hudood* Ordinances, the *Qanun-e-Shahadat* (Law of Evidence Order) and proposed laws regarding *Qisas* and *Diyat*, Islamic penal laws governing compensation and retribution in crimes involving grave bodily injury.

Briefly summarized, the *Hudood* Ordinances penalize theft, drunkenness, fornication, adultery, rape and defamation. They require the testimony of four male Muslim witnesses to impose maximum punishment for rape, adultery and fornication. In adultery, fornication and rape cases for married persons, the maximum punishment is stoning to death; for unmarried persons, it is 100 lashes in a public place. Women's testimony was excluded, which had the effect not only of protecting men accused of rape from maximum punishments (which in any case are considered cruel and inhuman under international law), but also of disfavoring women who were, in the absence of four male Muslim witnesses to the act of penetration, unable to prove rape. This made women victims susceptible to charges that, rather than having been raped, they had committed the crimes of adultery or fornication.

The Law of Evidence similarly relegates women to inferior legal status and, in some circumstances, renders the testimony of women equal to only half that of men. In addition, under the *Qisas* and *Diyat* laws proposed at the time, compensation for the death of a female victim was half that of a man. On the other hand, a woman charged with murder could receive the same punishment as a man.

Zia reinforced the legal strictures he imposed on women with a series of informal regulations and unwritten polices designed to curtail women's personal liberty and their participation in public life. In 1980, Zia required all government officials to adhere to Islamic dress codes. However, men were only required to wear national dress whereas women were expected to adhere to the stricter Islamic Code of Dress. In 1982, he followed this directive with another aimed solely at women, which required women teachers and students in government schools and all female government official to wear the *chador* over their clothes and to cover their heads.

Female members of the Foreign Service were recalled and

the Ansari Commission, set up by Zia in 1983 to "Islamize" Pakistan's political system, recommended that the office of the head of state be closed to women and that female members in the National Assembly be over 50-years-old and have the permission of their husbands to participate.

While the Ansari Commission's suggestions concerning women were largely ignored (with the exception of recommendations restricting the nature and length of women's appearances on television), they contributed to the chilling atmosphere of state-sponsored and -tolerated discrimination against women. According to Shaheed, the effect was to raise "an entire generation in Pakistan to distrust and dislike any woman deviating from...[the] norm of good, house-bound, veiled, self-effacing, self-sacrificing, second class citizen."

The Zia era produced a shift in the relationship between women's rights and religion in Pakistani politics. Until 1977, the constantly changing religious and political alignments mitigated against both conservative and progressive extremes and, with the help of a growing number of independent organizations, women were able to secure a steady flow of moderate reforms, although their impact on the majority of women was minimal. After Zia's coup, the politics of the army and the religious right were so closely aligned that the opportunity for reform disappeared, and women took a step backward. Increased social control of women was an important part of the Zia regime's appropriation of conservative religious values to legitimate state power.

Zia's Islamization campaign had the effect not only of legitimating the existing subordination of women in the eyes of the state but also of intensifying that oppression. Women who deviated from prescribed social norms thus faced not only social censure but also criminal penalties. This development gave the more powerful and legally favored members of Pakistani society — men — a punitive sanction to hang over the heads of women and, by extension, their families. This situation was amply suited to the martial law government's need to exert and maintain social control.

Pakistan's poorer women, who had gained least from the legal reforms previously secured by their better-off sisters, were the hardest hit by Zia's retrenchment. The number of women in prison at any moment — the vast majority of whom were illiterate and impoverished and, therefore, in no position to press for their rights — soared, from as few as 70 in 1980 to as many as 4,500 in 1990.

A 1985 study by the Pakistan Commission on the Status of Women, whose findings were suppressed by the Zia administration, concluded that women in Pakistan were treated as possessions rather than self-reliant, self-regulating humans. They are bought, sold, beaten, mutilated and even killed with impunity and social approval. They are dispossessed and disinherited in spite of legal safeguards [and] the vast majority are made to work for as long as 16 to 18 hours a day without payment.

In September 1981, women came together in Karachi in an emergency meeting to oppose the adverse effects on women of martial law and the Islamization campaign. They launched what was to become the first full-fledged national women's movement in Pakistan: the Women's Action Forum (WAF). WAF grew steadily in its first two years, opening branches in most of Pakistan's major urban areas and attracting endorsements from all the established women's organizations, including the APWA.

However, WAF's rise to national and international prominence did not come until February 12, 1983 when the Pakistan Women Lawyers Association organized a march on the Lahore High Court in which many WAF members participated to protest Zia's Law of Evidence. The march was the first public demonstration by any group against a martial law edict. Police broke up the demonstration using tear gas and batons, injuring some women and arresting nearly 50 others. Pictures of the courageous women being lathi-charged (88) by the police were plastered all over Pakistan, and WAF along with women's rights issues were catapulted onto the national scene.

WAF was to become one of the main voices of opposition to Zia and the leading opponent of his policies toward women. WAF staged public protests and campaigns against the *Hudood* Ordinances, the Law of Evidence, the *Qisas* and *Diyat* laws (temporarily shelved as a result), the Ansari Commission's report, and the proposed 9th Constitutional Amendment. The

Amendment, which was defeated in part because of effective opposition by women, would have placed the hard-won Muslim Family Laws Ordinance of 1961 under the jurisdiction of the Federal *Shariat* Court.

However, in challenging Zia's policies, WAF found itself challenging "Islam" and denounced as "un-Islamic," although nearly all of its membership was Muslim.

WAF's quandary went to the heart of the relationship between religion and women's rights in Pakistani politics. It raised the question of what is meant to be by "Islamic" and whether, in an Islamic country, women's rights should be founded in religion or secular law. From the standpoint of an international human rights organization, the provenance of women's rights in a given state is not of paramount concern — so long as those rights comport with accepted international principles of equality before the law and equal protection of the law.

Rather, it is abuses of women's rights by the state, no matter what the justification (religious, secular or otherwise) that warrant international condemnation. However, for women trying to obtain rights denied them by a particular state, the source of rights is often an important strategic issue. From its inception, WAF hotly debated whether to adopt a secular or religious approach to securing women's rights in Pakistan.

Some members promoted an understanding of Islam that supports and protects equality for women, and believed that this approach would be more persuasive to the majority of Pakistan's women. Other WAF members vehemently opposed this approach, saying that it would subject to religious interpretation rights that are already established as universal and fundamental, and that should not be modified in accordance with local cultural circumstances. In Pakistan, the two approaches have often been in conflict, yet WAF has attempted to use both — a flexibility which has helped it to survive in difficult times.

The coming to power of Benazir Bhutto in 1988 represented yet another radical shift in the history of women's rights in Pakistan. It amounted to an unprecedented alignment of state power with an apparently progressive women's rights policy. Bhutto's campaign pledge to repeal the *Hudood* laws, to release women imprisoned under *Hudood*, and to remove all other discriminatory statutes had great appeal. However, soon after Bhutto's election, it became clear that, once again, the protection of women's rights had been subordinated to the need to maintain a delicate balance between various political forces, including those representing conservative religious values. The PPP's failure to secure a majority in the national assembly made it necessary for Bhutto to strike political deals with smaller groups, including the Jama'at-e-Islami, and her campaign promises on women's rights gradually proved empty. Although Bhutto did release women sentenced under *Hudood*, she limited the amnesty only to convicted women. Pending-trial female prisoners, who constituted the vast majority, were not affected. Moreover, she never repealed a single one of Zia's Islamization laws.

When Bhutto's government was dissolved in 1990, the women's groups that had been lulled into inaction by the appearance of a female Prime Minister were discouraged. The appointment of Nawaz Sharif, appeared to provide little opportunity for progress. Sharif's political rhetoric was reminiscent of the Zia years. When he came to power in November 1990, he promised to adopt Islamic law as the supreme law of Pakistan, and in April 1991 he introduced legislation to that effect. Many women's rights activists, including WAF, feared that women would be forced to take yet another step backward.

Yet, despite Sharif's rhetoric, the political reality has shifted considerably since Zia's days. The interests of the state are not as clearly aligned with the religious right as during martial law; indeed, in some cases, they are clearly in conflict. In this context the implications of the *Shariat* Act remain unclear: on the one hand, after sustained lobbying by women's rights groups and the PPP, a clause protecting women's constitutional rights was incorporated in the act's language; on the other, the act as a whole has strong support from the religious right, even though it has opposed even the minimal guarantees added to the amendment.

Women are particularly concerned that the reaffirmation of constitutional rights in the *Shariat* Act may not protect reforms like the Muslim Family Laws Ordinance that are not spelled out in the Constitution.

Today, the role of religious interests at the national level remains uncertain, as does the direction of government policy toward women. Regardless of its direction, however, clear violations of international law on the rights of women occur daily in Pakistan without an adequate state response.

Women in Custody

Precise data on the number of women currently in police custody or prison in Pakistan are difficult to obtain. Police do not keep statistics separated by gender, nor do they compile national criminal statistics in any systematic way. However, available figures clearly indicate that, after a sharp decline in convicted prisoners during the tenure of Benazir Bhutto, the number of female detainees is rapidly rising.

A 1980 study of criminal justice in Pakistan documented only some 70 female convicts in the entire country. By 1987, the number had increased to 125 female convicts in the state of Punjab alone, and an estimated 91 in the state of Sindh. The number of pre-trial female prisoners is even more difficult to determine because of their dispersal in jails throughout the country.

However, according to police records for all of Pakistan in 1983, a minimum of 1,682 women faced trial for offenses solely under the *Hudood* Ordinances. That number increased to 1,843 in 1984 and has continued to rise ever since. In late 1988, according to a study conducted by Pakistani human rights attorneys Asma Jahangir and Hina Jilani, there were 503 female pre-trial prisoners in Punjab's 21 jails alone. By 1990, the number reportedly had reached 738. Sociologists Khawar Mumtaz and Farida Shaheed estimated that in 1990 there were a total of 4,500 women prisoners (both convicts and pre-trial) in the entire country. Compared to the number of men incarcerated in Pakistan these figures are extremely low.

However, they represent a vast increase in the involvement of Pakistani women with the criminal justice system that, before the passage of the *Hudood* laws in 1979, had been minimal. Women's increased involvement in the criminal justice system has in turn exposed them to more frequent violence by the police. Torture and abuse of prisoners in police custody — particularly in police lock-ups — are common throughout Pakistan, and abuses against women detainees are frequent. According to a 1988 survey of female prisoners in Punjab (both convicts and pre-trials), 78 percent alleged maltreatment while in police custody and 72 percent claimed they had been sexually abused by the police. Sexual abuses ranged from rape, including the insertion of foreign objects into the vagina and rectum, to beating and manipulation of exposed genital areas, to stripping and public exposure.

According to Lahore-based researchers quoted in a recent study of rape, "the official 1991 figure of 1,117 reported rapes in the Punjab [population approximately 50 million] is not even the tip of the iceberg. In Pakistan, the social stigma attached to rape and laws that often lead to the victim herself being prosecuted have resulted in most cases of rape going unreported."

The vast majority of Pakistan's female prisoners are poor and illiterate. A 1987 study of female prisoners in the Multan jail in Punjab concluded that the majority were from rural areas, 69 percent lacked any formal education, 26 percent could read only the Quran, and only a small proportion had some formal education. Seventy-one percent of the female prisoners came from Pakistan's lowest income bracket.

A 1988 study of the Multan and Lahore prisons in the Punjab revealed similar, more disturbing patterns. Eighty-two percent of the female prisoners came from rural areas, 88 percent were completely illiterate, and more than half came from families with a monthly income of less than 1,000 Pakistani rupees, or roughly 40 U.S. dollars. These attributes place female prisoners in a particularly precarious position when they are in the custody of the police.

Perhaps most disturbing is that many of the women detainees imprisoned under such circumstances do not belong in prison in the first place in that the law under which they were imprisoned is overtly discriminatory and, in any event, there is often no evidence to support the charge against them. According to a 1987 interview with the Inspector General of prisons, "[m]aybe 50 percent of the women in jail are innocent, but because they are unaware of their rights and are too poor to hire proper legal aid, they are convicted." He told researchers investigating conditions in the women's prisons that most women prisoners were victims of intrigues and vendettas pursued by males. A local human rights attorney, who frequently acts of behalf of indigent women charged with *Hudood* offenses, estimates that over the vast majority of such cases are not supported by the evidence and should never have been prosecuted.

The 1987 study of women in the Multan jail in Punjab, cited above, indicates that women are most frequently detained for spousal murder or for offenses under the *Hudood* Ordinances. Other less frequent offenses include theft, alcohol abuse, and possession of drugs or illegal arms. A large number of women from Bangladesh are also imprisoned in Pakistani jails, largely as a result of trafficking in women. Murder is one of the two offenses that account for the majority of the female prison population. A 1987 study of 100 female convicted and pre-trial prisoners indicates that 42 were incarcerated for murder, and of these, the majority were accused of murdering their husbands. In late 1991, of over 30 convicts in the Multan jail, half were convicted for murder and sentenced to death. Nine of these had been charged with killing their husbands. Until 1990, punishment for murder was governed by section 302 of Pakistan's Penal Code, which stated that "whoever commits murder shall be punished with death or imprisonment for life and should also be liable to fine."

According to the 1987 study cited above, nine of the women convicted of murder were sentenced to death. Another 25 murder convicts were sentenced to 25 years in prison and, in some cases, lashes or a fine or both. The remaining prisoners facing murder charges were sentenced to lesser punishment or were awaiting trial. However, preliminary research suggests that women who kill their husbands in Pakistan receive heavier sentences than husbands who kill their wives. Men accused of murdering their wives often received mitigated sentences pursuant to section 300 of the Pakistani Penal Code, which states that culpable homicide will not be considered murder if "the offender, whilst deprived of the power of self-control by grave and sudden provocation, causes the death of a person who gave the provocation." By contrast, women who kill their husbands are not known to benefit from this defense. According to preliminary research conducted by human rights lawyer Hina Jilani, most cases of "grave and sudden provocation" involve a man who has killed his wife because of marital infidelity.

Under the new penal law passed in 1990, murder and attempted murder along with the crime of causing grave bodily injury (both intentional and unintentional) are punishable by retribution (*qisas*) or compensation (*diyat*) for the benefit of the victim or his or her legal heirs. When these laws were first proposed in the early 1980s during General Zia's Islamization campaign, the testimony of women was not accepted in the execution of *qisas,* which meant that a woman accused of committing an offense requiring retribution would not have been allowed to testify on her own behalf.

Moreover, when the victim was a woman, the amount of *diyat* was halved. The current law does not distinguish between the sexes with regard to payment of *diyat,* but both the amount of the *diyat* and the validity of a woman's testimony have been left to judicial discretion "in accordance with the qualifications prescribed by the injunctions of Islam." This invitation to exercise discretion only with regard to women encourages judges to manifest their own prejudices and biases against women. The *Hudood* Ordinances account for much of the increase in the women's prison population since the early 1980s and are one of the major reasons why women are detained or jailed and why their complaints of police misconduct go unanswered. The *Hudood* Ordinances are Islamic penal laws introduced by General Zia ul-Haq in 1979 as part of his "Islamization" campaign. The Ordinances apply to all Pakistanis – Muslims and non-Muslims alike – and consist of five sections: the Offense of *Zina* (adultery, fornication and rape); the Offense of *Qazf* (perjury or defamation about fornication or adultery); the Prohibition (of Alcohol) Order; the Execution of the Punishment of Whipping; and the Offenses Against Property Ordinance.

The *Hudood* laws impose the death penalty and punishments deemed cruel and inhuman under international law and clearly discriminate on the basis of sex. The Offenses of *Zina* and *Qazf* and the Execution of the Punishment of Whipping Ordinance are the *Hudood* sections most relevant to the discussion of women in custody.

The Offense of *Zina* Ordinance repealed the previous rape laws in Pakistan's Penal Code, which defined rape as compulsory sexual intercourse. The new law adds to this definition that both a man and a woman may be guilty of rape, and dramatically narrows the circumstances in which rape can be said to have occurred. Statutory rape, previously defined as sex with or without the consent of a girl under the age of 14, is no longer a crime, making it possible for a minor girl (defined as one who is determined by the court to have reached puberty) to be charged with engaging in illicit sex.

In addition, the legal possibility of marital rape has been eliminated; by definition, rape is an extra-marital offense. One of the most important changes brought about by the adoption of the *Hudood* laws, which has had a profound impact on the rights of women, is that for the first time in Pakistan's history, fornication (extra-marital sex) is illegal and, along with adultery, is non-compoundable, non-bailable and punishable by death.

Once convicted of adultery, fornication or rape a person can be sentenced in one of two ways, depending on the religion and marital status of the accused, the witnesses and the evidence on which the conviction rests. The maximum sentence is known as *Hadd*, the singular of *Hudood*. It is a mandatory sentence that a judge may not mitigate.

In the case of fornication and adultery, if the accused is a Muslim and (a) confesses or (b) there are four adult, pious, male Muslim witnesses to the act of penetration, then the accused must be sentenced to death by stoning. If, on the other hand, the accused is a non-Muslim and (a) confesses or (b) the crime is witnessed as described above, the accused must be sentenced to 100 lashes with a whip.

Sentences vary according to the marital status of the accused: married offenders are to be stoned, while unmarried offenders (including widows, divorced women and prostitutes) are subject to 100 lashes. In any case, the maximum (*Hadd*) punishment for fornication, adultery or rape is identical. The testimony of four female Muslim witnesses is not adequate for the maximum (*Hadd*) punishment. To date, although *Hadd* punishments have been imposed, none has been carried out.

If the evidence falls short of what is required for

maximum punishment but the case is still proven, then the accused is sentenced to a lesser class of punishment known as *Tazir*. Evidence for *Tazir* punishment is governed by the standard evidence code (*Qanun-e-Shahadat*) which was introduced by General Zia in 1984. At both the *Hadd* and *Tazir* levels of punishment, the burden of proof is on the prosecution to prove rape or adultery/fornication charges beyond a reasonable doubt. There is a general rule that if there are two versions of an incident, the one favoring the accused should be accepted by the court. For example, in one 1988 *zina* case, the benefit of the doubt was given to the accused and he was acquitted when penetration was not positively proved. Other cases have also maintained that stains of semen or vaginal swabs do not necessarily mean that sexual intercourse has taken place; there must be positive proof of penetration or other corroborative evidence.

In practice, at the lesser *Tazir* level the courts continue to exhibit a bias against female testimony. The courts tend to see women as complicit in sex crimes, notwithstanding a lack of evidence or evidence to the contrary. While the courts extend the benefit of the doubt to men accused of rape, they set standards of proof for female rape victims that require extraordinarily conclusive proof that the alleged intercourse was forcible. Moreover, when women unable to prove rape are themselves charged with illicit sex, the courts routinely set a lesser burden of proof for the prosecution and fail to extend to female defendants the same benefit of the doubt that is commonly granted to male defendants.

The *Tazir* punishment for adultery or fornication is up to 10 years in prison, thirty lashes with a whip and a fine of indeterminate amount. The *Tazir* punishment for rape is up to 25 years in prison and 30 lashes. For the purposes of *Tazir*, no distinction is made between a married and unmarried offender. It is important to note that insufficient evidence to impose a *Hadd* punishment does not eliminate criminal liability. The accused may still be convicted for *Tazir*.

Most *Tazir* convictions result in a sentence of public whipping. While no *Hadd* punishments have been carried out, *Tazir* punishments of whipping, which constitute cruel and inhuman punishment under international law, do occur.

The *Hudood* Ordinances apply to Muslim and non-Muslim, male and female Pakistanis. A commentary on the Ordinances notes, "all Pakistanis, regardless of sex, suffer the rigors of the system." However, both in law and in practice the *Hudood* laws weigh most heavily on women.

First, in determining maximum punishment the law clearly discriminates against the testimony of women by disallowing it altogether. This means that women who have been sentenced to the cruel and inhuman *Hadd* punishments have been sentenced under a law that prevents them from testifying on their own behalf. Men have also been sentenced under these laws, but in general men accused of rape are effectively exempted from maximum *Hadd* punishment both because women victims cannot testify and because it is extremely unlikely that there would have been four male Muslim witnesses to the act of penetration.

Asia Watch and the Women's Rights Project oppose the maximum penalties as cruel and inhuman and, although we recognize that no such punishments have been carried out to date, are distressed that nothing impedes the government from implementing them in the future. The majority of *Hudood* cases involving *Zina* or *Zina-bil-jabr* are heard at the *Tazir* or lesser level of punishment.

While the testimony of women is admissible at this level, as noted that the courts continue to exhibit a bias against women victims and defendants and their testimony is not accorded equal weight with that of men. As discussed below, this bias has three main results: (a) women find it extremely difficult to prove rape and, if they cannot prove rape, are themselves vulnerable to prosecution for fornication or adultery; (b) men accused of rape often receive unfairly reduced charges; and (c) women are often wrongfully prosecuted for *Hudood* offenses and are provided with limited protection from such ill-founded accusations. It is under these laws that the majority of women prisoners in Pakistan are detained, and thus exposed to abuse by police authorities.

The criminalization of adultery and fornication in Pakistan, when coupled with the discrimination against women in law and in practice in Pakistan's criminal justice system, has created an extremely adverse and precarious situation for women, and in particular for women victims of rape. While Pakistani courts extend the benefit of the doubt to men accused in rape cases, they set standards of proof for rape victims that are colored by gender bias to such an extent that the woman victim must provide extraordinarily conclusive proof that her "participation" in impermissible intercourse was forced.

In one 1982 case in which a rape charge was changed into one of adultery for the purpose of mitigation of sentence, Sohail Iqbal was accused of rape and the charge was supported by medical evidence. He was convicted and sentenced to 20 years' imprisonment, ten lashes and a fine of 2,000 rupees. On appeal, the Federal *Shariat* Court reduced Iqbal's rape conviction to fornication, resulting in a lesser charge carrying five years' imprisonment, ten lashes and no fine. The Court said "there is a possibility that the victim might have been a willing party to the offense."

In a 1983 case, the Federal *Shariat* Court reduced a rape conviction to one of fornication on the grounds that "since no violence was found on her body, it could be reasonable to infer that she was a willing party to sexual intercourse." In 1987, the Federal *Shariat* Court overturned a lower court's conviction of rape on the grounds that medical examiners "did not observe any injury on the thighs, legs, elbows, arms, knees, face, back and buttocks of the victim," and held that "she was bound to sustain injuries...as she was supposed to put up resistance." Although victims such as the 94-pound girl raped by Iqbal may have no chance of fending off an attacker, Pakistani judges seem to require that they resist and also suffer visible physical injury if they wish to defend themselves against charges of consensual sex.

If a woman alleging rape cannot prove that the encounter was forcible or non-consensual, she may herself be charged with the capital crime of adultery or fornication. In practice, we found in such cases that the standard of proof beyond a reasonable doubt is not applied equally. While the courts generally require rape charges to be proven beyond a reasonable doubt, they often accept a woman's rape allegation – once disproved – as *prima facie* evidence that she engaged in consensual extra-marital sex, despite the fact that a failure to demonstrate rape (coerced sex) beyond a reasonable doubt does not automatically prove beyond a reasonable doubt that consensual sex occurred. Put another way, the benefit of the doubt that is rightfully accorded to men accused of rape often is not equally extended to women whose rape charges have been converted into charges against them of consensual sex.

The differing effect of available medical evidence often compounds this discrimination. Medical reports that show pregnancy or forced penetration introduced in support of the original rape charge can be used against the female victim to prove that impermissible sex occurred. However, medical evidence implicating the accused male is often lacking, so he may be released for lack of evidence while she is imprisoned pending trial. The most infamous case of this kind is that of Safia Bibi, an 18-year-old blind girl who became pregnant allegedly as a result of rape in 1983. She was unable to prove her allegation of rape and was charged with fornication, found guilty, and sentenced to three years' rigorous imprisonment, 15 lashes and a fine of 1,000 rupees. While her pregnancy was cited to prove that she had engaged in extra-marital sex, her assailant was acquitted due to "want of evidence." After national and international protest, the Federal *Shariat* Court acquitted Safia of fornication on appeal.

In another well-publicized 1983 case, 15-year-old Jehan Mina claimed her pregnancy was a result of rape. According to her testimony, she was doing domestic work for her aunt and was raped by her uncle and his son. Initially, her family members disbelieved and threatened to kill her. However, one uncle believed her charges and registered a rape accusation on her behalf. The court decided that her statement did not warrant a rape conviction because she had failed to register the complaint immediately. Instead, she was charged with fornication. In sentencing her to three years' rigorous imprisonment and ten lashes, the court stated that the case was not a case where merely her statement [alleging rape] can be regarded as a basis of conviction, but in fact the basis of conviction is her unexplained pregnancy coupled with the fact that she is not a married girl. In a 1987 report on human rights after martial law in Pakistan, the Geneva-based International Commission of Jurists concluded that "there have been many reported cases where a complaint of rape has been made and the court has convicted and punished both parties for adultery or fornication...." According to a 1988 study by human rights advocate Asma Jahangir, these sentences are often upheld by the superior courts.

A 1991 report by Amnesty International describes an August 1989 case in Pakistan in which two nurses were raped at gunpoint by three interns in a hospital. One of the women tried to lodge a rape complaint with the police and found herself charged with illicit sex. According to Amnesty International's report, the woman lost her job and her marital engagement was broken off as a result of the charges. In November 1991, a case in which a rape accusation brought by 18-year-old Majeeda Mujid was converted into a charge of fornication against her. Majeeda told us that she had been working with her family at a brick kiln for four months when the landowner and some other men abducted her. She was held by the landowner and others for over two months and raped repeatedly.

Ten days after her abduction, Majeeda's family filed a first information report (FIR) with the local police. Eventually, the landowner brought Majeeda to the Nawankot police station in Lahore and told her to tell the police that she was staying with them of her own will. She refused and told the police that the landowner had raped her. She was kept in the police station for six days without ever seeing a female police officer. On the sixth day she was taken to prison, having been charged by the police with fornication. She was held in the prison for over two months before being released pending trial.

As might be expected, the real possibility of criminal prosecution has a deterrent effect on women victims' willingness to seek punishment of rapists as provided for by law. In a 1985 decision, the Federal *Shariat* Court observed that it is extremely brave of women to complain of rape under Pakistan's legal system. As one Pakistani analyst told us, "women in Pakistan do not see the law as a mechanism for their protection. They are afraid of it."

Cases like those described above are not uncommon. However, more often *Zina* charges are not brought against the alleged rape victim by the courts. Instead, the woman victim is excused and, based on the possibility that she consented to the act, the accused is given the benefit of the doubt and the rape charge against him is converted to one of adultery or fornication to reduce his sentence. This occurs despite the fact that according to human rights advocates Jahangir and Jilani, "if the benefit of the doubt did exist, principles of criminal law require the court to acquit the accused and not to construe it as a mitigating circumstance."

While in such cases the female rape victim is not criminally punished, she must still suffer the social stigma that comes from consensually engaging in impermissible sex, since her alleged rapist was charged only with adultery or fornication.

Treatment of Women in Prison

Pakistan's prison rules – with notable exceptions – generally conform to the UN Standard Minimum Rules for the Treatment of Prisoners (SMR). Under the rules, the prison Superintendent is required to inform all prisoners at the time of admission how long they have to appeal their conviction, and to render all assistance necessary to allow prisoners to appeal. However, neither the SMR nor the prison rules require prison officials to monitor how long pre-trial prisoners have been incarcerated or to do anything about the status of their cases. Every woman admitted to prison must be examined by a woman warden within 24 hours of admission, under the direction of the medical officer of the prison, to discover unexplained injuries. If any injuries are discovered they must be reported to the district magistrate and to the police. Women prisoners may not be fettered and are allowed to keep certain items of jewelry and cosmetics with them in prison.

All women prisoners serving sentences of two months or more and all juvenile girls must be transferred to a woman's prison on conviction. Women prisoners must be kept separate from male prisoners at all times. The general rules about separation of pre-trial prisoners establish that under-trial prisoners may be separated at the Superintendent's discretion, while another rule says under-trial and convicted prisoners must be segregated. A third rule says women awaiting trial must always be kept separate from women convicts.

Women are allowed to keep their children with them

until the child reaches age three, when the child is supposed to be given to the woman's family or put in an institution. The SMR require pre- and post-natal care, but says nothing about whether children should remain with their mothers beyond nursing years or what should happen to the children if they do not remain in prison. The SMR do suggest that when nursing infants are allowed to remain with their mothers, the prison should have a nursery where the babies can be placed when not in their mothers' care.

Pregnant women are not provided medical attention or special food in prison. According to the LHRLA study cited above, five pregnant women were imprisoned in the Karachi Central Jail in October 1991. At the same time, the jail held 21 children from ages two-and-a-half months to eight years. Four of these children had never seen life outside the prison because there was no one else to care for them. Under the prison rules, the Deputy Commissioner of each district is supposed to visit jails located in his area at least once a month to inspect the facilities and determine whether the inmates have any complaints or are suffering any abuse. However, according to the LHRLA, "the Commissioners never bother to visit the jails."

The most common violation suffered by women in prison is lengthy detention without trial. Like overcrowding, this is a problem that affeacts all prisoners in Pakistan. However, women are particularly vulnerable to prolonged detention because of the difficulty they have in securing bail, surety and release. These problems are exacerbated by the degree to which women prisoners lack adequate legal counsel.

Discriminatory Police and Judicial Practices

Discrimination against women begins at the police level and continues on up through the superior judiciary. Police have both participated in and routinely failed to combat violence against women in custody. They also have often exhibited discriminatory behavior toward female victims of gender-specific abuse by private parties.

In November 1991, the Inspector General of Police of Punjab, who is responsible for investigating reports of police abuse, told human rights attorneys concerned with rising rates of custodial rape that "in 95 percent of the rape cases the women themselves are at fault." A superintendent of police, Shamim Khan, when asked about rising rates of abduction of women in Pakistan, stated that "in fact many women are the abductors. Women can easily entice and kidnap, you see."

The bias reflected in such attitudes is particularly disturbing because, as noted above, police are the "detaining, investigating and prosecuting authorities." Discriminatory attitudes towards women by the police not only contribute to the failure of the police to police themselves, but also to their willingness to prosecute women who have committed no offense. In theory, such abuses should be checked by the magistrates, who have the authority to order investigations into and to adjudicate cases of police abuse, or by the Sessions Courts, which are the courts of original jurisdiction in *Hudood* cases.

5

Women's Participation in Government

The Article 8 of the Constitution needs to be further strengthened with the addition of a specific clause saying in substance that all the provisions of the Constitution shall be interpreted so as to accord with the Fundamental Rights. An exception is made in Article 8 (3) in respect of conformity to fundamental rights of laws relating to the armed forces and police and of laws in the First Schedule. A proviso may be added here saying that these laws shall not in any case be immune to the requirement of non-discrimination on the basis of sex. The prohibition against 'slavery, forced labour, etc' in Article 11 should include a specific bar on all forms of sexual exploitation and prostitution of women. The phrase 'decency or morality' as a factor of restraints on freedom of expression in Article 19 should be deleted. Prohibition of discrimination under Article 22(3) (b) on the basis "only of race, religion, caste or place of birth" for admission to an educational institution aided from public revenues should include 'sex' and the word only be deleted.

It must, however, be clearly provided that in the light of Article 25(3), this Article will not be applicable to institutions especially set up for women and girls. From the bar against discrimination between citizens on the basis of 'sex alone' in Article 25, the word 'alone' should be omitted. Article 25(3) be amended to remove the word 'protection' in the context of woman and replaced with word which connote that special affirmative provisions be made to enhance women's status and rights towards the promotions of gender equality. Access to religious places on the basis of race, sex, caste or residence or place of birth should be restricted. From Article 26(1), which prohibits discrimination in access to public places on the ground only of ...." the word 'only' should be omitted. Article 26(2)(1) be amended to remove the word "protection" in the context of women and replaced with word which connote that special affirmative provisions be made to enhance women's status and rights towards the promotion of gender equality.

The council of Islamic Ideology should include members from various walks of life and an adequate number of female members, so that it is more representative in character. The Parliament should debate the impact of the various parts of the Eighth Amendment and repeal all such of its provisions which are found to be against the letter and spirit of the original 1973 Constitution or adversely affect the rights of women.

A conscious effort be made towards achieving gender equality at all ties of the judiciary. A special programme should be devised to sensitise judges early in their careers and to purge them of any subconscious prejudices that have become part of the social psyche. The oath of office of the judges prescribed in the Third Schedule of the Constitution should be amended to include in the last sentence, after the works "according to law," the following "without bias, without discrimination on the basis of class, sect, sex or creed..." Widowers of female judges should be made entitled to pension.

Daughters should be given their share of the pension until they are 21 years of age even if they are married before that. Pension should be transferred to children only on the death of the widow/widower of the deceased judge or if the surviving spouse remarries.

The principle of reservation of 33% of seats for women in an enlarged house of each of the elective bodies, from the local bodies up to the Senate, should be accepted. Necessary amendments in the Constitution and other laws should be initiated as speedily as possible to provide for women's reserved seats in all the elective bodies through any modality meeting the criteria of direct elections and joint electorate. The 33% reserved seats in the Senate should be filled through allocating the following number of seats for female Senators:

- five additional seats from each province;
- at least two out of the eight seats of FATA;
- one out of the three from the federal capital;
- one or two of the five seats for technocrats.

The five additional seats from each province can be filled through immediate elections, all others should be filled on a priority basis as the seats in those categories fall vacant.

The Election Commission should be authorised to conduct local body elections. Immediate steps should be taken to expedite the above, so that local body elections can be properly conducted. Elections to women's reserved seats in the National and Provincial Assemblies may also be held along with local body elections. Prompt and strong action under the existing penal provisions should be taken against parties, candidates, pseudo-religious and other categories of individuals and bodies acting to restrain women form voting or otherwise creating difficulties in the exercise of their right of franchise. Where the Election Commission finds evidence of large-scale non-participation of women in voting, it should declare the election null and void. Efficient updating of the electoral rolls is a high priority.

The process of issuance of identity cards should be greatly simplified and made prompt, especially in the rural and remoter areas. Photographs of women on identity card should be made compulsory, as it already is on passports. Cross-party consultation of all parliamentary and elective body groups should be held annually to review the state of women's representation and their political participation. An immediate process for this should be initiated through a dialogue on the modalities for reserved seats.

Citizenship

Section 4: Every occurrence of the words "his" and "father" be replaced with "his or her" and "either person" respectively.

Section 5: Every occurrence of the word "father" be replaced by "parent".

Section 8: Every occurrence of the words "father" and "father's father" be replaced with "parents" and "parent's parents" respectively.

Section 10: Every occurrence of the words "woman" and "women" be replaced with the words "person" and "persons" respectively.

Family Laws

Government should immediately set up a task force to

prepare proposals for reforms in the area of family laws for non-Muslims, this task force must be representative both along gender and along minority group lines.

The proposals for reforms must be discussed with the minority groups, particularly the women within those groups.

The legislature should give absolute priority in implementing the recommendations of the task force.

The *nikahnama* should include a column for the statement of the current marital status of the spouse, their existing partners' addresses, and the number of children, if any, from the earlier marriages.

Clause 17 of the *nikahnama* be amended so that where a statement of special conditions is required, a specific question be added to ask whether the wife shall automatically be delegated the right of divorce in case her husband contracts a polygamous marriage.

Clause 18 of the *nikahnama* should read as follows "Whether the husband has refused to delegate the power of divorce to the wife".

The task of registrar should be an educated person (at least with an intermediate certificate) so that he understands the importance and can acquire the skill of maintaining a crucial record that determines the legal status of people.

The penalty for the nikah registrar for violating the law, or misusing his powers, should be a rigorous imprisonment which may extend to three years and a fine of upto Rs. 50,000.

As no legal provision prescribing a time bar on registration exists, the Government should pass a law requiring all subsisting marriages solemnised after the promulgation of the 1961 Ordinance which are unregistered to be registered within the next three years. Further, a time limit should be prescribed so that all future marriages are registered within thirty days of solemnisation of the marriage. The Government must publicise the enactment of this law though the mass media and encourage personnel of the Union Councils to facilitate the marriage registration process.

Since the nikah registrar deals with question of family law where there is a substantial involvement of women, it is recommended that an adequate number of women be appointed nikah registrars.

A law be enacted to punish those who coerce nonconsenting parties into a marriage, and at the same time to declare that the consent of the wali to the marriage of an adult female is not required under the law.

A comprehensive law be enacted to provide for the following:

In case it is proved that the husband has willfully failed to provide maintenance for his wife for a consecutive period of six months or more, he shall be required to pay the entire amount, past, present, and a future amount for one year in lump-sum within a period of three months which may be deposited in the court; the law must also ensure that in case an appeal is preferred against the order of the family court the appeal shall only be heard if the husband deposits at least 50% of the decreed amount.

In case the husband fails to deposit the decretal amount awarded by the court (as above) within a period of three months, or after the appeal has been finally disposed of, whichever is later, he shall be liable to imprisonment for a term which may extend to one year.

Criteria for maintenance be laid down which must include food, clothing, accommodation, medical care, and other benefits appropriate to the financial status of the wife.

Criteria for maintenance of children be laid down which must include food, clothing, accommodation, medical care, educational expenses, and other benefits appropriate to the financial status of the family.

Provision for grant of maintenance to minors till they reach the age of 21 regardless of whether they are married or have become financially independent prior to that time.

Provision be made granting the family courts jurisdiction for ordering interim maintenance to the wife in case the suit is not decided within six months of its being filed, however, a proviso should be added that the same should only be done if the delay is not caused by the wife herself.

Provision be made granting the family courts jurisdiction for ordering interim maintenance for children at the earliest but certainly within a period of six months from the filing of the suit.

Schedule to section 5 of the West Pakistan Family Courts Act, 1964, be amended to delete "restitution of conjugal rights".

Rule 19 of the West Pakistan Rules under the Muslim

Laws Ordinance, 1961 be amended so that revisions against decisions of the Arbitration Council be heard by the Family Court.

Section 4 of the Muslim Family Laws Ordinance, 1961, be amended to provide the right of inheritance to spouses from the share of their predeceased partners on the death of a parent-in-law. Similar provisions be made for the parents of a predeceased child.

The *nikahnama* should include a column for the statement of the current marital status of the spouses, their existing partners' addresses, and the number of children, if any, from the earlier marriages.

A new marriage should strictly be subject to permission, and the authority for permission should be the family court.

Permission should only be granted on the following conditions:

the existing wife/wives have voluntarily and specifically consented to the additional marriage. Their statements should be recorded by the concerned family court.

The husband should be required to file details of his assets and income.

The family court should grant the existing wife/wives adequate provisions for maintaining their own residence/residences and ensure that her/their financial status in not affected by the additional marriage of her/their husband.

An application made by the husband for an additional marriage should include a provision whereby he must delegate his right of divorce to his existing wife/wives.

The husband be liable to pay a dower amount to the existing wife/wives which shall be fixed by the court keeping in view the financial status of the parties.

The grounds for granting permission for an additional marriage should exclusively be where:

- the insanity of the wife is established
- the wife is declared physically unfit to have conjugal relations
- the parties are issueless and the wife has been medically declared unable to bear children and where in the opinion of two competent medical practitioners she has no chances of recovery.

Where an appeal is preferred to the district court, the

decision of the family court shall only take effect after the appeal has been disposed.

A complaint against violation of the law can be made by an aggrieved person or any of her blood relatives.

Penalty for violation of the law should be imprisonment of five years and a fine of Rs. 200,000 to be paid to the aggrieved wife.

A provision be made imposing a penalty for mis-stating any facts in the *nikahnama*.

Where the husband mis-states his pre-existing martial status, the aggrieved wife should have the same rights as those applicable to the existing wife, for example, the court should grant her the delegated right of divorce, adequate provisions for maintaining her residence and financial status, and a dower which is equitable in light of the financial status of the parties.

Amendments be made to section 2 of the Dissolution of Muslim Marriages Act, 1939 as follows:

In section 2(i), the words "the whereabouts of the husband have not been known for a period of four years" should be changed to "the whereabouts of the husband have not been known for a period of one year" further, the proviso to this section should be deleted since it gives the husband a six month period to appear before the court prior to the final judgment.

The proviso to section 2(v) should be deleted as it requires the husband to prove his potency within one year after the court has decreed dissolution on the grounds of impotency. Section 2(vi) be amended so that the wife can seek dissolution if a husband is insane for a period of six months rather than two years.

Section 2(viii)(a) be amended to expand the definition of cruelty by dropping the word "habitually".

A new sub-section be added in section 2 to include incompatibility and irretrievable breakdown of marriage as a ground of divorce.

The law be amended to provide for the dissolution of those marriages where the parties have been separated for over a year and reconciliation efforts have failed.

Khula should be granted by the courts after making due efforts at reconciliation and by simply recording the statement of the wife making out a case of *Khula*.

The family courts be empowered to issue restraining orders

against the husband where the wife is separated from him.

The law be amended to provide for granting ma'ta on the termination of marriage either through talaq or otherwise, where under the law the wife should be provided adequate maintenance till she remarries or dies.

It is important that every divorce, including an oral one, is officially registered. The record is needed, among other things, for subsequent legal decisions, as on maintenance, custody of children, settlement of mutual obligations, etc. Thus the law should be amended to give the Family Courts powers to terminate the marriage and to decide all other connected matters at the same time.

Every notice of *talaq* received by the Union Council must also be sent to the family court.

The family court should decide all the matters arising out of the termination of the marriage within ninety days, failing which talaq may be granted after ninety days having received the notice of Talaq. However, proceedings regarding other related matters shall continue and be heard on a day-to-day basis. As family courts will be deciding all family disputes effecting marital disputes (as mentioned earlier), therefore such judges be appointed with care and be sufficiently experienced.

The law be amended to require the Union Council to notify the Family Court as soon as it receives intimation from the husband that he has pronounced divorce upon his wife.

Women and men should have a right of equal inheritance on the principle mentioned in Section 4 of the Muslim Family Laws Ordinance, 1961. Spouses should also inherit from the share of their predeceased partners on the death of a parent-in-law.

The West Pakistan Family Courts Act, 1964 should also be extended to the Tribal Areas.

Schedule to section 5 of the Act be amended to delete "restitution of conjugal rights".

The law be amended to allow for the transfer of family cases from one District Court to another, as in Punjab, and from one province to another.

The law be amended so that a special hearings should not be prescribed for affection reconciliation, the same should be done during the course of the trial.

The law be amended to require the consolidation of all

issues - for example, custody, maintenance, dower, ma'ta, and jactitation of marriage - arising out of the same divorce proceeding.

Family courts be set up in necessary number, and they should deal exclusively with issues concerning the Family Laws.

The judges of these courts should be given special orientation in dealing with family disputes.

The courts should hold hearings on a day-to-day basis and except for the display of dowry or the ostentatious display of wealth in any manner.

The Pakistan Penal code, 1860 be amended to add a new section providing punishment for cruelty on a wife. The law should say "whoever being a husband or relative of the husband of a woman, subjects such a woman to cruelty which may be mental or physical shall be punished with imprisonment which may extend to 3 years and shall also be liable to fine."

The law should prescribe a ten year sentence where such cruelty leads a women to suicide.

Section 174(3) of Code of Criminal Procedure, 1898 be amended to empower the police to investigate and report cases of unnatural or suspicious deaths of women. The following situations be specifically covered

— Involving suicide by a woman within 7 years of her marriage.
— Death of a woman within 7 years of her marriage in any circumstances raising a reasonable suspicion that some other person committed the offence in relation to such woman.
— Death of a woman within 7years of her marriage and any relative of the woman has made a request in this behalf.

Where there is any doubt regarding the cause of death of a woman.

A new section 198-A be added to the Code of Criminal Procedure, 1898 to provide that no court shall take cognisance of an offence punishable under section 498-A of the Pakistan Penal Code, 1860 unless the complaint is made by the aggrieved person, or a close relative or the guardian or a neighbour of the aggrieved person.

In section 6 of the Act the words "European-British subject" should be deleted.

Section 9 be amended to say that the jurisdiction in matters covered by the Guardians and Wards Act, 1890 shall be the same as prescribed under the West Pakistan Family Courts Act, 1964.

Section 15 be amended to include that the mother of the minor should always be considered for the guardianship of the property and the person of the minor at par with any other person.

Section 17 be amended so that the only consideration for the court to determine guardianship should be the welfare of the minor.

Section 19(a) be amended so that the husband of a minor female should not be given preference for appointment as a guardian.

Section 19(b) be amended to replace the words "whose father is" with "where either of the parents are".

Section 21 be deleted as it permits a minor to become the guardian of his wife or children.

Section 26 be amended to allow some flexibility so that a guardian of the person of the minor can temporarily remove the minor anywhere within the province without leave of the court but shall not remove the minor outside the jurisdiction of the Province of Pakistani territory without the permission of the guardian court.

Section 41(d) be amended so that it does not automatically make the husband of a female ward her guardian. In section 41(e), all occurrences of the word "father" should be replaced by "parents".

Pakistan should become a Contracting Party to the Hague Convention in order to protect children who habitually reside in one contracting State and who have wrongfully been removed from, or retained in, another contracting State.

The application of this Act should be extended to other religious communities where their own personal law allows such marital union. This law be repealed.

The prescribed minimum of 16 years of age for the marriage of girls should be strictly enforced. The offence against this should be non-cognisable and anyone should have the right of complaint. The parents/guardians, the groom if adult and the person solemnising the marriage should be liable to punishment. If the girl's age at marriage is less than 12 the punishment should be a maximum of five years of imprisonment and a fine up to Rs. 25,000, if above 12, the maximum sentence should be three years and Rs. 20,000 fine. Sections 4,5 and 6 of the Child Marriage Restraint Act, 1929, should be accordingly amended, but the proviso in section 6, prohibiting imprisonment for any woman, should stay.

Later, the age of the girl too should be raised to 18 with the proviso that a minor between 16-18 years may in exceptional circumstances be married with permission of the family court and after ascertaining that the marriage has the girl's voluntary consent. A child marriage should be liable to be dissolved or annulled if contracted in violation of the law and if the child complains. This right may be exercised by the child till she/he attains the age of twenty one.

Forced marriages of minors should be made a punishable offence under the Pakistan Penal Code, 1860. They violate both the fundamental rights and the tenets of Islam.

Labour and Service Laws

The Commission strongly recommends that a firm commitment to the rejection of gender as a classificatory device underlie a review of all existing labour legislation and new legislation, where necessary, be drafted in conformity with this approach.

Parliament should give clear voice to a strong mandate for affirmative action in order to give women a fair chance to participate in all facets of national socio-political and economic life.

In drafting legislation, special care should be taken to ensure that laws which genuinely increase the opportunities available to women and "operate favourably" toward them are enacted; laws which claim to "protect" women while, in fact, depriving them of opportunities, should be struck down.

Disparate impact should be the doctrine used to test whether a law is discriminatory toward women.

The use of the word "workmen" should be substituted for the gender-neutral and more inclusive word "workers".

Women should be classified separately only where it is necessary to do so because constitutionally permissible reasons have been established to demonstrate that they are unable to perform the task required. Everywhere else, the use of gender as a classificatory device should be barred.

Several parts of the labour laws of Pakistan discriminate against women. These laws must be modified to operate more equitably.

The provision restricting women's receipt of compensatory payments should be deleted.

All restrictive provisions regarding women should be deleted, every occurrence of the word "workman" should be replaced with the word "worker".

The government should require employers to provide child-care for their worker's children.

A special minimum quota should be fixed for apprenticeships for women in order to ensure that they have access to training opportunities.

The number-of-hours restriction on the work of both men and women should be completely eliminated.

Women should be compensated on the internationally recognised principle of equal pay for equal work.

Additional workplace security, strict penalties for sexual harassment as well as other crimes against women, and unrelenting enforcement must be put in place to protect working women.

Women should be classified as workers if they work at least 20 hours a week.

The condition in the proviso under which maternity benefits are made available to women should be changed to require that the social security contribution has been paid or payable any time during the three months prior to confinement; employers should be required to provide their female employees with pre-natal and post-natal care.

Women should be represented on the executive bodies of the trade unions of the establishments in which they work.

Female representation on these bodies should be commensurate with the percentage of the workforce that they comprise but at least large enough to ensure that they have a meaningful voice on all issues of import to them, women should also be represented on the executive bodies of collective bargaining agents.

Pension should be given to all children, male of female, till they attain the age of 21.

Strong legislation mandating substantive affirmative action programmes, including quotas if necessary, for women should be introduced.

The Commission recommends the addition of agricultural and domestic workers into the definition of "workers" in order to bring them within the purview of all laws applying thereto.

See relevant recommendations in chapter on Criminal Laws.

Employers who comply with stringent affirmative action targets for female workforce membership should be rewarded, possible with reduced corporate taxes or other incentives.

Employers, or other establishment (including institutions of higher learning) who are found to actively discriminate against women should be strongly penalised with fines as well as other punishment.

The recommendations of the Task Force on Labour on streamlining the Labour Judiciary should be implemented.

Labour inspectors should check on gender discrimination regarding pay and sexual harassment and to ensure extenuation of statutory benefits extended to women such as child care and maternity benefits.

All advertisements for government and private sector jobs must specifically state that men as well as women are eligible for the posts offered.

In order to achieve gender parity, fresh recruitment should give preference to women where their qualifications are similar to those of male applicants.

If the Government believes that a job can only be performed by a man or a woman, it must expressly state the constitutionally and legally admissible reasons for such a classification Otherwise, all jobs must be open to both sexes on a fair and equitable basis.

The performance of each government department, and of all statutory bodies which are controlled, administrated, or established by the government, on the hiring and promotion of women be a matter of public record and that this data be reported annually to the ministry of which such department is a part, the Cabinet Division, and other governmental and statutory bodies (e.g. the Pakistan Law Commission). In addition, the Commission recommends that the government must make concentrated efforts to ensure that the percentage of women in all of the above entities is enhanced each year across the board both horizontally and vertically. A 5% quota for women on these bodies, which was introduced in 1988 be increased accordingly and implemented effectively.

The Government must ensure adequate participation of women in, and on the boards of semi-autonomous bodies, advisory boards, committees, banks, PIA, Zakat and Ushar committees, etc.

Where promotions are linked to field duties or training programs, the government must ensure that women avail these opportunities in order to seek advancement.

The government should withdraw the reservations made to the United Nations Convention on the Political Rights of Women.

Criminal Laws

Parliament should examine in depth the question of evidentiary requirements in the Holy Quran and Sunnah and develop principles that are fair and non-discriminatory. It should then spell these out for the courts in ways that make them clear and easy to interpret.

The first proviso should be amended to read "Provided that an exchange of a female as badal-i-sulh is prohibited and shall be illegal".

A law should be enacted providing for punishment for handing over of a female as badal-i-sulh or part of it.

In section 313 (2) (b) the words 'father' and 'paternal grandfather' wherever they occur should be replaced by 'parents' and 'grandparents'. Similarly in section 337 O, the words 'father or paternal grandfather' should be replaced by 'parents or grandparents'.

Parliament should clearly spell out the principle of diyat. That principle should be based on parity and non-discrimination between men and women.

The main provision should be amended to read that diyat will be disbursed among the direct heirs in equal shares with a discretion to the judge to allocate up to 25% for minors or any handicapped members of the family.

A woman's right to obtain abortion by her own choice within the first 120 days of pregnancy should be unambiguously declared an absolute legal right.

Subject to the consent of the mother, courts should have the power to permit abortions beyond the 120 day period only if the pregnancy is the result of rape, if the mother is seriously disabled, if there is danger to the mother's life or a serious threat to her health, or, if there has been exposure to disease or other hazards which may result in abnormality. Only where, due to disability for example, the mother is incapable of giving consent, should the court's permission alone suffice.

Abortion or miscarriage carried out without the consent of the expectant mother should be a criminal offence and be punishable as follows:

with imprisonment of either description for a term which may extend to two years, and a fine to be paid to the mother, if the abortion or miscarriage is carried out within 120 days of the conception.

With imprisonment of either description for a term which may extend to seven years, and a fine to be paid to the mother, if the abortion or miscarriage is carried out after 120 days of conception.

Provided that permission for carrying out an abortion on a mother incapable of giving consent, due to mental illness, for example, be granted by the court.

The law be amended to raise the punishment to seven years imprisonment.

The law be amended to include all sexual offences within the description of punishable conduct.

The law be made applicable to all women regardless of age.

The law be amended to make all sexual offences punishable.

The law should distinguish a forcible act from a consensual one. The maximum punishment for the first be life imprisonment. The second be liable to a sentence of five years or less. Offence against a minor should always be regarded as an act of force and a minimum limit of the sentence also be prescribed. The same principle be adopted in matters of rape.

The punishment be enhanced to rigorous imprisonment and extended to a learn of five years.

The law be expanded so that written material,

photographs, and all forms of vulgar displays are made punishable.

The law should make it clear that honour killings will be punishable as qutl-e-amd.

The following proviso should be added at the end of this section "provided that where the arrested person is a female, her medical examination, if needed, shall as far as practicable be performed by a registered female medical practitioner".

The first proviso in this section be preceded by the following one "Provided that in relation to any offence the investigation and interrogation of women, as far as practicable, be conducted by a woman police officer regardless of whether the female is a witness or an accused. Wherever possible, the investigation or interrogation be carried out at the female's house but always in the presence of a family member or a person chosen by the female. Provided further that if the alleged victim is less than sixteen years of age she shall be questioned only at her residence and in the presence of her parents or guardians and the questioning shall be as brief as possible."

It be provided that in the case of women accused, if the challan is not submitted within 14 days the investigating officer will merit an adverse entry in his ACR.

In rape trials the name and address of the victim should not be published and if the victim so requests the proceedings be held in camera.

The present facilities for medical examination, especially of rape victims, and the reporting in that and in the medico-legal areas, have to be examined and stringent new provisions made. There is need for more and better-trained staff and greater competence, professional and freedom from gender-bias in the reporting.

The punishment for rape on a minor female must prescribe a minimum of at least seven years imprisonment.

The second proviso in section 497(1) be amended to add that a woman who is accused of an offence punishable with death be granted bail if she has been detained for a continuous period of one year. Where she is accused of an offence not punishable with death, a woman be admitted to bail if she has been detained for a continuous period of six months.

The law should allow a woman to be admitted to pre-arrest

bail even if a case is not registered against her or if she is unable to be present in court or is not in custody.

Women and children be allowed to access the facilities of bail and surety liberally, for these groups, surety should not be made conditional on other factors since such constraints can work to virtually deny the facility to women and children.

The law be amended to grant powers to the trial court to refer any case to either the Session Court or the High Court where, in the opinion of the trial court, the accused in genuinely mentally disabled and not likely to recover.

On reference to the Session Court or the High Court, where the court is satisfied that the accused is mentally disabled, the court should acquit the accused.

The words "for any unlawful purpose" be deleted.

Instead of the District Magistrates, Sessions Judges be vested with the powers conferred by this provision.

The laws should be followed and be publicised specially amongst members of the legal profession so that women may avails of this advantage.

In all future convictions of women, the state counsels be instructed to ensure that the courts consider the release of female convicts on parole and the government may issue necessary instructions to the Advocate Generals of the Provinces.

The law be amended to allow prisoners including females who are presently undergoing imprisonment to apply for release on parole and necessary instructions be issued by the Home Department so that applications of female convicts for release on parole are filed in the courts.

The Commission is convinced that all the Hudood laws were conceived and drafted in haste. They are not in conformity with the injunctions of Islam.

Secondly, these laws have come into direct conflict both with the country's Constitution (such as of Article 25) and its international commitments (as made at the World Conference at Beijing and under the UN Convention on the Elimination of All Forms of Discrimination Against Women).

Thirdly, in practical terms too, these laws have demonstrably failed to serve their purpose. They have not been any deterrents against crimes. And they have only led to proliferation of complaints in the courts, which, as it happens, have mostly been false or unjustified and have caused undue hardship.

Therefore, it is necessary that:

The *Hudood* laws are repealed.

The repealed provisions of the Pakistan Penal Code are re-enacted with an amendment to make marital rape a penal offence and to impose a severer punishment for rape on a minor wife.

If the Parliament considers it necessary to make any further laws in this area, it should to do so after serious debate and by reaching a consensus that the proposed laws are in accordance with the injunctions of Islam.

Qanun-e-Shahadat, 1984

The provisions of the old laws be revived and if the Parliament considers it necessary to make any further change in this area, it should do so after serious debate and by reaching a consensus that the proposed laws is in accordance with the injunction of Islam.

The offending clauses of this article [128(a)] and 128(2) be repealed so that a child has the right to legitimacy.

This provision of the law be widely publicised by NGOs and amongst the bar associations. The Government should issue directives to the Advocate Generals of all four provinces to instruct state counsels to ensure that this provision of the law is followed in every case, where a woman is being examined, but more particularly in sex related cases.

The provision should be repealed. The criminal justice system around the world has been recognising the unfairness of it. There is no support for it in Islam either.

Violence Against Women

Specific legislation on domestic violence by husband or in-laws should be enacted, after further deliberation, clearly spelling out cruelty as a criminal offense. Such definition should include mental cruelty, continuing harassment, threats and simple injuries, as well as the more serious forms of violence.

Immediate and clear directives should be issued to the police that all cases of domestic violence must be registered and prosecuted. There should be a monitoring body to check on effective implementation of this directive, as well as a media campaign to inform people about it.

Legislation should be enacted in accordance with the directions of the Lahore High Court judgment (KLR 1991 Criminal Cases 380) including recording of the statement by doctors, mandatory reporting of incidents to the police by hospitals, free medical aid, creation of special cells to investigate cases of death by oil stoves, criminal liability of manufacturers/ distributors of defective oils stoves; and exemption of court fee in suits for damages for injuries/death by negligent manufacture.

The procedure for investigation by the police should be clearly laid down and closely monitored.

Policies for provision of legal support and financial responsibility of the state in oil-stove burning cases must be clearly articulated and followed.

More burn units should be immediately set up and the existing facilities expanded and improved.

Legislation should be enacted making it mandatory for all employers to respond to and monitor incidents of violence and harassment in the workplace.

Strict legislative and implementation measures should be enacted for penalising the police and other members of law-enforcement agencies for any instance of violence against women, as well as for ensuring effective monitoring punishment meted must also be publicised, both to serve as a deterrent as well as to restore the confidence of the public in the law-enforcement agencies.

Citizen-police liaison committees should be made mandatory for all police stations (see also relevant recommendations in Chapters on Institutionalisation)

Since this is an area which has been virtually ignored in Pakistan, much more concerted efforts are required to develop a sensitive policy and enact special legislation, with regard to what has been done in other countries. Child sexual abuse should be clearly defined and harsher penalties introduced in law.

As a preventive measure, the topic should be introduced in school curricula or special programmes run for school children, to ensure sensitive treatment of the victims. Nurses and doctors must be educated about it and trained how to handle cases, and, most importantly, cells must be opened in government hospitals to deal with medico-legal issues of child sexual abuse.

Trafficked women and prostitute should be recognised as

victims of a depraved society, not as criminals, efforts should be seriously made towards rehabilitating them and protecting them, and the agents and pimps should be made financially liable for all costs incurred in their rehabilitation.

To ensure that the real criminals are prosecuted, trafficked women and prostitutes should be made witnesses in cases instead of accused, and also afforded protection in the process. Pimps and trafficking agents should be prevented from meeting the victims in jail.

Attempts must be made to reach agreements with countries to share repatriation costs, otherwise the trafficked women will never be able to get out of jail even after serving their sentences.

The option of providing temporary amnesty to trafficked women and children should be considered, with the option of permanently legalising their status in Pakistan.

There should be no forced sterilisation. However, in the case of mentally handicapped girls and women, permission for sterilisation should be sought from court. Required legislation be enacted in this regard.

There should be no mitigation of sentence in any case of 'honour' killings. The Home Department, Commissioners, Deputy Commissioners and other senior police officials should take notice of reports in newspapers and through other sources and ensure that all the criminals are prosecuted. The Home Department and senior police officials should monitor the progress of such cases.

Developmental Rights

The Women's Division be upgraded to a Ministry again. A clear and comprehensive policy for women's development in the country be formulated after extensive and intensive deliberations with women at all levels, and the government publicly own this policy as an indication of its commitment to uphold and enforce women's rights.

The policy be geared towards integrating women's perspectives into all sectoral programmes and policies. Draft policies prepared in the past and the national Plan of Action, as well as other reports should be taken into account for preparing the policy.

The Women's Division/Ministry be made a permanent member of important policy-making forums like the National

Economic Council (NEC), Executive Committee of the NEC (ECNEC), Central Development Working Party (CDWP), Agricultural Credit Advisory Committee etc.

Women's concerns be integrated into all sectors of the Ninth Plan, with requisite financial allocations, clear targets and effective implementation and monitoring strategies.

The CEDAW document be widely publicised and intensively discussed, particularly at all decision-making levels.

The educational and health needs of women should be given top priority.

All governmental schemes/programmes must be geared towards removing all gender-disparities in education facilities, all existing schemes or programmes should be immediately converted into programmes for girls, till parity is achieved. Incentives of food, scholarships etc. should be introduced for lower-income families.

Mechanisms should be developed for enforcing compulsory primary education.

The financial allocations for education should be enhanced to 4% from the existing 2.3%. At least 50% of the entire education and training budget at all levels should be for girls and women.

Provision should be made for opportunities for women in new technologies and training based on market needs.

Allocations to the health and population sectors should be gradually increased to 6% of GDP, in keeping with the WHO philosophy.

Outreach of all health, nutrition, hygiene and sanitation programmes should be extended, with a particular focus on rural women, urban slums, squatter settlements and women with disabilities.

Regulations should be amended to ensure women the right to avail of tubal ligation without the husband's permission.

Women's right to obtain an abortion by her own choice within the first 120 days of pregnancy be unambiguously declared an absolute legal right.

Women's right to obtain an abortion beyond the 120 day period be made permissible only in the event of pregnancy due to rape, in the case of seriously disabled girls and women, in case of danger to the woman's life or serious threat to her health, and in the case of any exposure to disease or other hazards which may result in abnormality of the child.

Serious attention should be given towards providing reproductive and maternal health care facilities, according to several recommendations made earlier, along with sufficient financial allocations.

Family planning programmes should begin to target men both as users and for awareness-raising. Information should be widely disseminated highlighting the fact that a vasectomy for a male is far less serious operation than tubal ligation for a woman.

Media should play a more constructive role in raising awareness about women's reproductive health issues.

Tax or other incentives for families with three or less children should be considered.

Working women's hostels, at inexpensive or subsidised rates, should be immediately set up in larger towns and cities in relatively safe and populated areas, where public transport is available.

Low-cost housing scheme for different levels of lower-income women should be immediately undertaken in larger towns and cities, where they can collectively rent a house with a common-kitchen and toilets, providing both security and companionship for them. Once again, these must be in relatively safe and populated areas where public transport is available.

Day-care centres should be set up on a priority basis in larger towns and cities, as well as rural areas where a sufficiently large number of women are taking up employment, with reasonably low charges on a sliding scale. The idea of more informal home-based day-care arrangements at the houses of lower-income women seeking employment should also be explored.

Public transport facilities for women should be immediately improved, whether through providing funds for special transport schemes for women or through increasing and improving existing transport schemes and ensuring sufficient space for women in them. Penalties should be imposed on the staff of public transport for any misbehaviour with women or for allowing men to take their seats.

Public toilet facilities for women must be specially set up in reasonably crowded public places along roads and highways and in all offices and working places which hire women. Pension rules be changed to ensure that widows get the full pensions of their husbands. With regard to children's rights in pension or any other financial scheme entered into by their parents the shares of sons and daughters should be equal in all respects. There should also be no cut-of-dates in terms of widows' rights to enhanced pension rates. Inheritance cases of widows and orphans should be taken up on priority basis by courts and settled within six months, as has been directed by most high courts with respect to family court cases.

Property in the name of women be recognised as their property and the law relating to benami transactions, which generally affects women adversely, be done away with through statute.

In the case of transfer of property by whichever means or issuing of general powers of attorney by women, their personal presence before any registration office or revenue authority, or any other office or authority, as well as locally well-known witnesses be made mandatory. Intimation of all such transactions be sent to some central district location, so that information in this regard can be collated.

Women's share in all property and assets acquired after marriage (but excluding inherited property, marital gifts and other financial contributions due to her from her husband) in the name of either spouse, based on her paid and unpaid contributions, be legally recognised and secured for her in case of divorce or her husband's death. Rules for calculating her share be carefully and sensitively developed.

A special committee/commission be set up by government to explore ways of improving women's economic status on the basis of earlier reports/recommendations and studying what other countries have done in this regard. The issue of unequal inheritance must particularly be kept in mind while suggesting financial mechanisms to empower women. For example, Morocco, recognising the current realities, has recently declared the wife a partner (40%) in rural households with reference to property and enterprises, to ensure her due share. The terms of reference should include training needs, enhancement of employment opportunities and special financial and credit schemes for women, with a particular focus on the lower income groups, widows and the disables.

Women's access to ownership and control of assets, particularly government distributed land and property, be increased through the registration of title-deeds of all state lands allotted for lease or home sites, jointly in the name of the husband and wife, and in the case of female-headed households, to the primary earner.

Campaigns should be run to motivate people to make just economic provision for wives, sisters and daughters and informing them on ways of doing so through wills, gifts, trusts, insurance policies, financial and saving schemes etc. (see other relevant recommendations in the Chapter on Labour and Service Laws).

Institutionalization

Separate facilities should be built for female prisoners everywhere, these jails should be designed to accommodate without overcrowding.

Basic facilities such as food, could water, medical care, and toilets etc. should be adequately provided for.

Prison staff should be adequately trained and penalties for deviations from prescribed procedures should be imposed, in particular, demanding bribes to give what is owed under the law, and maltreatment should not stay uncorrected.

Access to competent counsel for inmates should be facilitated.

Access to educational facilities as well as appropriate child care should be secured for the innocent children of inmates who live with their imprisoned mothers.

As used to be given to foreign nationals in Pakistani prisons since they frequently have literally no one to plead their case and may also face a language barrier as well as racism.

Laws to protect juvenile inmates and provide separate facilities for them, especially female ones, should be studied, enacted, and enforced.

Female prisoners and mothers of juvenile prisoners must be allowed to visit their children regularly.

The present ratio of women personnel in the police force should be gradually enhanced through a phased programme. In due course of time, women's cells headed by senior police officers be established in each station.

The present women's police stations should be converted into training centres for imparting appropriate orientation/ training to the serving and newly recruited personal. The training should be comprehensive and cover all aspects of police functions. These should gradually be set up every district, as was planned for the police stations.

In the short terms, till such transition takes place after making appropriate arrangements, women police stations should be as independent and autonomous as other police stations and should offer provisions equivalent to those available there including ready access to forensic and media experts as well as overnight detention facilities. They should be given special jurisdiction to entertain complaints within territorial limits as well as from suburban areas.

Such women's police stations or training centres should have linkages with shelter homes, NGOs legal aid offices, and other professional groups so as to be able to provide appropriate help a support to victims of violence and abuse.

Gender-sensitisation should be undertaken throughout the police force with respect to behaviour towards both policewomen and female witnesses as well as accused persons; severe penalties for sexual harassment should apply.

Meritorious policewomen should be promoted to all levels of hierarchy within the police.

Shelters, whether set up by NGOs or the government, should be run as a wholly volunteer recourse for women, their purpose should be only protective and neither custodial nor reformatory. Thus redefined, shelters should be set up throughout the country. They should collaborate with and be linked to, legal aid, social welfare and vocational training facilities for necessary assistance and ongoing support.

The government should made certain rules regarding such institutions. Their purpose being protect both the residents from being exploited and the management from being harassed by families of the residents. Such institutions should be registered have a proper board of management notify its address with the magistrate and the deputy commissioner of the area be provided adequate security by the government where requested. Adequate resources should be provided to women's shelters in order to ensure appropriate accommodations, basic facilities and necessary amenities.

The Government should consider setting up a network of care homes for girls and children who have been abandoned, who do not wish to return home or whose mothers are in prison, after due deliberation.

The Pakistan Law Commission should immediately move towards appointing a number of women (preferable one-third of its current strength) as its members. The Law Commission should also set up a panel of experts in various areas relating to women's development.

The immediate task of the women members, in consultation with the panel, should be to develop the structure and terms of reference for a permanent Commission on the Status of Women as well as an Equality Ombudsmen. Till such time as these institutions are set up, the Law Commission should undertake the responsibility of examining all laws or proposed laws from the gender-perspective.

The Government should, in collaboration with expert groups and individuals, develop a comprehensive policy for gender-sensitising educational and training programmes in all governmental and public-sector training institutes. The police training academies and schools, as well as the judicial training institutes for fresh entrants and in-service subordinate judiciary, are of particular importance.

Chiefs of different institutions should work our a modality for regular interaction and dialogue with women's groups. Discussions towards this end may be initiated with immediate effect.

A media policy for women's development should be designed with the collaboration of the government and concerned civil society organisations and representatives of women from all walks of life. The role of media should be guided and developed on the basis of the 'right to know' of citizens, for their better participation in development and governance. This will create space for the needs of the disadvantaged groups, especially for women. A code of ethics and other self regulatory mechanisms should be developed with the collaboration of the private sector media, business community and the human rights organisations to enable a balanced and progressive portrayal of women, and to discourage the unnecessary and vulgar display of the female body.

Women's access to information on health, population, sanitation, environment, education, law, finance, productive opportunities, agriculture, politics for decision-making in their daily lives should be encouraged through programmes over the electronic and print media.

The Allama Iqbal Open University and other educational organisations should be facilitated to collaborate and address women's development needs in training and increasing their productive skills.

Information focal points or centres should be set up at the village level or at the mohalla level in the urban areas to ensure that the information transmitted through the media actually reaches the grassroots level women. These focal points should be linked up with the Open University, to enable women and girl's access to education and information. To enable women to participate in governance and political processes to influence decisions affecting their daily lives, specially designed media programmes and regular overage of the issues should be encouraged. Private sector initiatives to set up radio stations for the objective of increasing women's access to information should be encouraged. A media campaign should be promoted to democratise family norms and promote a sharing of household responsibilities. Awareness and sympathetic understanding about women's concerns should be developed among senior media managers and media reporters. Women professionals' representation in the media should be increased especially at the decision-making level. Monitoring of the media should be done with the collaboration of civil society organisations and a special cell should be instituted under the Equality Ombudsman to receive and address complaints. Alternative media forms for supporting women's development should be given encouragement.

6

National Policy

Preamble

The first Bill of Rights for women was laid out (in the Quaranic Chapter on Women Al-Nisa and Other Quranic Chapters/verses), nearly fourteen hundred years ago. It may be said that no document is more gender sensitive than the Quran itself. In all references to roles and responsibilities, it addresses women and men, at all and specific times. In fact, women's roles and responsibilities as engendered in Islam, accord them a high status in the family and society.

The founder of Pakistan Quaid-e-Azam Muhammad Ali Jinnah in an address to students and at the height of the Pakistan Movement unequivocally stated the following. "It is a crime against humanity that our women are confined within the four walks of their homes like prisoners. They should stand side by side with men as their companions in all spheres of life." These words found life in the principles of equality as enshrined in the 1973 Constitution of Pakistan.

Even while religious and constitutional provisos exist, Pakistani women have had to face the challenge of being the neglected and discriminated half of society, and have done so resolutely. On the positive side, it can be stated, that a small segment of women have succeeded in carving a niche for themselves, and have made a mark on national development.

However, this progress is generally considered as one step forward and two backwards. The overall situation analysis for women's development shows, that this has generally been constrained by a number of factors, including prevalent negative attitudes, lack of commitment and interest in investing in and building the capacity of the overall human resources of the country, and women in particular. And even while opportunities exist, one a few women are able to access these. Thus the status of the large majority of women, the invisible half of society, remains low on the global human development rankings, poor literacy rates, poor health ratios, with little or no participation in the decision-making process. Their work in the productive sectors, remains un-recognised, with 'Pakistan's GEM (gender empowerment measure) ranking being second to last'.

Successive governments have adopted measures to improve the status of women, however, these have been adhoc, isolated and limited. In the absence of a comprehensive WID/ GAD policy, most measures have impacted negatively, as government policies remained inconsistent.

However, since 1995, there has been a paradigm shift towards women's / gender and development issues. This has to a large extent been due to the global focus on women's issues, with an impetus, being provided with the convening of the Fourth World Conference on Women held in Beijing '95, in which Pakistan participated.

Pakistan accession in 1996, to the Convention on the Elimination of all forms of Discrimination against Women (CEDAW). Has created further focus. The National Plan of Action (guideline document listing strategic objectives/actions) in 12 areas of concern, launched at the highest level in 1998, has also been instrumental in accelerating focus on women's issues. Other developments that have impacted positively include: Publication of the reports of earlier Commissions set up, including the Commission of Inquiry '97, as has the setting up of the present Permanent Commission on the Status of Women in 2000.

Many documents and reports on women, (Pakistan's National Report presented at the Fourth World Conference on Women'95, the National Plan of Action, 96-98; the WID Working Group Report for the Ninth Five Year Plan'97. Pakistan NGO Reviews, February 2000); have clearly emphasized and exhorted the need for a policy for women. One which provides a framework for undertaking affirmative action and other measures.

The Government of Pakistan accepting its national and international commitments and cognisant of the need to maximise the capacity of nearly half its population, that is women, is therefore building upon this need by enunciating a clear WID/GAD policy. Such a policy would facilitate all Pakistani women, irrespective of caste, creed, religion etc., in utilising their full potential in all spheres of life (home and the work place), and to participate in decision-making processes as well as to take decisions for and about themselves, in an enabling environment.

With this in views, the policy for women will therefore be comprehensive and encompass the 12 areas of concern that have been globally recognised as "areas of particular urgency that stand our as priorities for action". It will be guided and abide by the principles of gender equality and equity at all times.

It will also cover all Socio/economic and other sectors which impact women and men. In particular, this policy will address affirmative actions needed in all 12 areas of concern and in the sectors outlined in the five year plans, with special emphasis on budgetary allocations. The policy will overall advocate and highlight Islamic/religious rights/obligations of society, towards women and girls in all spheres of their life.

The Beijing Platform for Action

Given the fact that (policies for Health, Education, Population and other sectors are already in place, the National WID/GAD policy will facilitate these by reaffirming measures in place and by continued review and evaluation of such measures. It will address gender inequities in the all areas of National development including Education and Health, through existing Govt. mechanisms and policies. It will support all measures that take into account the benefits of educating girls and women, on the principles that educating girls and women means educating a whole family.

Recognising that poverty affects women and children more adversely, the policy will advocate measures for adequate provision of social safely nets. It is intended that policy will held in bringing about a focus on the needs of the rural poor, especially rural agricultural women.

The policy would place a strong emphasis on women's employment issues, skill development, vocational training, self employment, entrepreneurship, credit, marketing, labour laws, trade unionism and other related concerns.

The policy would advocate that female house holds heads/bread earners, women with disability in particular, women in general have priority accessing credit facility on soft terms from FWB and the Khushali Banks and other financial institutions, for setting up of business or for buying properties, especially for house building.

The policy would advocate special/beneficial measures for all disadvantaged women's groups particularly, aged/elderly women, women and girls with disability, women in detention, abused women.

On the issue of violence against women, the policy would advocate stringent measures by the Govt. Through concerned agencies in order to reduce the prevalence of violence against women in all its forms, whether domestic or at the work place.

The WID/GAD policy would place emphasis on and ensure:

- A positive portrayal of women in all media
- Representation of women at all decision making levels and in legislative bodies.
- Existence of strong and effective mechanisms for WID/GAD, within the Govt. machinery.

The role of the Ministry of Women's Development at Federal level and the role of the women development department at provincial level be reviewed and restructured, to enable them to act as catalysts rather than Project implementers.

Rights of women and girls are protected through positive legislation and that all discriminatory laws are reviewed and repealed. In addition, the National WID/Gad policy would support measure for protecting women" traditional knowledge related to resource use and management of the environment.

Achievement of gender equality and equality in the 21st century as well as the social, political and economic empowerment of Pakistani women at all levels of society. This to be made possible through an enlightened and progressive policy on women and through its committed implementation by the federal, provincial and all tiers of local government, with support of all segments of civil society and NGOs.

Aims:

The overall aim of the policy for women would therefore be to:

Tap the immense human resource potential and capacity of half of Pakistan's population, and to make them equal and visible partners in the country's development by undertaking new and diverse initiatives.

Empower the women of Pakistan by providing them equality of opportunity in an enabling environment.

In addition:

Sensitize the population at large, by creating and increasing awareness on women's rights, roles and responsibilities in the 21st century.

Ensure that women's concerns and perspectives are reflected at all stages of development and subsequently, institutionalized.

Mainstream women into the developmental process

Ensure integration of a gender perspective (including gender budgeting/gender impact analysis/gender auditing) in all national development programmes and projects.

Develop multi-sectoral and inter-disciplinary approaches for women's development with horizontal and vertical linkages at every level.

Sensitize government agencies in adopting a gender sensitive approach to development, by preparing need based and implementable programmes and projects.

Ensure the social, political and economic empowerment of women, by including them indecision-making processes and through representation in local government and in provincial/ national assemblies.

Address both the practical as well as strategic needs of women through affirmative action.

Enabling Environment:

A conductive and enabling environment is one in which women do not face discrimination at any level - whether at home or at work. Efforts will therefore be aimed at:

Ensuring that prevalent negative attitudes, customary practices and harmful tradition; that constrain women are changed, through committed efforts at every level.

Ensuring that all discriminatory laws are reviewed and subsequently repealed.

Ensuring that all forms of violence against women is eliminated.

Principles:

This policy will be guided by the following:

Principles of equality as per Islamic/Quranic injunctions and as enshrined in the 1973 Constitution of Pakistan in particular. Articles 25 and 34.

The strategic objectives and actions listed in the National Plan of Action (officially adopted as a guideline document at the highest levels in 1998 to date).

Reports/recommendations of all four Commissions on Women and of the National Commission on the Status of women set up in September 2000.

The Convention on the Elimination of all Forms of Discrimination against Women-Pakistan acceded to CEDAW in March 1996 and is bound by the Articles of this Convention.

Also by a recognition of:

Women's rights as human rights.

Women's work and worth

Efforts made by Pakistani women at all levels, to impact national policies and institutions and to create a niche for themselves.

The fact that women and men as equal partners, together can create a better society and family and can accelerate the pace of development for a greater Pakistan.

Coordinator Mechanism:

The role of the Ministry of Women's Development (MoWD) will be key for implementing the WID/GAD policy. It will act as the focal ministry and facilitate coordination between other ministries at national level and line departments at provincial level as well as between these and civil society and NGOs.

MoWD will regularly brief Cabinet on progress of implementation

MoWD to act as a catalyst for promoting Gender and Development

MoWD to facilitate gender sensitisation and training programmes for all other Ministries, WDDs at provincial level to do the same.

The National Core Group (NCG-comprising government officials from various line Ministries. NGOs, individuals and civil society representatives) set up in 1997/8 will be re-activated to act as the monitoring body. It will undertake the following:

Oversee policy implementation at national level, through setting up of area (12 areas) specific committees with a focal point from relevant ministry. Similar committees to be set up at provincial and local government levels.

Hold bi-annual meetings to review progress of implementation.

Regularly brief the National Commission on the Status of Women on Progress of implementation and vice versa.

Review the WID/GAD policy from time to time, suggest amendments to Government, as needed.

Regional Steering Committee on Asia Pacific for Advancement of Rural and Island Women (RSC-AP)

The Regional steering Committee on Advancement of Rural and Island Women for Asia Pacific Region, known as RSC-AP was established under one of the recommendations of 4th World Conference on Women held in Beijing on 5th September, 1995 and its Secretariat was setup in Kuala Lumpur Malaysia. RSC-AP was formed in response to the call of International Steering Committee as follow-up of the implementation of the Geneva Summit for Women 1992. The main objective of RSC-AP is to monitor the implementation of the objectives of the Geneva Summit at Regional level.

First Ladies, RSC-AP is one of the five regional committees to follow-up and implement the Geneva Declaration/Plan of Action adopted at Geneva Summit in 1992 on Economic Advancement of rural and Island Women. An International Steering Committee (ISC) comprising 15 First Ladies 3 from each of 5 World Regions (America, Africa, Europe, Asia Pacific, Near East / N. Africa) reviews implementation world wide. RSC-AP comprises 16 countries with 3 sub regions e.g. Central, West and South India (India, Maldives, Mongolia, Pakistan, Iran, Kazakhstan, Krygyzstan, Uzbekistan, South East Asia and Far East (Indonesia, Malaysia, China, Philippines, Vietnam) and Oceania Australia, Papua New Guinea, Tonga). RSC-AP was setup in September 1995 and Dr. Siti Hasmah Binti Haji Mohammad Ali First Lady of Malaysia was elected Chairperson for 3 years and re-elected for another term 1998-2001. First meeting of RSC-AP was held in Kuala Lumpur in October 1997 where the then First Lady of Pakistan led a delegation. Theme of the meeting was 'Poverty Eradication through Micro Credit'.

Second meeting of RSC-AP (25-28 September, 2000) held at

Kuala Lumpur had "Poverty and Empowerment of Rural & Island Women" as the main theme, with four sub-themes'.

Resource Mobilization, Access to Productive Resource and Empowerment of Rural Women.

Rural Women Health and Empowerment (with special focus on HIV/AIDS);

Environment and Poverty: Empowering Women for Sustainable Development; and

Empowering Rural and Island Women for Power Sharing and Decision making Position.

Follow up of implementation of decisions of 2nd RSC-AP meeting Kuala Lumpur 25-28 September, 2000 was undertaken and first meeting was held on 31.10.2000 at Army House under Chairperson-ship of Mrs. Sehba Pervaiz Mushraf.

Mrs. Sehba Mushraf, First Lady, has been elected as Chairperson of RSC-AP for a term of 3 years form 2001 to 2004. The Secretariat of RSC-AP has been shifted to Pakistan and established in MoWD. The meeting of First Ladies RSC-AP in Pakistan has been fixed as 10 November, 2001. The Aims and Objectives of RSC-AP are enclosed.

Aims and Objectives

To promote Rural and Island Women's social and economic advancement within the framework of national plans for social and economic development; and

To make public opinion and policy-makers and implementers aware of the importance of the multiple roles of women in ensuring sustainable national development and progress;

To mobilize political will at the national, regional and international in order to target rural and island women as participants and direct beneficiaries of all development policies, programmes and projects;

To ensure that the economic needs and well-being of rural women are taken into account of in all sectoral polices and programmes by brining into sharp focus the role of women in household' productive and community work, in the design of development interventions and the adequate allocation of resources;

To improve rural women's access to resource through alternative policy instruments that ensure more equitable gender-based distribution of land, labour, capital, technology, social services and infrastructure;

To launch initiatives essential for raising productive capacities of both men and women, with special attention to rural women from disadvantaged households, female-headed households, young rural women, disabled women, and migrant and displaced women;

To promote national and household food security by supporting the critical role of women in food production and income generation;

To alleviate women's heavy workload, which often involved long hours spent daily gathering fuel, collecting water, producing and preparing food, maintaining their homes, nurturing their children and, in addition, earning incomes that are essential to the survival of their families;

To improve the health and nutritional status of mothers and their children and thereby the quality of life of the family;

To reorient the information, communication and educational systems so that they meet the specific needs of rural women while preserving and promoting their cultural identify;

To optimize the role of rural women as agents of change and create conditions for their social, political and economic empowerment;

To create opportunities for rural women's to assume leadership positions in the decision-making process;

To promote strengthen and disseminate rural women's organizations in order to establish effective channels for their access to decision-making bodies at all levels;

To develop a constructive partnership between men and women in rural areas, based on social mobilization and an enhanced understanding of women's multiple roles and economic needs;

To adopt all the strategies stated in the Geneva Declaration for Rural Women and any other measures helpful for the implementation of our aims and objectives; and

To cause Governments, national institutions, non-governmental organizations, private sector agencies, United Nations agencies and other implement strategies to promote the economic and social advancement of rural and island women.

Women Rights - Major Activities Initiated/Undertaken

The women comprise more than 50% of the population of this country. It is the responsibility of the Ministry to improve the quality of life for the women and to coordinate efforts for women's development in the country. Major activities initiated/ undertaken in this area are as under:-

Restoration of Women Seats in National and Provincial Assemblies.

Ministry of Women Development is continuously pursuing with Ministry of Law, Justice and Parliamentary Affairs, proposals for amendments in the Constitution so that women seats can be restored in Provincial/National Assemblies as well as Senate. Presently the Minister of Women Development, Social Welfare and Special Education has initiated a process of national consultation on the same.

33% Increase in Women Seats in Local Bodies.

The Ministry has succeeded in enhancement of women seats in the Local Bodies. In the first phase election in 18 District were held. 4000 Women were elected.

Five percent quota in Employment

As per Cabinet Decision, this Ministry has issued instructions to all Provincial and Federal Governments/ Departments, Autonomous Bodies and attached Departments to provide employment to women's in their organizations. According to latest Census of Federal Employees, Women have 5.35% share in Federal Government.

U.N. Convention on the Elimination of all Forms of Discrimination against Women (CEDAW).

Government of Pakistan acceded to the UN Convention on Elimination of All Forms of Discrimination Against women (CEDAW) on March, 12, 1996. Pakistan's 1st Country Report on implementation of CEDAW is in the process of final revision.

Report of the Commission of Inquiry for Women

The Federal Government set up a commission of Inquiry for Women, in October, 1994 to review all the existing laws which affect the rights, living conditions and social and legal status of Pakistani women and suggest measures to bring them in conformity with the injunctions of Quran and Sunnah. The Commission was headed by a judge of the Supreme Court of Pakistan as its Chairman. The commission has finalised its report in August, 1997.

Crisis Centre for Women in Distress

The Ministry has set up "Crisis Centre for Women in Distress" in Islamabad and Vehari. This is a pilot project which aims at providing medical and legal aid to the women victims of violence. The Centre is being run round the clock by an NGO. The Management Committee comprises NGO and the Government servants. A team of volunteer doctors, lawyers and social workers have been associated with the Centre to help women in distress. Another identical Centre has been set up at Vehari so that this facility is availed by the rural women as well. Later on this experience will be replicated in other cities.

Fund for Women in Distress & Detention under the control of Ministry of Law

The main objective of the fund is to provide relief to the women victims of Violence. The fund is managed through a Board of Governors chaired by the Law Minister. Efforts are being made to streamline the procedure of disbursement so that release of funds to women in distress may be expedited.

Micro Credit for Women

Ministry of Women Development is one of the equity holder of First Women Bank and is a Director on its Board of Directors. In addition, the First Women Bank has been given a credit line of Rs. 48 Million to be given as micro credit up to the limit of Rs. 25,000 at 12% mark up rate with out collateral on personal surety basis or group guarantee.

Family Protection Project

A Family Protection Project has been launched under UNDP funded Gender Equality Umbrella Project (GEUP). Family Protection Project aims at to combat crime and violence against women and correlate law administration institutions like Women Police Stations and jails, and refuge/ counselling facilities like Darul-Amans, Crisis Centres and Police-Citizen Committees. The project is shortly to commence with a survey at the community level to identify current trend and incidence of crime/violence against women and the services/facilities provided;

Project for Women's Representation in Local Government

A project for women's representation in local government is underway with the objective to ensure women's participation in the Union council elections. It is an initiative under UNDP's ongoing Gender Equality Umbrella Project (GEUP). The project aims to motivate women in all provinces to file nominations as candidates and to vote in the ongoing Union Council elections in which 33 per cent of seats have been reserved for women as per the Government's Devolution Plan. A coalition of NGOs led by Aurat Foundation is implementing the project. Results of pools for the first phase show that 4857 women have been elected leaving 859 seats vacant. This amounts to an average coverage of the reserved women's seats of 84.70 per cent. Vacant seats will be filled through by election;

National Commission on the Status of Women

The Government of Pakistan is firmly committed for improving the status of women in the country. Government have taken a number of measures to release the women from the factors that hold them back and to speed up their progress. The Government has set-up a National Commission on the Status of Women in July, 2000. The main objective of the Commission is to examine the policy, programmes and other measures taken by the Government for women development and gender equality to assess implementation and make suitable recommendations to the concerned authorities where considered necessary for effective impact.

Anyone interested in learning about health conditions in Pakistan would probably start by reviewing the published health statistics. Impressive numbers of hospitals and doctors, and rapid growth in facilities and personnel in the past decade would be obvious. The researcher might conclude that improving conditions were at the root of the increased life expectancy and improved infant and overall mortality rates. However, comprehension of health conditions and health care cannot be gained from these data, for ultimately health conditions refer to whether or not people perceive that they are well and health care refers to the kind of assistance they seek when they feel poorly.

The basic concepts of health and illness that Pakistanis employ differ from those common in the West, as do the available treatment options and the criteria people use when they select a treatment source and later evaluate the care they received. Fundamentally, these differences are rooted in the fact that most Pakistanis view the world from a predominantly religio-moral as opposed to secular-scientific perspective. Their sense of welness is holistic, including emotional and spiritual as well as physical dimensions; their search for treatment is ultimately a search for contact with healing power conceived primarily in Islamic terms and understood through reference to the hierarchical structures of power they experience in society.[1]

During the 1980s, the population of Pakistan grew at a high annual rate of 3.1 per cent, increasing from 82.58 to 112.05 million.[2] Life expectancy increased dramatically, from 52.0 years for men and 51.0 for women to 59.3 years for men and 60.7 for women.[3] In this period also, the crude death rate fell significantly from 16.2 deaths per thousand to 11.6, and the infant mortality rate continued a striking, pattern of improvement, dropping from 124.0 to 104.0 infant deaths per thousand. The crude birth rate increased slightly, from 43.7 births per thousand to 44.4 per thousand.[4]

From these data one might properly conclude that the nation has recently entered the demographic transition from high to low fertility and mortality rates. In a period of very rapid population growth, death rates fall first and some years later birth rates also decline, possibly as a result of people realizing that their children have a much greater chance of surviving to adulthood than before. A slight drop in total fertility rate[5] from 7.0 to 6.7 starting in 1982 through 1987[6] would support this conclusion.

In the same decade, the number of physicians increased from 10,777 to 51,883 reducing the number of patients per physician from 7,549 to 2,127 . The number of nurses rose from 5,336 to 16,948 and the number of dentists increased from 928 to 2077. Also, the number of hospitals increased from 4,068 to 4,447, while the number of beds in them expanded from 47,412 to 71,897. From 1980 through 1987, the number of pharmacists increased from 1,673 to 3,153 and between 1980 and 1988 the number of midwives grew from 3,537 to 12,011[7].

One might hypothesize that the reductions in mortality are a reflection of the increased numbers of trained health workers and facilities, and conclude that health conditions are improving significantly in Pakistan. But this would be overly hasty, in part because the statistical information reviewed thus far is minimal, revealing nothing about the distribution or quality of personnel and facilities. More important, the inference of causal relationship between health conditions and demographic statistics is fallacious.

Where the demographic transition is an abstract statistical about large populations and can therefore be demonstrated with such data, human response to disease is extremely complex and cannot be reduced to an enumeration of personnel and facilities—availability cannot be used to predict utilization, efficacy or satisfaction.

Review of additional statistical data in itself raises doubts about the suggested relationship between health care and demographic change. For example, the number of people for each hospital bed was only slightly reduced from 1,716 to 1,535 during the 1980s despite the very significant increase in the number of beds.[8] Also, in reporting the number of hospitals in 1980, the United Nations appears to have combined the number of hospitals (602) and dispensaries (3466) (excluding those operated by the armed forces and private doctors), but had not added the numbers of maternity and child welfare centers (812) reported by the Government of Pakistan.[9] The total (4068) thus included many ill-equipped and poorly-staffed health stations as well as small hospitals in rural areas. Financial data raise additional questions. GNP per capita was only US$ 350 and the total (public and private) per capita expenditure on health care was US$ 8.46 in the mid-1980s. Only one per cent of the national budget, or US$. 81 per capita, was allocated to health.[10] It seems improbable that the significant improvements in mortality rates could be attributed to health care at a time when such small allocations had to cover the great expansion of facilities and personnel, as well as the cost of actual health services.

No data are available on morbidity, though the National Health Survey of Pakistan is now preparing a baseline health profile for the country.[11] No data are published concerning the distribution of facilities and trained health workers between urban and rural areas and among various regions within the county, other than by province.[12] No data are given about the numbers of male and female doctors and nurses, nor the percentage who are actively practicing. Nothing is reported about the allocation of bed space for men and women in hospitals, or about the availability of health care for women outside urban areas. Nothing is revealed about private clinics, care provided by practitioners of non-biomedical traditions, or about public health and sanitation programs. Finally, and of great import, no information is available concerning the quality of medical training, the facilities, or the available medicines, either as assessed by international health specialists or by those who rely upon the health care system.

A more fundamental problem with these statistics is the fact that they are motivated by pervasive assumptions about the possibility of accurately assessing social behavior through quantifying selected information. One assumes not only that a hospital is a building of significant size, but that it is supplied with specialized equipment, stocked with an array of medications, and staffed by various qualified workers, including fully trained doctors and nurses, who provide services day and night. Further, one assumes that the men and women who seek care there respect and trust the institution and its employees to treat their maladies competently and completely. Therefore, one assumes that by counting the number of hospitals, one is obtaining an estimate of the available health care, and that if one had utilization data, one would know a great deal about the health of the population in the area. Unfortunately, these assumptions amount to an arbitrary imposition of cognitive and affective meanings from one cultural milieu to another, for the buildings, equipment and supplies are poor or missing; the workers, mostly paramedics in rural areas, are frequently absent; and the quality of their work is distrusted.

Full appreciation of the nature and dimensions of contemporary health problems of Pakistan requires understanding the manner in which Pakistanis themselves conceptualize and feel about health, illness and proper treatment, and choose among and evaluate sources of care, and regard the health conditions in their country.

Plural Medical System

Pakistanis rely on many folk , religious, and professional sources of health care, not just upon physicians and hospitals. They commonly seek help from practitioners of several different types of therapy simultaneously or serially. The alternatives include home treatment with herbs and diet, Yunani Tibb (Galenic medicine resystematized and elaborated by Muslim physicians), and an array of religious therapies, from sole reliance upon prayer to use of amulets, exhalation of blessings following recitation of the Quran, visits to shrines; and exorcism rituals. The concepts and vocabulary Pakistanis employ to analyze and describe the body in health and illness, while primarily those of Yunani Tibb, include elements of the Ayurvedic humoral system as well. Homeopathy is also taught and practiced by some practitioners too. Popular expectations of the structure of clinics and the interaction between practitioners and their patients; of the significance of signs and symptoms; of the types of prescriptions and other advice healers give; and other speed and efficacy of treatment, are variously derived from and applied to experience with different types of medicine.

Home Treatment

Much attention is lavished upon someone who is considered sick in Pakistani society. In villages relatives, friends and neighbours discuss someone's ailment and offer numerous remedies. Women readily share suggestions about foods to eat or avoid and about herbs (prepared in various ways, singly or in combination) that are thought to be efficacious. They also discuss the practitioners they have had experience with, when the possibility of moving outside the home and the immediate community are considered. Men likewise converse about health problems and speak with women in their own families. As urbanization and literacy increase, people are much more likely to know and repeat the names of specific medicines, but the pattern of attention in the form of suggested treatments and referrals to specific healers is the same.

Throughout the country there are people whose recommendations of herbal remedies are respected and sought our. Some older women are revered for their knowledge of herbal treatments. I noticed that it was from men, including widely famed *hakims* (practitioners of Yunani Tibb), rather than from women, that I heard the greatest praise for these older women's skills and how these were gleaned through years of trial and error treatment of sick children. Women themselves tend to denigrate home based herbal treatment and are very modest about their abilities. Some are very reluctant to discuss the topic and deny any knowledge of herbal medicines, apparently because of their association with some forms of evil magic. I concluded that the manner in which adult men lauded older women's skills reflected not only the women's knowledge but a more tolerant attitude toward older women.

The Biomedical System

Within the biomedical system, services are available at many levels from different types of institutions. Hospitals range from large general hospitals in provincial capitals and other major cities to regional hospitals in smaller cities and towns and institutions with very few beds in more isolated areas. Small dispensaries are scattered throughout remote regions of the countryside in major villages. In addition there are specialized hospitals at which treatment for TB or mental illness may be obtained. The government also maintains a network of military hospitals that serve the armed forces and some government officials. Christian missions also run hospitals, some general and some specializing in the treatment of specific ailments such as leprosy and eye diseases. The Agha Khan also sponsors numerous community clinics, and one of the country's most modern hospitals located in Karachi.

In rural areas biomedical care is often most readily available through private sources, starting with shopkeepers who stock a few aspirin tablets. In larger villages and towns there are often pharmacies that are run by men who have served the required time as dispensers or worked as medics in the army. Physicians who serve in government hospitals often work outside clinic hours in private practice, and others who have completed the required national service have established private practices, primarily in cities.

Dispensers have one or two years of training following matriculation at the end of ten years of school . Some, at least, are very competent at handling routine problems, suturing wounds, giving basic medicines and referring patients when they require more sophisticated treatment. Dispensers are no permitted to charge for the services they provide, but some villagers reported that they did pay a small fee, possibly for the medicines they receive. Like the doctors in small hospitals, they are responsible for supervision of the stock of medicines, and reports of missing supplies were common to both levels.[13]

After five years in a rural post, a dispenser may compete for licensing as a pharmacist. Those who succeed may establish lucrative businesses, so ambitious if not-too-well connected young men are attracted to becoming dispensers. Older pharmacists served in the armed forces, as apprentices or had other types of training. Pharmacists diagnose and prescribe as well as sell medications, though their licenses permit only the latter. May compete to demonstrate their competence or power, so they tend to dispense broad spectrum antibiotics and pain killers, as well as vitamins, iron supplements and laxatives liberally. A few also prescribe homeopathic remedies, which, though popular in India , are commonly regarded as Western medicine for those too poor to pay for biomedical prescriptions. Seeking immediate relief of symptoms, patients may see a series of pharmacists and receive an assortment of medications, all in improper dosages, over a short period of time, for pharmacists do not inquire about prior treatments and their patients would be unable to give useful responses in any case. The pharmacist's shop in the bazaar often has a counter or display case, posters distributed by pharmaceutical companies, and a side room where truncated examinations, especially of women, may be conducted.

"Doctor" is the term used for anyone who appears to have competence with biomedicine. The dispenser, the pharmacist, the itinerant trader with a supply of iron tablets to sell, like the physician, are all honored with this title. Physicians in Pakistan hold the MBBS degree, the equivalent of the MD in the British system. To qualify for this five year program, a student must first do Cambridge A-levels (requiring one year of classes following matriculation), and an F.Sc. (a two year preliminary degree in sciences).

Admission to medical schools is widely known to depend upon cash and *Safarish*, connections or influence (which may also depend in part upon cash). It is very rare that a student performs so well on examinations that his position cannot be given to a better-connected candidate. Thus, being in medical school is primarily evidence of prior and future family influence rather than of unusual intelligence or dedication to helping people. When political activity is permitted only in colleges and universities under martial law regimes, medical schools become highly politicized. I was told that one year in the 1970s medical students were not tested in anatomy of physiology because their political protests severely threatened the stability of the government. Under the administration of Zulfikar Ali Bhutto, several new medical schools were opened, and complaints that these were set up in locations to reward supporters or appease opponents were common in the early 1980s. (President Zia ul-Haq chose to support Yunani Tibbia Colleges, see below.)

Consciousness of status difference generally pervades the work of most physicians, and they are widely viewed as greedy and inhumane. The disadvantaged complain bitterly that doctors would not treat those who could not pay, and that they would only give weak medicines to the poor and uninfluential who could never repay favors with further introductions.

While doctors are reassigned after some years, functionaries in hospitals are poorly-paid members of the local communities. They chafe under the attempts by successive physicians to establish proper bureaucratic order in the smaller hospitals and demand fees from patients for every service they perform.[14] The lack of comfortable, family-based patterns of relationship in government clinics fosters discord and contributes to the distrust patients feel toward these institutions.

For the physician, assignment to a rural area poses special problems as well. He envies those of his classmates who arrange a better position, again through connections. The appointment means that he must leave family, including his wife and family, behind, because living conditions are so unsatisfactory in rural posts. Transportation may be so difficult that days are required for a round trip. He loses out on opportunities to build and expand his social network in an urban area, and these connections are essential for continued influence and future opportunities for himself and his children. He is isolated from colleagues, expected to work with limited equipment and supervise a resentful staff. He may well not speak the same language as his patients who often come so late in their illness that he is unable to do much to help; and he may not have the supplies that would allow him to try. Even salaries in rural areas are (or were) much lower than in cities.[15] Small wonder that absenteeism is high! Yet the losses for citizens the physicians are intended to serve are far greater .

Women physicians, or "lady doctors," whose training emphasizes obstetrics and gynecology, face particular problems. Their professionalism is subordinate to their roles as women in the families into which they marry (see below). Responsibility for their choices and safety rests with their husband's family, so few ever practice far from home, or at all after starting to bear children. In a sense, the greatest benefit of an MBBS degree for a woman is that her marriage prospects improve and the opportunities for her children may be enhanced. Though there were three positions for female physicians in the districts of Mansehra and Kohistan in the early 1980s , only one of these was ever filled, to the best of my knowledge. Thus, up to three million women were dependent upon a single female Physician in the public system and she, obviously, could not begin to fulfill their needs. Fortunately a few female MDs were on the staff at a regional Christian missionary hospital, but they were also overburdened with patients.

Throughout the biomedical care system, non-availability of soap and water for hand washing between patients is the rule, and carelessness with sterilization of syringes and other equipment, for example, repeated use of needles and auriscopes with little or no cleaning, probably leads to spread of infection among patients. In 1981 there were no proper storage facilities for blood in the country, so only 20 per cent of the amount needed was available and reputedly 80 per cent of that was defective.[16]

Drugs are purchased by the central government for the entire country using the British formulary rather than a simpler generic list. Several international drug companies operate local plants where medications are produced and sold throughout the country side by networks of salesmen, Nonetheless, the Minister of State for Health and Social Welfare reported that 20 tons of medicines had been wasted during 1980 because there was no adequate system for their distribution.[17] The information about activity, dosaging, counter-indications etc. supplied with the medications was negligible if present at all. Medicines in Lahore General Hospital were said to be either sub-standard or expired,[18] and I often found old medications in pharmacies. Patterns of prescribing are also problematic. Typically, several medications are given simultaneously, including some to control the side effects of others. For example, rather than recommending oral rehydration for a diarrhea patient, a doctor will prescribe one medicine to quell peristalsis, an antidiuretic, a pain killer for cramps, medicationcs) to control the nausea that is caused by the first three, and perhaps an injection of streptomycin. Part of the reason for this is that patients expect such polypharmacy and suspect that they have not been treated fully if they are not given an array of substances. Also, proper dosages of antibiotics are commonly prescribed for insufficient periods of time. Patients rarely complete the courses that are prescribed before seeking new prescriptions from other healers as noted above, so they may receive several different antibiotics in improper amounts, and possibly all for a condition for which they are not required in the first place. Biomedical substances are prescribed by untrained or undertrained persons, from itinerant traders to pharmacists. Like these practitioners, some Yunani Hakims, those from the Delhi school rather than the conservative Lucknow school that advocates reliance solely upon native herbal (*desi*) treatments, substitute biomedicine for tonics for particular organs, apparently without knowledge of potentially dangerous interactions among them, and also give herbs to counteract their heating effects. Many are concerned about the side effects of the strong medications.

Hospitals are distressing places in Pakistan; many people think of them as places to go to die, or at least as places to be avoided if you are not willing to risk dying. A small percentage of beds is generally reserved for women, and others may be set aside of members of one or another branch of government service. Much of the nursing and care is provided by family members who may stay there around the clock. When someone is hospitalized, it is incumbent upon the patient's friends to visit, so family members must entertain these guests and worry about the cost of providing tea and sweets. Hospitals are notorious for serving only those who can pay and reports of atrocities were common in the Urdu press during the August, 1981. I found three reports of family members having to run around hospitals to locate physicians treat patients who were left unattended while bleeding seriously in emergency rooms.[19] One author titled his piece" Hospitals or Slaughterhouses?"[20] and others called for shutting down hospitals if they were intended solely for the profit of physicians.[21] There were complaints that sewage and filth was left to fester in clogged drains,[22] of food so dreadful as to be inedible,[23] and reports of operations being done on the wrong patients![24]

In short, the statistician's assumptions about the meaning of "hospital," "doctor," and "nurse" are all inappropriate for Pakistan. While it would certainly be wrong to assume that no physicians are conscientious and work hard to help their patients, the career pressures under which many struggle, the quantity and quality of equipment and supplies available to them, the conditions of the hospitals, and the problems they face in supervising permanent staff make their profession a very different one than that of medicine in the West. Most corrosive perhaps are the difficulties they have communicating with patients who commonly mistrust their profession and the government sponsored services, speak different languages, and employ different concepts to analyze health problems, and their expectations of care.

Yunani Tibb

Yunani Tibb (Greek medicine or wisdom), or Islami-Tibb, is Galenic medicine, itself a revision of the system of Hippocrates and

Aristotle, augmented and resystematized by Muslim scholars. The most influential text in this tradition, still in use today in Pakistan, is *al-Qanun fi al-Tibb* (Canon of Medicine), written by the Persian, Ibn-Sina(Avicenna) during the 13th century. Derived from an analogy with the separation of blood that has been heated in a crucible into four parts, Yunani medical theory centers around the notion of four humors which constitute the body: blood, phlegm, bile, and black bile or *sauda*. These are constituted of the four elements earth, air, fire and water, which are composed of the four fundamental qualities of heat, cold, dryness and moisture. Each is associated with a temperament or personality type as well: sanguine, phlegmatic, bilious or choleric, and melancholic, respectively.

Individual health is conceptualized as proper balance amount the humors and the qualities they represent. Every person has a unique point of balance that represents health, and hence a unique constitution or temperament. This varies with age and sex, occupation, etc. Imbalance, due to excess or deficiency of one or more humors, is the equivalent of disease and the restoration of balance is the aim of treatment. The system is allopathic: when an individual suffers from excess heat, for example fever, proper treatment consists of consumption of foods and herbal medicines that have a cooling effect on the body. Cooling (or Sun-) baths, bloodletting or cupping, and herb-induced purging are other main forms of remedy.

Causation is also split into four categories. First the material cause, the substance itself: second the efficient cause, which moulds the material, including age, sex, mental and physical activity, sleep, habits, etc.; third, the formal cause which determines the shape and quality of a thing; and fourth the final cause, that which governs the function of the material in question.[25] Yunani Tibb is thus a holistic medical system that recognizes innate and environmental, congenital and acquired, organic and functional, and physical and emotional dimensions.[26]

Diagnosis depends upon careful observation of mental function, pulse and respiration, stools and urine, and the appearance of everypart of the body including tongue, skin, hair eyes, etc. Questions about likes and dislikes, sleeping, occupation, dreaming, emotionality, etc., also are asked.[27] Symptoms are identified and the underlying imbalanced state determined.

Diseases may be internal or external , and simple or complex (affecting simple or complex organs) depending upon the number of underlying disturbances.

In the first centuries of Islam there was controversy about the acceptability of Greek medicine within the religion, due to the notion of vital force as the fundamental motivating factor for life. Theologians distrusted this concept because it appeared to contradict the primacy of divinity. In recent years in Pakistan, however, precisely this factor has contributed to the renewed acceptance of this medical system. The fact that a non-physical force or entity is held responsible for life itself in Yunani Tibb means that it is not perceived to be in contradiction with religion in the way that secular biomedicine is. Soon after taking power in 1978, Zia-ul-Haq announced as part of his program to Islamicize the country that he would be promoting Yunani Tibb because it was better suited to the Muslim temperament of the people of Pakistan.[28]

Pakistan speak highly of hakims, stressing that they treat the whole person, not just the patient's body, and that they give personalized treatment. They are aware that hakims are motivated by human sympathy, *hamdardi*, rather than greed, and point to the fact that they accept no payment for their services, though they may sell the substances they prescribe for their patients. These beliefs are propagated by hakims themselves, in part, at least, in their competition with biomedicine. The hakims generally inquire about a person's residence and occupation as well as their physical complaints, but their examinations were so short.[29] in popular city clinics that, even though much might be deduced from this information, a comprehensive understanding of the patient's personal situation and individual temperament could hardly have been attained. Those who practice in villages and are well acquainted with those who seek their help probably do have a good sense of their individual patients. The verifiability of the hakims, claims about their work is not essential; rather, the function of the claims is to assert the moral basis of Yunani Tibb and legitimate its practitioners as healers in this society where religious consciousness and awareness of dangerous side effects of (often misprescribed) biomedicines are both increasing.

Religious Healing

Belief in religious healing, in one form or another, is ubiquitous in Pakistan. Few would question the idea that birth and death are the responsibility of Allah, and many assume that much of what occurs during life is predetermined. The existence of a hierarchy of beings, including some who may be responsible for illness or misfortune, is set forth in the Quran, so the truth of their existence cannot be questioned by the faithful. Also, the Prophet Mohammed recommended certain preventive practices and herbal remedies, and sometimes healed by praying over a supplicant, as recorded in the Hadiths. Thus, medicine is undeniably a dimension of religion.

A variety of forms of practice are encountered under the rubric of religious healing: reliance upon prayer; prophetic medicine; and numerous types of popular practice. Those who propound exclusive reliance upon prayer generally reject the legitimacy of the latter forms , claiming that by relying upon mundane substances, from herbs to ink and paper, while attempting to manipulate blessing power, people are demonstrating lack of faith in Allah or even being idolatrous. Similarly, biomedicine is commonly regarded as non-religious and imure and thus denigrated in comparison with religious healing and Islami Tibb. Those who support Prophetic medicine argue that if Mohammed employed certain techniques to prevent or cure disease, they must be acceptable within Islam.

Others who sanction the use of all forms of treatment note that even though certain remedies were not discovered until recently, they were part of Allah's creation and must therefore be acceptable to Him.

Prophetic Medicine

The Hadiths, the recorded sayings and actions of the Prophet, include commentary on the nature of health and illness, the responsibility people bear for nursing the sick, and relevant ideas about purity and pollution, as well as a record of specific treatments the Prophet used. Care of the seriously ill is a compulsory religious duty (*farz*). Failure casts responsibility upon the entire group, just as widespread calamity reflects the degradation of society because people forget to exchange moral advice.[30] In the case of routine sickness, care is less compulsory but in accord with the actions of the Prophet (*sunnat*) and will be rewarded by angles who pray for the care giver.[31]

The Prophet recommended moderation in all things to preserve health of the body and mind.[32] He ate honey every month and had cupping (bloodletting) done every season to maintain internal purity. He also stressed diet for good health, as the stomach is the fountain of health. For treating various ailments he prescribed black nigella (presumedly black cumin), for several others he suggested sea costus. Henna and juice of truffles had limited use. Branding or cauterization was mentioned but condemned for all but treatment of wounds.

Popular Religious Healing

The line between Prophetic and popular healing is quite blurred. Preparation of amulets (*tawiz*) based on passages in the Qur'an, exhalation of blessings immediately after recitation from the Qur'an (*dum or dua*), and multiple repetition of certain Qur'anic phrases for an extended number of days (*wazifa*) are among the most common methods of popular religious healing. Certain passages in the Hadiths condone such practices, but others that appear to reject them have been stressed by theological conservatives in the recent past. Similarly, visits to shrines, formerly much more common (or at least publicized), are condemned as heretical.[33] The line between medicine and 'magic' -- the deliberate manipulation of nonhuman force--is very slim.

The concept of *jinns* is syncretized with varieties of indigenous spirits in each society where Islam has been adopted. In Pakistan *bhootna* or ghosts are recognized to be just like jinns but less powerful. *Churrail* are vengeful spirits of women who died in childbirth. They are recognized by their eyes and are known throughout North India. In the Himalya, powerful *perian*, or fairies, dwell in remote high places above communities that they previously ruled, notably Hunza. They generally leave people alone, but they have been propitiated by the Shina peoples of Gilgit as part of their ancient religion.[34] Also in the Hindu Kush and Himalaya, people acknowledge the existence of wild, aggressive bestial women (like a *ghuul* or male *yeti*) who may apprehend a lone male and attack him fiercely.

Religious healing, in its various forms, provides explanations and remedies for a variety of common, chronic physical and psycho-social problems. It permits attribution of cause, displacement of responsibility from the victim, and the opportunity for actions to be undertaken to counteract the situation, and these are among the major elements of healing.

Discussion: Choosing a Healer

The search for competent help when one is sick involves

multiple discussions among family and friends about possible causes and explanations for the problem, use of home treatments, and complicated decision making about whom to consult. People view health and illness holistically and seek resolution of both physical and mental aspects of distress by consulting practitioners of different types of medicine. To address various possible etiologies and to maximize the possibility of obtaining the appropriate countermeasure which will result in immediate relief, people seek help from practitioners of different therapies simultaneously or serially.

The individual practitioner, rather than the medical theory to which he subscribes, is paramount in most dicisions people make about where to seek help. The familiar (family-based) structure of the hakin's clinic, and its strong religio-moral legitimation contribute to the appeal of this type of practice but the practioner's reputation for piety, generosity, and success are most important. For some problems, notably physical presentations of psycho-social conflict and convulsions, religious forms of healing are recognized as the only correct ones. But in another sense, religion is always the sole appropriate form of treatment for all health and other problems in life, and few would challenge the idea that without the blessing of Allah no one will be healed by any form of treatment. Secular, scientific medicine is thus devalued as a theory, and physicians are commonly thought to be greedy and inhumane, and terrible hospital conditions are openly deplored. Yet people, particularly men (see below), flock to pharmacists and doctors their friends have recommended hoping to receive through biomedicine the power that will restore them to proper, balanced functioning.

Women and Health

Full comprehension of the health and health care issues facing women in Pakistan requires an understanding of the way women are viewed, the significance of Islamic precepts in popular perceptions of them, and the roles they occupy in social life. Wide class differences separate a very small number of well-off, educated women in urban centres from the vast majority who have little or no education, virtually no independent mobility, and extremely limited control over property or productive resources. Economic and social constraints result in great restrictions on women in much of the North west Frontier Province, Boluchistan, and the poor in rural areas and urban slums in other parts of the country.[35] These class differences aside, women throughout the country are affected by widely shared notions about the nature and capacities of women.

Women are believed to be fundamentally different from and in many ways inferior to men. In what might be seen as a subconscious yet deliberately self-fulfilling prophecy, men regard women as intellectually and emotionally weak and thus incapable of making reasonable decisions or exercising responsibility for them. I was told "women are unable to think!" by a man who insisted that it was unnecessary, inappropriate, and useless to have women respond to a felt needs survey in a rural development project intended for their benefit. For him, any participation in public life was by definition male, so the prospect of women's involvement broached a categorical as well as a moral impossibility.

Women's sexuality is commonly perceived to be insatiable and thus threatening to men and the public order they strive to maintain. Where a woman simply meeting the eyes of a man outside the immediate family is often understood to be blatantly promiscuous, supervision of women's movements and contacts is felt to be necessary to ensure their obedience and chastity, and preserve the *Izzat* (honor) of the men and the family. Purdah, or concealment of women, correlates with social status, for the very poor rely upon women participating in agricultural or other work which precludes complete seclusion. The upwardly mobile stress concealment of women is an indicator of sufficient wealth to afford their release from labor. Highly educated urban women have superficially greater freedom. Women's personal names are not used outside the most intimate circles, and reference to women in another man's family is scrupulously controlled, or might precipitate fighting. To protect their identity and family dignity, men expend great effort to make sure that all other men know that they are properly controlling the women in their families. At the same time, consciousness of sexuality is pushed to the foreground, and opportunity for illicit contact is sought as ardently as effort is made to preclude it.

Expectations of women are primarily determined with reference to their bodies. It is a woman's duty of care for her husband and his home. Production of children especially sons, for his family is her most important task, and hence her most treasured goal. Ability to become pregnant, to deliver a healthy baby, to have a son, and to keep children alive through childhood all reflect on the quality and character of the woman. In an infertile marriage the woman is most abjectly miserable, for she must personally bear responsibility for a situation that may not be her fault. Pseudocyesis, false pregnancy, was reputedly common where I conducted research, suggesting that the psychological pressure on women to reproduce is intense. Grown sons who remain emotionally dependent on their mother permit a mature woman to achieve so status and power in life. She may exercise considerable control over her sons' wives, but is unlikely to ever control productive resources or exercise authority outside the home. An older, post-menopausal and thus no longer threatening, woman may be highly respected as an idealized, caring, motherly figure by many men in a small community who yearn for the special closeness they had with their own mothers.

A woman's health is likewise thought to depend largely upon her sexuality. Postpartum depression and related disorders are often attributed to misalignment of the uterus. Hysteria is conceptualized as a woman's emotional disease related to the condition of her reproductive organs, much as it was in late 19th century Europe. Stress and strain are thought to make a woman irritable and sick, so strenuous physical exercise or mental exertion is best avoided. Thus in the early 1980s , many conservatives argued against permitting girls to study math and physics on the grounds that their fragile health, specifically proper hormonal balance, might be disrupted by the effort required. Again, the possibility of influence from 19th century Europe, where women were required to take rest cures to force them into docility, is evidenced.[36] Menstruation is referred to as sickness and widely believed to require rest because the loss of blood is thought to induce weakness at the time. In the long run, *Khun-Ki-Kami*, or insufficiency of blood, is a great concern of women. The humoral notion of lost heat contained in this important humor, is central to understanding a common Pakistani view of woman's bodies and their reproduction-dominated dynamics.

Women in remote areas must typically perform demanding physical tasks such as carrying all the family's water up steep hills in heavy containers even in severe weather conditions. Those in families with greater resources may be forced to stay within the compound walls, and get far too little exercise. Early and frequent pregnancies, widespread severe iron deficiency and generally poor nutrition seriously undermine many woman's strength while they are still young. Thus, women are typically either drawn, hollow-cheeked and grew-skinned with deep lines from worry and exposure to sun and wind, or very plump, flaccid and unfit.

Women's access to health care is very limited due to standards of family honor and economic constraints. Purdah places constraints on interaction between women and care givers. Depending on the status of the family, the type of complaint a women has, and the closeness of the healer to the family, she may or may not be permitted to seek help. If an amulet (*tawiz*) is sought from a close relative, the patient, in the company of another close female relative, may be able to directly ask for help. If her ailment is internal, especially reproductive, she will not be able to consult any male practitioner anywhere near her home. Instead her husband may purchase medicines from a doctor or at a pharmacy at a distant location when on a trip for some other purpose. The expectation that a competent doctor will be able to identify the problem without seeing the patient or asking man questions facilitates prescription under these circumstances.

Only when it is apparent that special help is required, often far too late for minimally comfortable travel or successful treatment, and only if the family can afford to arrange and pay for the trip, will the woman be seen by competent biomedical personnel. At least one other woman must accompany the patient to be present during the examination and help care for her if she must stay in the hospital. For each woman who travels approximately one man must accompany the group to ensure the safety and honor of the women. Thus, for residents of remote regions, a trip to a hospital when a woman is severely ill requires that many family members leave home and is thus often prohibitively costly. A healer close to home may be too close to the community to be allowed to learn about the woman's problem. The result is that women frequently are denied access to medical care by circumstances that are considered to be beyond the control of men.

Other locally available care for women is poor or undressed. Though the dispenser had ferric and folic tablets for pregnant women, propriety prevented him from educating men about their advisability. Men might have been offended that their wives were being obliquely retered to in conversation, and very probably would have been reluctant to request the tablets because that would have amounted to an inappropriate public announcement of their wife's condition. Pregnancy is not regarded as a special health condition in any case; people rarely mention it when seeking medication for apparently unrelated complaints, so women undoubtedly consume dangerous drugs while pregnant. Birth control pills are available though a completely separate network of offices. My efforts to obtain pills at the request of older village women who generally already had ten living children were met with grossly offensive ridicule from the men in these offices.

Doctors sometimes vacationed where I worked and I asked them about their perceptions of the health conditions. Since they were approached for help only by men, they were aware of the great problems villagers faced, but they remained oblivious to the difficulties encountered by the women who were unable to seek their help. They realized that men sometimes complained about problems they would expect to encounter during the winter, for example, chest pain and cough, in order to obtain medicine for use when needed. Their comments suggested that, perhaps naturally, they regarded women's health problems in a similar light--as potential or abstract rather than pressing and severe..

Improving the availability of women health-care workers would seem to be an obvious remedy. However, a woman who agrees to serve away from her home is viewed with great suspicion by the men in the region where she is sent to work. Since they would never permit the women in their own families to train as nurses or midwives and thus be involved with the defilement of childbirth or dealing with people's bodies , or to work out from under their supervision and away from home, they readily conclude that the woman who does so is from such a dishonorable family that they would permit this, or personally of such reprehensible moral character that the men in her family have thrown her out. A " lady doctor' whose education evidences high family status who serves in rural area is in some ways even more perplexing The woman's presence proves her disrespectability, men consider her a fair target for sexual advances, and her opportunities to help women are limited. I was taunted with lewd hilarity and derision when I purchased medication for leukorrhea at a pharmacy in a regional town at the request of a woman friend; a female health care worker would have been unable to maek this or any purchase. Her requests for resupply through appropriate channels might be greeted with similar responses.

Nonhuman agents are often considered responsible for women's problems. Hot flashes and other symptoms of menopause are commonly attributed to jinns. At least in the area where I conducted field research, women seemed unaware that menopause was a normal part of life. Instead some told stories of repeated episodes of possession, and others begged me for medicines to restore their periods Since knowledge about menstruation, pregnancy and chid birth as well as menopause is not disseminated but only learned through experience, their lack of awareness was plausible. They were also reluctant to accept my assertion of its normalcy, for, as an unmarried woman, I could not be expected to know such things. The women's tendency to suspect nonhuman causation was often derided , publicly if not privately, by men who overlooked women's lack of access to other forms of explanation and treatment and claimed that this further proved that women were supersitious or less rational than men.

In sum, I found there to be a rigid conception of womankind in which body type was assumed to define intellectual capacity and emotional character, and to dictate social role. Men most earnestly declared it to be their religiously-defined responsibility to ensure the perpetuation of moral order, including overseeing of the appropriate activities of women, even though local customs might in some ways deviate from religious prescriptions in some details. As a whole, the entire nation seems to diminish, conceal or ignore women's health issues. Like women themselves, they are largely kept out of sight and public consciousness lest anyone's honor be offended. Very few hospital beds are reserved for women, and very few highly trained women health workers are stationed outside urban areas. Islam, rather than being cited as a compelling force for social policies that will ensure the well-being of every citizen, is instead referred to as the source of honor-indexed constraints on public speech, mobility, and access to care that result in great suffering for the half of humanity that gives birth, prepares food, and stays out of the public domain lest their pollution contaminate and disrupt the world.

Conclusion

The uninformed researcher who depends upon published statistics for information about health and healing in Pakistan is easily misled into believing that good and improving services are amply provided in the nation. This is primarily a consequence of uncritically transferring assumptions about the definitions of health, doctors, and hospitals, and about standards of quality from Western society when interpreting the available data. Instead, health conditions and the accessibility of health care are severely prejudiced against half of the population on the basis of sexual identity, and the quality of services and supplies is often poor.

More fundamental is the fact that many different types of health care based on widely divergent medical theories are available in Pakistan. People make judgements about the nature and severity of health problems, defined holistically to include psycho-social as well as physical conditions, and then seek treatments simultaneously of serially that will address all of the contributing factors--from practitioners of Yunani Tibb and religious healing as well as biomedicine. They are most comfortable in clinics with a familiar hierarchy in which the healer exercises paternal authority over subordinates. The concepts and vocabulary they most commonly use when analyzing the body and its well-being are primarily derived from Greco-Islamic humoral theory. They evaluate the care they receive and the practitioners with whom they have interacted largely in religio-moral rather than secular, scientific terms.

The Evolution of Islam in Politics

> The teaching of the Quran that life is a process of progressive creation necessitates that each generation, guided but unhampered by the work of its predecessor, should be permitted to solve its own problems.
> *Allama Iqbal*, 1932
> 'FOR GOD'S SAKE LEAVE ISLAM ALONE'
> *Baluchistan Times*, 1977[37]

The Muslims first arrived in India in the eighth century and established their rule in the thirteenth century with the Sultanate of Delhi. After that time most of India came under Muslim dominance, though numerically the Muslims remained a minority. With the advent of the Moghal Empire between the sixteenth and the eighteenth centuries the political influence of the Muslims spread to encompass virtually all of the sub-continent. Moghal authority was potently challenged only by an alien force, the British, whose victory in the Battle of Plassey (1757) marked the beginning of the decline of Muslim supremacy in India. A century later the disintegration of Muslim rule in India was complete. The glories of the past were not forgotten however, and from the Muslim point of view, the 1857 Rebellion, when both Hindu and Muslim elements of the British Indian Army rebelled against the British, was an attempt to re-establish Muslim rule.

The failure of the predominantly Muslim-led rebellion against British colonial power and the subsequent discrimination against Muslims, who were held responsible by the British, forced the Muslim intelligentsia to reassess its community's position in society and to redefine its future. There was, however, no consensus on what that future should be or how to achieve it, and various trends of thought emerged.

One trend was inspired by Sir Syed Ahmad Khan (1817-98). Sir Syed saw the problem of Indian Muslims as being one of a withdrawal from the economic and political spheres of life. A withdrawal that was at once voluntary and involuntary-voluntary in that after the 1857 British policy deliberately removed Muslims from positions of power or decision-making. Sir Syed was concerned with lifting the Muslims out of their internalized and isolated condition so that they could actively participate and compete with Hindu in the prevailing system. To achieve this, he felt that it was essential for the Muslim population to espouse modern education. To overcome any reticence that may have existed in the Muslim community, he set about proving that there was no contradiction between Islam and the selective adoption of western ways in order to 'modernize'. Sir Syed's reform movement aimed at bringing Muslims into the mainstream of Indian political and social life took root, and the establishment of the Mohammadan Anglo-Oriental College at Aligarh in 1875 was a manifestation of his efforts. The college had a far-reaching impact on the Muslims of the sub-continent. It attracted Muslim youth from and distant areas and imparted modern education without ignoring or excluding Muslim culture, and thus prepared them to work within the British system.

It was Sir Syed's unstinting efforts for Muslim education combined with Syed Amir Ali's (1849-1928) endeavour to expose the Muslims to practical politics that revived the community's awareness. Amir Ali contributed not only in practical terms by providing the Muslims with a model in the judicial and legislative fields but also made a mark as a scholar and writer. He wrote extensively on Islam and history and made a strong impact on the Muslims of India.

The second major school of thought to emerge after 1857 was the religious one which flourished in the scholastic centres of the *Deobands* and *Berelvis*. Unlike Sir Syed, these centres were not looking for immediate social and economic solutions to a political problem. They were concerned instead with what they viewed as the psychological, cultural and spiritual disintegration of the Muslim community in India. Their aim was not to recapture a share in state power, but to pursue the goal of an integrated Muslim identity in India. For this they advocated an inward looking strategy divorced from the structures of British colonial rule. Whereas differences occurred between the Deobandis and Berelvis (as well as amongst adherents of each school and other traditionalists) they shared in common a doctrinaire and dogmatic approach to Islam.

These two divergent trends of Muslim thought developed concurrently, but with little cross-fertilization. The trend initiated by Sir Syed was to evolve a socially progressive ethos which was particularly relevant for women, and it is among Sir Syed's followers that we find the first advocates of women's education and of an enhanced status and role for them. On the other hand the traditionalist trend was socially conservative, especially with regards to women. Yet it was this trend which resulted in the *Khilafat* movement—the first movement to mobilize women on a political platform.[38] Both trends of thought contributed to the general reawakening of the Muslims in the sub-continent, which coincided with the growth of Indian nationalism as a whole. But, whereas both were active in raising the consciousness of the Muslims, they were diametrically opposed to each other on the question of Muslim nationalism vs. Indian nationalism.

The Muslim awareness created by Sir Syed's followers led to the formation of the All-India Muslim League in 1906. In its early years the League failed to attract members and it was only much later with the intensification of Muslim nationalist sentiment that it became a viable party. In this period Sir Allama Mohammad Iqbal (1887-1938) came to the fore as an outstanding intellectual, philosopher and poet of the region. Iqbal's early writings advocated Hindu-Muslim unity and reflected Indian nationalism. But by 1909 his views had undergone a marked change and he now saw the Hindus and the Muslims as separate national entities. Extremely anxious about the future and destiny of the Indian Muslims, who he feared would be completely subsumed by the Hindus, he was seriously concerned about the preservation of their identity. Therefore, at the same time as spreading consciousness about Muslim identity, Iqbal projected practical and modern view of Islam-Islam not as a vehicle for eternal salvation after death but as a principal of social functionalism. He strongly believed that a revitalized Islam, in consonance with the real world, was the sole mobilizing force for the Muslims of India and that it could only develop in a free Muslim state.

Needless to say, Iqbal's ideas were in direct contradiction with those of the traditionalists. The *ulema,* both of the *Deoband* and *Berelvi* school of thought, opposed his brand of Muslim nationalism. The *Deobandis*, headed by Husain Ahmad Madani, who was an anti-imperialist, believed in Indian nationalism as opposed to Muslim nationalism. Madani urged the Indian Muslims to set aside the issue of faith, to consider themselves part of a larger Indian nationhood and stand united to overthrow colonial rule.

On the other hand, Maulana Abul Ala Maududi, a recognized and important scholar of Islam (and later head of the Islamic fundamentalist political party, the Jamaat-e-Islami) saw India as composed of various religious entities each with the right to pursue its own beliefs and rules of conduct. He rejected both Indian as well as Muslim nationalism as un-Islamic and seems to have ignored the anti-imperialist struggle going on in India.[39] He vehemently opposed the creation of Pakistan and accused the leaders of the Pakistan Movement of misleading the Muslims and of carrying out a nefarious plot to undermine the cause of Islam in India.

It was Iqbal's vision that 'the formation of a consolidated North-West Indian Muslim State appears to be the final destiny of the Muslims, at least of North-West India' that ultimately caught the imagination of the Muslims.[40] So much so that in 1933, three Muslims students studying in Cambridge demanded the partition of the sub-continent between Muslims and Hindus and one of them (Barkat Ali) coined the name Pakistan of the proposed Muslim state. The name was formally adopted by the Muslim League in 1940.

The Pakistan Movement (1940-47)

That there was confusion amongst the Muslims and that their forces were scattered between 1930 and 1940 was clearly evident from the results of the elections for the provincial legislatures in 1937.[41] Of the 484 Muslim seats the Muslim League, which claimed to represent all the Muslims of India, captured only 108 seats and failed to win a majority even in the Muslim majority areas. This depressing state of affairs seems to have jolted the Muslim League leaders, especially Mohammad Ali Jinnah, into focusing attention towards organizing the Muslims and articulating their fears and aspirations.[42]

In the following years Jinnah completely re-organised the Muslim League. Travelled from province to province and made mass contacts with the Muslims. In March 1940 he presented the two-nation theory in his presidential address at the annual meeting of the Muslim League in Lahore. This became the famous Lahore Resolution demanding independent Muslim states in the sub-continent on the basis that Muslims and Hindus belong to two different religious philosophies, social customs, literatures... they belong to two different civilizations which are based mainly on conflicting ideas and conceptions... They have different epics, different heroes and different episodes... Musalmans are a nation according to any definition... and they must have their homelands, their territory and their state.[43]

In his efforts to mobilize Muhammad Ali Jinnah did not only appeal to the Muslim males. He focused equally on women, recognizing that they represented and untapped force and source of strength. He supported women's rights and deplored the oppression of women in his speeches and at public rallies. His most quoted and remembered speech is the one delivered in Aligarh in 1944 in which he said :

> It is a crime against humanity that our women are shut up within the four walls of the houses as prisoners. There is no sanction anywhere for the deplorable conditions in which our women have to live. You should take your women along with you as comrades in every sphere of life.

As a symbolic gesture, he took his sister, Mohtarma Fatima Jinnah with him wherever he went. He also encouraged the organization of women's wings of the Muslim League in every major city. The women responded to the Muslim League with fervour and enthusiasm, especially the younger one, who had hardly ever stepped out of their homes and now showed their organizational potential and capacity to work.

As the Pakistan Movement gained momentum it polarized the Muslim population into those supporting the formation of a separate homeland and those opposed to it. Both the supporters of the movement and those in the leadership were adherents of the Sir Syed school of thought. Of those who opposed the movement the most prominent were the *ulema* (religious scholars) and their extreme right wing 'Islamic' parties who viewed it as an impediment to the spread of Islam. The *maulvis* (preachers) were against Muslim nationalism and castigated the Muslim League for demanding a separate country. Among those opposed to the idea of Pakistan was Maulana Abul Kalam Azad, who viewed the Pakistan Movement as a source of weakness for India, and for whom Indian nationalism was paramount.

Post-Independence Developments

The Pakistan Movement was steered by politicians who, after having achieved an independent state, were faced with the formidable task of building the infrastructure for the state, almost from scratch. Pakistan, unlike most post-colonial states, did not inherit functioning administrative, political, economic and military structures from the withdrawing colonial power (i.e., the British).[44] The demand for Pakistan had been conceded in June 1947 at the tail end of the Indian people's struggle for independence, and the transfer of power to Pakistan was hurriedly made in August 1947. Consequently, most of the assets and states machinery went to India. At the time of Independence, therefore, Pakistan's political as well as economic structures were fluid and ambivalent. That the opportunity for remodelling the structures in accordance with the needs and requirements of the people existed, and was allowed to pass, merits a separate discussion not within the scope of this study.[45] It is sufficient to state here that the attempt by the succession elites to resolve the problems of political and economic development was complicated by the entry of the orthodox *ulema* on the political scene almost immediately after independence. This element, which has found itself completely by-passed and isolated during the Pakistan Movement, now presented itself as a contender for power using 'Islam' of its political rationalization. Opposed to each other prior to independence, the politicians and *ulema* remained antagonistic in the period following. If previously they had clashed over a separate homeland, after independence the two groups contested the Islamic nature of that homeland.

In the years that followed two important factors emerged; one was the phenomenon of Islam becoming central to the political debate in Pakistan and the other was the formation of new economic and social structures. Both these factors not only had direct bearing on the political ethos that developed in Pakistan but also had an impact on women's position in society.

The Early Years : 1947-58

The arrival of the *ulema*-including those of the *Berelvi* and *Deoband* schools and the Majlis-e-Ahrar-in Pakistan, and their demand for positions of power and importance in all branches of the state system, was initially dismissed by the political leadership as being inconsequential. The politicians viewed the *ulema* as irritants. Liaquat Ali Khan, the first prime minister of Pakistan, denounced them as 'enemies of Islam' who meant only to 'disrupt and destroy Pakistan'. Mian Iftikharuddin, an urban-based landlord, called them 'stooges[' of the British. Others considered them uneducated and narrow-minded.

Jinnah's vision of a non-theocratic Pakistan, and Liaquat's aspirations for building a liberal, democratic political system, were not viewed by the political elite as being antagonistic or contrary to Islam. Democracy, right of speech, freedom of conscience, emancipation of women, human dignity, tolerance, etc., were all considered Quranic principles and very desirable in a modern democratic state. Furthermore, the interpretation of Islamic injunctions according to the needs of changing times and conditions was considered that right of Muslims at large and not the exclusive prerogative of the *Ulema*. The politicians emphasized Islamics principles and not Islamic law. They viewed Pakistan as a state of Muslims who, being in the majority, had the freedom to practice their religion without fear of persecution.[46]

The *ulema* had a different though well-defined position on the nature of an Islamic state. In January 1951 they held a convention in Lahore and passed a resolution prescribing the principles of an Islamic state which they insisted should be incorporated in the constitution of Pakistan. These included: absolute sovereignty of God; Quran and Sunnah to be the basis of all law; state to have no right to repeal any Islamic law; and banning of preaching and propagation of any ideology not in consonance with Islam. In 1953 the *ulema* held another convention at which they reiterated their earlier position and added the demand for the appointment of five *ulema* to the Supreme Court. These *ulema* would periodically review specific laws and determine whether the laws were repugnant to

Islam or not. They further demanded that Islamic studies be made a compulsory subject for all Muslim students and that tribal, ethnic and linguistic differences of the provinces should not be recognized.

Maulana Maududi, the most vocal opponent of Jinnah as well as of a separate Muslim state, chose to migrate to Pakistan as early as August 1947, whereupon he declared that his party was the guardian of Islam and that he would launch an Islamic revolution and seize state power. In addition to the points incorporated in the resolutions of 1951 and 1953, he advocated that voting rights should be extended to all adult males and only to educated females. He expounded that women should not be allowed to take up any public office where they were likely to come in contact with men. Important public offices including that of head of state could only be held by pious and learned males. He recommended a separate assembly of women to advise legislatures on issues relating to women. The entire emphasis of the *ulema's* contention about the Islamic state centred on the sovereignty and supremacy of the laws contained in the Quran and Sunnah, which could only be applied and interpreted by themselves. They were thus hoping 'to recapture the prestige and prosperity they had traditionally enjoyed in Muslim states until recent times'.[47]

While it is true that in the early years of Pakistan's life (1947-1958) the orthodoxy was looked upon with disdain and irreverence by the political leadership, it is equally true that measures to pacify it were also taken. These were exemplified by the concessions made to the *maulvis*. For instance, Pakistan was declared an Islamic Republic under the 1956 constitution, and the *ulema* were provided with an advisory role in the legislature. However, most of their demands regarding the functioning of an Islamic Republic, such as excluding women from contesting or participating in elections, or for a Ministry of Religious Affairs and separate electorates for Muslims and non-Muslims, were ignored by the Constituent Assembly and eventually the ulema accepted the constitution of 1956 as being Islamic.[48]

The question that arises is why these concessions were offered at all. Several explanations seem possible. One is that the founding fathers saw themselves as pragmatists and modernists, whose immediate concern focused on the procedural problems of running the state and who did not see Islam as being an obstacle. They were the educated elite who did not have the tie to investigate and arrive at a philosophical rationalization of dynamic Islam, nor did they consider this necessary. As a result they were put on the defensive when labelled 'un-Islamic' by the protagonists of 'purist' Islam. Instead of responding with a worked-out counter-argument the politicians gave in to the blackmail of the *ulema*. They conceded on points which in their view were not important in the overall pattern or system or governance.

The other reason for making concessions was the ability of the religious elements to create tensions and law and order situations on a religious and sectarian basis. The anti-Qadiani movement engineered by these forces in 1953 is one such example which resulted in Martial Law being imposed for the first time (in Lahore).[49]

Another possible explanation is that the ruling groups viewed the rightist element as having the potential of being used in their internal power struggles either as an ally or for exerting pressure. This rationalization is not entirely misplaced or incredible for there is no doubt that if those in power had so wished, they could have dealt with the *ulema*, quite summarily at that point. For their part the *ulema* having been granted a certain leeway, continued to use Islam to pressurize those in the government to give them a share in power.

With the passage of time and the notifications of internal contradictions within the ruling group, which consisted of landlords, politicians, bureaucrats and professionals, the political use of Islam augmented and with it the *maulvis'* capacity to manipulate and gain for themselves a place in the system. The *maulvis* made systematic efforts to publicized and propagate their brand of Islam and to make inroads at the institutional level within educational institutions and the armed and civil services.

By 1956, when Pakistan's first constitution was finally promulgated, a very fundamental change had occurred in the politics of the country. From the situation at the time of Independence, when a broad-based heterogeneous ruling group had tried to share power, Pakistan had arrived at a position where the civil bureaucracy, supported by the army and the emerging national comprador bourgeoisie, was in complete control. In this period no elections were held and no effort at starting a genuine political process was made. Consequently the political leadership found itself isolated from the mainspring of its support, the people, and pitched against West-trained administrators and Sandhurst - trained army officials. These new elites also considered themselves as pragmatists concerned with the development and modernization of Pakistan and were not preoccupied with Islam at any level (philosophical or intellectual). While both the old and the new leadership had similar outlooks on Islam and Pakistan, they were at opposite ends in the power struggle. As a result the old political leadership found itself trying to forge alliances with the forces that had opposed it during the Pakistan Movement, i.e., the right wing. The Muslim League by this time was no longer a political force, new parties were created and party-changing vacuum the order of the day. In this setting the religious parties were presented with the opportunity of becoming active competitors in the politcal arena.

Ayub Khan's Period (1958-69)

The year 1958 marked the change-over of power from the civil to the military bureaucracy. General Muhammad Ayub Khan assumed through a military coup and force all political activity by banning political parties, thus sounding the death knell for political institution-building in Pakistan. During Ayub's period (1958-1969) it became evident that it was not possible for any government in power to work outside the Islamic cultural framework, for even Ayub, a military dictator of the liberal-west tradition, made use of Islam for political ends.

Ayub Khan's period was significant for being the period of reversal for the Islamic advocates. Ayub challenged the medieval thinking of the *ulema* and saw them as divisive and retrogressive elements in society. Many of the *ulema* were jailed by him, including Maulana Maududi in 1963. He also decide to drop the prefix 'Islamic' form the official name of the country when he promulgated the new constitution in 1962 (according to which Pakistan was to be the Republic of Pakistan).

Ayub's constitution did provide for the Advisory Council of Islamic Ideology to recommend ways for organizing life according to Islamic concepts and principles, but denied it power to examine laws for their Islamic content. He also set up the Central Institute of Islamic research which, in his view, was aimed at liberating Islam from the clutches of the obscurantists. Ironically, even his hand-picked National Assembly of 1962, as one of its first actions, ameneded the constitution to change the name of the country back to the Islamic Republic of Pakistan. Later, when faced with growing

Bengali national consciousness, Ayub Khan responded by invoking Islam for the greater unity of Pakistan while ignoring the actual resentments expressed by East Pakistanis.

Finally, in the elections of 1965, when Jinnah's sisters Fatima Jinnah was put up as the presidential candidate by the Combined Opposition Parties (COP) he condemned her candidature as un-Islamic on the grounds of her being a woman. He had various *maulvis* give *fatwas* (edicts) to condemn Fatima Jinnah for contesting the election. And Maududi, who found himself allied with the opposition, revised his position on female heads of state, obviously for reasons of political exigency, and supported Fatima Jinnah's candidature.

Other significant aspects of Ayub Khan's years of military rule were the bolstering of the capitalist class, which had *comprador* links with international capitalism, and the increase in the repressive powers of the state. The emerging *comprador* bourgeoisie was one of his pillars of civilian support, the other being the bureaucracy. He also singled out the members of the landed aristocracy who were willing to serve within his system. These included the Nawab of Kalabagh and Zulfiqar Ali Bhutto. The Nawab served as a ruthless governor of West Pakistan and Bhutto as minister of industries and subsequently as foreign minister in his government. Measures to close all avenues of political expression included banning of trade unions, promulgation of a University Ordinance curbing students' activities and the taking over of independent newspapers by the state.

As a result of Ayub Khan's policies, the inequalities between different sectors of society, and between provinces, increases alarmingly, and great concentration of wealth ensued: 66 per cent of the country's industrial capital was in the hands of 22 families.[50] Disparities increased and in the countryside living standards declined due to the introduction of capitalization in agriculture : tenants were ejected and landless labour grew. The size of the working class in the cities grew, but wages dwindled. Besides creating stark class differences, the economic and developmental policies (planned with US advisers) also heightened the disparities between East and West Pakistan.[51]

The above factors contributed towards the movement against military regime. From November 1968 to March 1969, the country experienced popular upheaval. The people of both East and West

Pakistan were united in their rejection of Ayub Khan. Students, industrial workers, teachers and lawyers faced bullets and arrests. Troops were called into quell the agitation but met with little success, forcing Ayub to negotiate with the politicians, who had earlier been barred from participating in political activity. He agreed to the restoration of parliamentary democracy and to direct elections on the basis of universal adult franchise. These concessions notwithstanding, on 26 March 1969 Ayub had no option but to step down and hand over power to General Muhammad Yahya Khan, Commander-in-Chief of the army, who promulgated martial law once again and promised general elections very soon.

The anti-Ayub agitation had spread to most large and small urban centres of Pakistan. It remained largely male-dominated and female participation was negligible. Nevertheless, there were instances of women political prisoners. One such prisoners was Alkhtar Baloch, a young middle-class woman, arrested in Sind in 1970. She and her sister spent several months in Sukkur gaol with women criminals. Her diaries were later published. [52] Zulfiqar Ali Bhutto, who had fallen out of fabour with Ayub Khan after the 1965 War and who had formed his own political party in 1967, emerged as the most prominent leader of the anti-Ayub movement.[53] Ayub's downfall in 1969 and the first general elections in 1970 saw a polarization between the political left and the right in Pakistan. The right wing parties, which included the Jamaat-e-Islami, Jamiat-e-Ulema-e-Islam (JUI) and Jamiat-Ulema-e-Pakistan (JUP) joined ranks with the Muslim League to contest elections with the solgan 'Islam in danger'.

The Bhutto Era (1969-77)

Bhutto assumed office as head of state in January 1972, but his impact on the polity of Pakistan began with the anti-Ayub agitations of 1969 and the election campaign of 1970. Emerging as the leader of the downtroden and oppressed during the anti-Ayub movement, he fired people's imaginations with the hitherto unknown slogan of Islamic socialism. He held out the promise of *roti, kapra* and *makan* (food, clothing and housing) for every Pakistani. He promised everybody the right to vote, a representative government and equal opportunity. He talked of redistribution of land and nationalization of industry. His charisma mobilized hundreds of young people, intellectuals and women. Whereas very few or no women were visible during the anti-Ayub movement, during Bhutto's election campaign many were actively involved.

Bhutto and his Pakistan People's Party (PPP) emerged victorious in the elections. Of the 138 West Pakistan seats PPP own 81.[54] Jamaat-e-Islam won a dismal four and the other Islamic parties managed a total of 14 seats. The various factions of the Muslim League had a combined strength of 18. Mujib-ur-Rehman's absolute majority, however, threw the military government of Yahya, which was not prepared to hand over power to the Awami League, into a quandary. The tensions and mutual distrust between East and West Pakistan had already reached breaking point during the elections. Bhutto's refusal to attend the opening session of the Assembly in Dacca triggered widespread political protest in East Pakistan and the Bangladesh flag was hoisted in any places. General Yahya Khan responded with armed action in March 1971, which resulted in a bloody civil war that raged till almost the end of the year. Armed Indian intervention then led to the third India-Pakistan war and secession of East Pakistan in December 1971.

When the military transferred power in January 1972, Pakistan was both reduced in size and demoralized. There were about 90,000 prisoners of war in India, and Pakistan's international prestige was perhaps at its lowest. Internally, the people were shocked, hurt and humiliated. The country had anenormous foreign debt and Ayub Khan's policies had left the urban workers and rural poor in a state of extreme poverty. Bhutto's immediate task was to provide a viable political structure, revive the people's morale and rebuild the economy.

Bhutto's failure to fulfil people's expectations, and the reasons for this, havc been discussed in great detail by analysts.[55] It is not necessary to go into a discussion of all the complexities of Bhutto's period of power, but there is a need to point out the significant contributions—tangible and intangible—made by his to the polity.

Firstly, Bhutto's most important contribution was giving the downtrodden an awareness of their own dignity and self-respect. The deprived sections of society in Pakistan had been suffering under a centuries-old oppressive social and economic system, and until recently they accepted it as their fate. Cutting across class differentiations, Bhutto managed to instil in them a sense of worth, generating a confidence buried in years of servitude. Equally important was his appeal to women to participate. For the first time women experienced some freedom of movement and expression—

they were being singled out and addressed. That self-respect has remained and cannot be eliminated by repression.

The other contribution was the Constitution of 1973. Based on principles of federalism and parliamentary democracy, it was arrived at through a consensus of all political parties and representatives of the four provinces.

The Constitution, for the first time in Pakistan's history, gave equal rights to men and women and provided for equal opportunities for all. It prohibited discrimination on the basis of sex, class or creed, and had most of the provisions of a secular and egalitarian document.

Another important aspect of Bhutto's period was the legitimacy that he gave to left ideology. In Pakistan, as early as 1954, the Communist Party had been banned in the wake of an alleged plot, known as the Rawalpindi conspiracy, to overthrow the government and capture state power. Socialism and Marxist thinking were viewed as a major treat by the various governments in power and were discouraged by the establishment. Against this background Bhutto's slogan of Islamic socialism enabled a large number of younger intellectuals and students to be exposed to a different ideology to express their allegiance to it and not be persecuted of adhering to it, at least in the initial years.

It is ironic that Bhutto, winning the election with the populist slogans of socialism, *roti, kapra* and *makan*, perceived the need for Islamic symbols. For instance, his socialism was prefixed with Islam, the name of the country as the Islam i.e. Republic of Pakistan was retained, Islam was declared the state religion (Article 2) etc.[56] In foreign affairs Bhutto initiated an active policy of establishing and nurturing Muslim links, especially with progressive Muslim states such as Libya. The Islamic Summit organized in Lahore was an extension of this policy.

Within the country, the measures that Bhutto introduced : social reforms, nationalization of banks, insurance companies and educational institutions—did not come up to the possibly exaggerated expectations of those who supported him. Quite early in his years of power (1972-73) he ruthlessly crushed labour unrest in Karachi and Multhan, and the disillusionment of the masses increased proportionately to his shifting class alliances. Having mobilized the masses along class lines, Bhutto seemed to have subsequently forsaken them. Most of his reforms were attempts at breaking the power of the dominant classes; not in favour of the masses, but to the advantage of the small entrepreneurs, small farmers and low - and middle - income urban workers. The big landowners were left more or less untouched. His land reforms, delayed until 1967, which proposed lower land ceiling, were never properly implemented. Similarly, while he purged the civil service of senior bureaucrats and introduced reforms, he did not reduce the power of the bureaucracy; in fact it burgeoned with the nationalization policy, as enterprises were taken over by the civil servants.

Bhutto had chosen to keep the military bureaucracy intact when he assumed power in 1971, and he did not hesitate to deploy the armed forces whenever it suited him, for example, in Baluchistan in 1974. He also created his own special security force (FSF) and it is an irony of fate that the murder of a political opponent by members of the FSF (stated to be done for sycophantic reasons) was instrumental in Bhutto's implication in the crime for which he was executed in April 1979.

Over the years Bhutto became increasingly a victim of his own policies. The progressive and radical element of his party soon found itself out of place. By 1975, most of the left intellectuals had either left him or had been forced to do so. In fact the wrath of Bhutto and the establishment came down with more force on the radicals, who found themselves being persecuted. The People's Party, in the meantime, was transformed into a party of feudle landlords.

During his time in office Bhutto also became increasingly vulnerable to pressure from the political right. This element, completely routed and humiliated in the 1970 elections, kept up an unabated diatribe against Bhutto and his 'un-Islamic' policies. Initially, Bhutto tried to win over the reactionaries by measures such as that of 1974 declaring the Qadiani/Ahmedi sect as non-Muslim through an Act of Parliament, which overnight converted thousands to a religious minority. By 1976 the denunciation of his policies became so intense that Bhutto was constrained to introduce more Islamic reforms, though largely symbolic in nature. For instance, he switched the weekly holiday from Sunday to Friday, banned the sale of liquor and all forms of gambling, closed night clubs and placed copies of the Quran in first class hotels and government rest houses.

By the time Bhutto announced general elections for early 1977 he could not have been more isolated. He had nationalized flour and rice-husking mills, and cotton-ginning factories, a measure probably designed to elicit mass support which ended up alienating the landowners who were the only supporters he had left.

The elections saw the entire opposition, from the Islamic fundamentalists to the centrist and liberal left-of-centre parties, coming together in a nine-party Pakistan National Alliance (PNA). The PPP was returned victorious but the opposition refused to accept the results and alleged widespread rigging.

An urban-based PNA movement was launched, demanding a return to Prophet Mohammad's Islamic order. From March to July 1977 the country was faced once again with political upheaval. Landowners, traders and merchants all pitched themselves against PPP. According to Alavi the PPP had alienated itself not only from the dominated classes, i.e., the industrialists, landowners and the military civilian bureaucracy, but also from the subordinate classes.[57] The emerging trader/merchant class, educated in Pakistan with an indigenous idiom and inherently conservative in nature, also opposed him while his former supporters remained silent observers during the PNA movement. This does not mean that grass-roots links forged between 1970 and 1971 were completely annihilated. Later events prove the contrary.

General Zia's Coming to Power : 1977-

The anti-Bhutto PNA movement culminated in Bhutto's arrest on 5 July 1977 and the imposition of Zia-ul-Haq's Martial Law. To judge from Zia's own take-over speech, Islam did not appear to have been in any great danger. On the contrary, Martial Law had been imposed in order to 'avert a national crisis'; elections would be held within 90 days; the army would return to its barracks and the country revert to civilian rule. Other than to mention in passing that he considered 'the introduction of an Ismic system a prerequisite for the country', Zia made no other allusions to Islam. Whether Zia originally intended to hold elections within the stipulated time, or whether he had already formulated plans for 'Islamizing' the country, is a matter of speculation. What is clear is that, initially, none of the political parties took Zia very seriously. The 'simple soldier' image that he projected encouraged politicians to dismiss him as incapable of presenting a theatre to their own ambitions. Equally clearly, Bhutto's release and the delirious enthusiasm with which he was greeted, first in Lahore and then in Karachi, left no illusions as to the outcome of elections if held within 90 days. Consequently, Bhutto was re-arrested and elections postponed until a 'process of accountability' could be completed. 'Accountability' meant that all grievances against Bhutto's PPP and its members, whether real or imagined, would have to be processed before elections could be held.

The political parties who had formed an opposition alliance against Bhutto and the PPP while they were in power were initially relieved at the postponement of elections. The popular support received by the nine-party Pakistan National Alliance during the anti-Bhutto PNA movement had left the component parties ill-prepared for the rekindled enthusiasm shown for Bhutto and the PPP once they were out of power.

Elections had been scheduled for March 1978. Instead, nine months after assuming power, Zia-ul-Haq voiced his intentions to Islamize the penal code of Pakistan as a first step towards establishing a truly Islamic state. Suddenly Islam was endangered and it had become imperative to ensure the supremacy of Islam before the country could be entrusted to civilian rule and political parties. Islam was being used to justify the continuation of Martial Law while most political parties were demanding an end to it. Having assumed power without authority, the army was looking for a means to justify itself and prolong its rule, and it found the perfect excuse in Islam. The only political party to express approval was the Jamaate-e-Islami, for reasons discussed below.

In the spring of 1978, at the same time as he had announced his intention of Islamizing the Penal Code of the country, Zia had co-opted various politicians into his government, notably form two political parties: the Jamaat-e-Islami and the Pakistan Muslim League. The PML is a right-of-centre party of no particular ideological significance, and being splintered into three different and independent groups, it poses no serious threat to anyone in power. This, in conjunction with its historical relevance as the party of Mohammad Ali Jinnah, founder-father of Pakistan, made it a natural choice for co-option. The choice of the Jamaat-e-Islami is another matter.

The Jamaat-e-Islami, self-appointed guardian of Islam in Pakistan, is an extreme right wing political party, Having constituently lost, and lost badly, in all elections, the Jamaat jumped at the opportunity of being co-opted into a position of power, particularly when it saw a good chance of pushing through all its plans for Islamizing the country—an opportunity hitherto denied it under both democratic and martial law regimes. The innumerable fillip-turns executed by Maududi and his followers in the pursuit of their avowed aim of Islamizing the state and people of Pakistan is a separate discussion, and falls outside the scope of the present study. Suffice to say that what was deemed 'Islamic' at one point world suddenly be considered un-Islamic, if it no longer suited the Jamaat. Similarly, what was un-Islamic at a given point was miraculously converted into being Islamic when it suited.[58]

In contrast to the vote-faces in other fields, the one area in which the Jamaat has shown absolute consistency is in its attitude towards women. Maududi's stand on women has been based on two axioms derived from his understanding of Islamic principles: first, that a truly Islamic society is based on complete segregation of the sexes, and second, that Islam subordinates women to men. Hence the Jamaat-e-Islami, and the like-mided persons and parties, have advocated inferior status and complete segreation of women who should preferably be confined to their homes, but otherwise heavily veiled from head to foot; and the total exclusion of women from any decision-making bodies or processes. While the exigencies of time, economic necessity and a growing political awareness among women has forced the Jamaat to tone down its attitude, there has been no substantial change in its position.

In 1977 the manifesto of the Jamaat-e-Islami may have paralleled the PPP's in other matters of economic and political significance, but it differed in its definition of Islamic principles. The Jamaat's manifesto called for the abolition of coeducation and the establishment of separate institutions of higher education for women which would be 'according to the needs of women', and the enforcement of total segregation of the sexes in places of work. The party opposed the Family Low's Ordinance (1961) that restrains polygamy and regulates divorce, and avowed the banning of extramarital sex, drinking and gambling. It also promised to put an end to birth control, which it saw as being un-Islamic, and to launch a campaign against obscenity and pornography. The clauses of this manifesto that pertain to Islamic principles are of particular relevance, since they appear to have been the guidelines for Zia's process of 'Islamization'.

General Zia-ul-Haq's legal measures truncated to usher in an Islamic order are discussed in detail later in the book. The point that needs to be made here is that most of the steps taken were no more than symbolic gestures. Firstly, Zia revitalized the Council of Islamic Ideology, which under the 1973 Constitution had the mandate to review existing laws and make recommendations for bringing them in line with Islam. The CII was expanded and packed with conservation *ulemas*. Subsequently, the most reactionary suggestions, especially regarding women, came from this body.[59]

Zia's symbolic moves included orders for saying afternoon prayers in all offices; for women in government service to wear *chadors*; to begin all office correspondence with the Quranic words '*Bismillah-hir-rahman-nir-rahim*' (I start this work in the name of Allah); and investing ceremonials with similar symbolically Muslim acts.

The orders were, of course, not strictly followed but the impact of the official campaign did pervade society in insidious ways. The fanatical elements within society suddenly assumed they had been given a *carte balanche* to become self-styled moralists. Incidents of vigilante groups taking initiatives to prescribe their version of Islam became frequent (discussed in later chapters).

The obvious objective of these measures was to give legitimacy to a government which had over-extended its stay. The cosmetic changes did not attempt structural overhauling, and therefore the real ills of society remained untouched; corruption, bribery, black-marketing, smuggling and drug-trafficking flourished. Women became the scapegoats. The vast majority, i.e., the rural women, were of course not touched, living in centuries-old drudgery as they were, but the urban middle- and lower-middle-class working and professional women became targets of the socalled Islamization.

Zia's accession to power and his starting of the Islamization process marks the culmination of the growth of the political usage of Islam. Beginning with the 'modernists', the cycle seems to have come full circle. Those whose philosophy and ideology were opposed to Pakistan have now come into positions from where they can steer the destiny of the country. In this period the bureaucracy and the army, already over-developed, have consolidated themselves. Their ranks are now filled with the locally educated and bred new intelligentsia. This intelligentsia is alienated from the earlier West-educated elite, and for its roots looks not to indigenous historical and cultural traditions but to religion. The only version of Islam that has developed and flourished at all is conservative, bigoted and fanatical, and it is from this that the emerging elites attempt to derive their plilosophical bearings. In the absence of any serious work towards progressive interpretations of religion, of distinguishing between its spirit and symbols, Pakistan seems to be in the grip of the unenlightened and the closed-minded. And since the political process has been subverted, the masses, whose belief may be Islam, but whose concern is not religion but the real issue of existence, have been by-passed.

References

1. See Anne T. Sweetser, *The Power to Heal: Medicine and Society in the Pakistani Himalayas*, Ph.D. Dissertation, Harvard University, 1992.
2. United National, *Statistical Yearbook for Asia and the Pacific, 1991*. p. 293. The World Bank gave slightly higher numbers than the United Nations for 1988, so they would no doubt indicate a somewhat greater total population in 1990 as well (The World Bank, *World Tables, 1989-90 Edition*, p. 437).
3. United Nations, *Statistical Yearbook for Asia and the Pacific, 1991*, p. 293. World Bank figures show a higher life expectancy at birth in 1980 of 53.0 years for both sexes combined, and also a higher figure in 1987 (the last available year) of 56.5. For that year, the United Nations figures were. 53.7 for males and 51.9 for females (The World Bank, *World Tables, 1989-90 Edition*, p. 439). Except for Nepal and Bangladesh, Pakistan was the only nation where male life expectancy at birth exceeded that for females in the late 1980s (The World Bank, *Women in Pakistan*, 1989, p. XV, note 6).
4. United Nations, *Statistical Yearbook for Asia and the Pacific, 1991*, p.293. The World Bank shows a steady drop from 144.0 infant deaths per thousand in 1968 to 109.0 in 1987 (The World Bank, *World Tables, 1989-90 Edition*, pp. 438-439).
5. The total fertility rate is the number of children women might expect to have by age 49.
6. The World Bank , *World Tables, 1989-90 Edition*, pp. 438-439.
7. United Nations, *Statistical Yearbook for Asia and the Pacific, 1991*, p. 307.
8. United Nations, *Statistical Yearbook for Asia and the Pacific, 1991*, p. 307.
9. Federal Bureau of Statistics, Statistics Division, Government of Pakistan, *Pakistan Statistical Yearbook, 1985*, p. 310.
10. Griffin, Charles C., *Health Care in Asia: A Comparative Study of Cost and Financing*, World Bank Regional and Sectoral Studies, 1992, pp. 158-159.

11. See Malik, Iftikhar, Gail Fisher, Gregory Pappas, and Akhtar Qureshi, "Prospects for the National Health Survey of Pakistan: Goals and Objectives," in *The Pakistan Journal of Medical Research* special supplement devoted to the survey, forthcoming, 1993. (The present author has an article in this supplement about survey methodology," Getting the Right Answer by Asking the Right Way: The Importance of Speech Patterns for Eliciting Accurate Survey Responses.")
12. Federal Bureau of Statistics, Statistics Division, Government of Pakistan, *Pakistan Statistical Yearbook, 1985*, p. 311.
13. Theft of medicines by staff in Lahore General Hospital was reported as common in *Mashriq*, July 7, 1981.
14. Similar complaints appeared in the Urdu press, for example, *Nawa-i-waqt*, August 8, and 14, 1981 and *Mashriq*, August 18, 1981.
15. In the early 1980s, physicians posted to rural assignments received half the salary of their urban counterpart and no travel allowance. There was discussion of raising their salaries so that they could afford to visit their homes without losing their entire income.
16. *Mashriq*, July 31, 1981.
17. *Mashriq*, June 32, 1981.
18. *Mashriq*, July 7, 1981.
19. *Nawa-i-waqt*, August 8 and 14, 1981 and *Mashriq*, August 18, 1981.
20. *Nawa-i-waqt*, August 14, 1981.
21. *Mashriq*, August 18, 1981.
22. *Nawa-i-waqt*, August 8, 1981.
23. *Mashriq*, August 18, 1981.
24. *Nawa-i-waqt*, August 14, 1981.
25. Shah, Mazhar H., *The General Principles of Avicenna's Canon of Medicine*, Karachi, 1966, Naveed Clinic, p.19.
26. Shah, *Avicenna's Canon*, p. xxviii.
27. Shah, *Avicenna's Canon*, pp. 213-216.
28. F. No. 5-2/80-NCT, National Council for Tibb, 46 Bazaar Road, Islamabad, Paragraphs 2 and 3.
29. In one clinic I timed the consultations for several hours, I found there to be a bimodal pattern of 40 seconds and 110 seconds per patient!
30. Karim, *Al-Hadis*, Vol. 1, p. 281.
31. Karim, *Al-Hadis*, Vol. 1, pp. 281-82.
32. Karim, *Al-Hadis*, Vol. 1, pp. 656-57 and 424-426.
33. This echoes the positions taken by schools of Islam that developed in India approximately a century ago. The Barelwis accepted local practices, the Ahl-i-Hadiths rejected all but strictest adherence to the Shari'at, and the Deobandis, while stressing restoration of Shariat law, were willing to accommodate their followers' desires for spiritual counsel in the indigenous manner. Today in Pakistan

the term "Wahhabi " (from the early 19th century fundamentalist movement in Arabia) is used for religious and political conservatives, including the Jama'at-i-Islami. Many who espouse Deobandi interpretation are in fact closer to the latter than to the original Deobandi formulations.

34. Jettmar, Karl, *Der Religionen des Hindukusch*, Kohlhammer, 1975, especially p. 219 ff. I read a draft English translation prepared by Adam Nayyar.
35. The World Bank, *Women in Pakistan: An Economic and Social Study*, 1989, p. xxii.
36. See Barbara Ehrenrich and Deidre English, *For Her Own Good: 150 Years of the Expert's Advice*, Doubleday Anchor, 1978.
37. Iqbal as quoted in Syed, p. 47. The Baluchistan Times as quoted in Mortimer, *Faith and power- The Politics of Islam*, p. 220.
38. The Khilafat movement started in the wake of the Balkan Wars, in which the Turkish Ottoman Empire was brought to its knees by the Western Christian powers—Britain being prominent among these. The Muslim population of India, which had been trying to reassert itself as a community in different (and often contradictory) ways, found in the defeat of Turkey (the only Muslim entity possessed of any power) a uniting factor. The architects of the Khalafat movement were the Ali brothers (Maulana Muhammad Ali and Shaukat Ali) and Abul Kalam Azad. They demanded that the British change the terms of the peace treaty to give the Turkish Empire more power, since Turkey was the seat of the highest Muslim authority of Khilafat (from the term Khalifa, meaning 'successor', applied to the successors of the Prophet Mohammed). The zeal with which the Khilafat movement was greeted in the Indian sub-continent demonstrates the extent to which the Muslims felt the need to forge a united identity. It was the first mass-based movement in the sub-continent and drew in both peasants and intellectuals. (It was also the high point of Muslim-Hindu cooperation against the British. The Khilafat movement was espoused by Mahatma Gandhi, who felt that if the Hindu helped the Muslims, they in turn would co-operate for Hindu rights.) The Khilafat movement was doomed from the start, for the Turks had already accepted the terms of agreement with the British, and must have been as surprised as the British were that people in India were that people in India were up in arms against the treaty. The confused ideology and impracticalit of the demand led to the movement's disintegration amidst violent communal riots.
39. In his view Indian nationalism would lead to a non-Muslim majority ruling over the Muslims, which in turn would influence the life and morals of the Muslims, by either prescribing laws which would be contrary to God's laws, or be legislating on issues

selected in Islam. Thus it would be a thoroughly un-Islamic state of affairs. Maududi's position on Muslim natinalism was somewhat similar, based on the premise that Muslim nationalists had no commitment to Islamic principles and therefore Muslim nationalism was also un-Islamic. He did not consider the cultures that flourished during the zenith of Muslim rule in the sub-continent or in Turkey, or elsewhere in the Islamic world, as being examples of Islamic civilization to be glorified.

40. Iqbal's presidential address to the 1930 annual session of the Muslim Lengue in Allahabad, as quoted in Anwar Syad, *Pakistan: Islam, Politics and National Solidarity,* Lahore, Vanguard Books Ltd. 1984, p. 46.
41. The British under the Government of India Act. 1935, held these elections as a first step towards transfer of power to the Indians. The elections held under a system of separate electorates showed the dismal position of the Muslim League.
42. Jinnah had returned from a 14-year self-exile in English in 1934, and despite his effort, the Muslim League had not fared well in the 1937 elections.
43. Anwar Syed, *Pakistan : Islam, Politics and National Solidarity,* p. 51.
44. In a relative sense the military and the bureaucracy were the more organised ot the institutions that existed at the birth of Pakistan.
45. For a discussion of the failure of those coming into power to remodel structures and the way they expanded the institution of the army, police and the civil services instead, suggested reading is: Hamza Alavi, 'Class and State' in Gradezi and Rashid (ed.) *Pakistan: The Roots of Dictatorship,* London, Zed Press 1983, pp. 40-85.
46. Pakistan had non-Muslim citizens, who also needed to be assimilated within the polity for the country to progress and develop. Theocracy was therefore not considered an acceptable systems of state, as that would exclude large number of non-Muslims from the mainstream. In fact, Jinnah declared that non-Muslims had equal rights as citizens and that religion did not come in the way of running the state. He also said that religion would be a matter of personal faith of each individual and that Pakistan would protect and promote the political, economic, cultural and religious interests of its people.
47. Anwar Syed. *Pakistan: Islam, Politics and National Solidarity,* p. 68.
48. The constitution of 1956 provided for a conventional parliamentary system with fundamental equal rights for men and women. Interestingly, the constitution of 1973 made by Bhutto's Parliament was also accepted by the *maulvis.* After the coup of 1977, in an open debate sponsored bya newspaper on the appropriate political system for Pakistan, the right wing Islamic parties delcared the

Parliamentary system as the best system for Pakistan.

49. A Court of Enquiry under Chief Justice Mohammed Munir was appointed to look into these disturbances. Once of the more interesting points that came to light during the proceedings was that no two *ulema* agreed upon the definition of a Muslim.
50. For further details, see Rashid Amjad, *Industrial concentration and Economic Power in Pakistan*, Lahore, South Asian Institute, 1974.
51. The people of East Pakistan resented what they saw as the exploitation of their resources to aid development in West Pakistan, to be viewed as a market for West Pakistan's industrial goods, to have disproportionate representation in the country's administrative and military services. After the 1965 war with India, there was also the feeling the East Pakistan's borders were not adequately defended.
52. See Akhtar Baloch, "A Journal of Sorrows", *Guardian*, 17 Jan 1977.
53. The party he formed was the Pakistan People's Party (PPP) which at the time of its creation had not received much attention.
54. The total strength of the Constituent Assembly was 300, of which 162 were elected from East Pakistan, where Sheikh Mujib-ur-Rehman's Awami League swept the polls getting 160 seats. Awami League's six-point election programme was that of provincial autonomy.
55. See, for example, Khalid Bin Sayed, *Politics in Pakistan*, New York. Praeger, 1980; Hamza Alavi, Gardezi and Rashid, and others in Gardezi & Rashid (ed.) *Pakistan : The Roots of Dictatorship*, Shahid Javed Burki, *Pakistan under Bhutto*, 1971-1977, New York, St. Martin's Press, 1980; Lawrenace Ziring, *The Enigma of Political Development*, Folkestone, Dawson Westview, 1980.
56. Anwar Syed lists a number of symbols of Islam that Bhutto incorporated in the 1973 Constitution, which went beyond those in the constitutions of 1956 and 1962. For instance, freedom of speech, expression and press, subject to the consideration of (among other things) the 'glory of Islam' (Article 19); oath of office prescribed for the president and the prime minister required the affirmation of belief in God, Qur'an and finality of Mohammad's prophethood; obligation to bring all laws into conformity with the injunctions of Islam: Syed, *op.cit.*, pp. 145-151.
57. Alavi, 'Class and State'.
58. For instance, having said that no true Muslim could pledge allegiance to any state, and could not hold any office in anything less than a truly Islamic state, Maududi abruptly changed his standpoint when he realized this would keep him and his followers outside the realm of politics and power in Pakistan. Similarly, having said that no true Muslim could canvass votes, when elections came around, Maududi suddenly had to devise a means for

condoning his own election campaign.

59. The CII had to perform this task in a period of seven years and the Parliament was empowered by the Constitution to accept or reject the recommendations within two years after these had been submitted to it.

7 Women in Politics

Since the introduction of the separate electorate system in 1985, there have been separate electoral rolls maintained for Muslims and non-Muslims in Pakistan. According to the 1997 General Elections Report, the total number of registered voters was 56, 615, 667, of which 55, 068, 024 (97.27 per cent) were Muslims and 1,547, 643 (2.73 per cent) were non-Muslims. With several additions, deletions and amendments made over the years, there is some doubt about the absolute accuracy of the electoral rolls. According to one study, they still contain the names of those who have died, left the country or moved out of the constituency. The Election Commission of Pakistan (ECP) is aware of these problems, and is currently in the process of vetting and updating the electoral rolls. This is important, particularly with regard to women, since several instances of malpractice or denial of the right of franchise can be attributed to errors on the electoral rolls. Almost half the eligible voters in the country are women.

Of the total number of registered voters for the 1997 Elections, both Muslims and non-Muslims, about 55.4 per cent (31, 382, 633) were men and almost 44.6 per cent (25, 233, 034) women. There were, thus, more than six million fewer women than men registered as voters, or a difference of about 11 per cent. The same proportions were reflected among the total number of registered Muslim voters (55, 068, 024), of whom 30, 533, 349 were male and 24, 534, 675 female. However, the share of women was marginally higher among the total number of non-Muslim voters registered (1, 547, 643), of whom 849, 284 (54.9 per cent) were male and 698, 359 (45.1 per cent) female. The highest proportion of women were registered in the Punjab

46.2 per cent), followed by Islamabad (45.4 per cent) and Balochistan (45.2 per cent), while the lowest proportion were registered in FATA (25.2 per cent).In 1994, the number of women registered in the Peshawar (NWFP) constituency was less that half the number of males registered, while only two constituencies (in Sindh) had more women than men registered as voters. In 1997, the gender difference in three FATA constituencies was above 90 per cent. A 1999 NWFP study presents some other interesting findings. While pointing out that the widest gap between registered male and female voters out of the provinces (excluding FATA) was in NWFP (about 180-19 per cent), it also notes that the province has the maximum and minimum gender differences with respect to registered voters. In Abbottabad, Karak, Haripur and even Chitral there is a minimum difference, while the maximum is in the Peshawar rural district. It suggests the possibility, without making any finding, that this may be due to the fact that the Hindko-speaking, non-tribal population of the province is less conservative than the Pushto- speaking Pathan tribes. The provincial assemblies in the whole country, that every Muslim constituency has a lower registration of women than men, excluding two constituencies where more women than men are registered; that there are 11 non-Muslim constituencies with gender equity in registration; and 17 non-Muslim constituencies with marginally higher female registration.

Male-Female Ratio

Even in FATA, where the male-female ratio for the Muslim community was 75:25, the ratio for the non- Muslim community was 55:45. Whether this has been due to a growing political consciousness since the imposition of separate electorates, or because the non-Muslim community has relatively fewer gender biases, is yet to be ascertained. While the barriers to women' registration have been discussed in greater detail in a later section, there are several instances both of indifference as well as active resistance to women's enrolment by male family members and local influentials, sometimes resulting in total prohibition. This obviously excludes a significant proportion of eligible women from their right to be registered as voters. While this restriction may be more common or intense in some areas, examples of it exist across all provinces, as referred to in different reports.The proportion of registered female voters has increased overall since the first general elections held on the basis of universal adult franchise in 1970, but showed a decline in the 1990s.

For the 1970 elections, women comprised 43.7 per cent of the voters' list, the percentage going up to 46.3 per cent by the 1988 elections. But the percentage decreased marginally to 46.1 per cent for the 1990 elections, to 45.5 per cent for the 1993 elections and even lower to 44.5 per cent for the 1997 elections. This decline appears to be due to the fact that fewer women than men have been registered as new voters in recent years. Between 1993-1997, there was a 7 per cent increase in the list for new male voters, only 3 per cent for new female voters. If this pattern continues, the difference between registered male and female voters will become even more marked. There has been a general downward trend in the overall voter turnout in Pakistan. In 1977, the reported turnout of voters was 61.9 per cent, declining to 43.07 per cent in 1988. In 1990, the national voting average went up slightly to 45.46 per cent, then declined again to 40.28 per cent in 1993 and further to 35.42 per cent in 1997. Similar trends are repeated in provincial voting patterns for the Provincial Assemblies elections, except for Sindh where the turnout was higher in 1997.

The voter turnout during the 1990s (38.5 per cent) ranked Pakistan as 146th in the global listing of 163 countries. The declining trend in the turnout of voters appears to indicate people's loss of confidence in the political system due to the growing corruption and criminalisation of politics in Pakistan, disillusionment among the general public because of the inability of the political parties to deliver; and a lack of faith in the electoral process itself. A far smaller proportion of voters from upper/middle class backgrounds actually vote as compared to those from lower income backgrounds. This perception finds reflection in the fact that political parties and candidates generally tend to ignore upper/middle class neighbourhoods in campaigning during elections. Voter turnout figures from Lahore (Punjab) during the 1993 elections ran counter to this generalisation, showing a similar turnout from wards categorised in the concerned study as upper, middle and industrial (43.8, 44.8, and 42.9). However, the sample is too small to reach any definite conclusions and other factors could also have contributed to this. It is difficult to accurately assess the turnout of female voters in elections, since the Election Commission does not maintain gender-desegregated data in this respect. Nor is there any national -level study on the subject. However, female voter turnout is generally thought to be lower than that of male voters, a fact borne out by the few smaller studies and data-collection exercises on 25 per cent of the total polling stations in the 1990 elections, revealed that 48 per cent of men and 30 per cent of women cast their votes, a difference of 18 per cent. One, based on male and female voter turnout data collected from constituencies in Lahore (Punjab) during the 1993 elections indicated a 46.9 per cent turnout of male voters, and a 40.4 per cent turnout of females, a difference of almost 7 per cent. Yet another, based on data collected from 3 villages of Hafizabad (Punjab) during the same election showed a male turnout of 56 per cent against a female turnout of 48 per cent, a difference of 8 per cent; while data collected from 10 women's urban polling stations in Rawalpindi (Punjab) indicated a 43.86 per cent voter turnout against an overall turnout of 46.2 per cent.

There are several reasons for a lower turnout of female voters in elections. But is apparent that they are often prevented from exercising their right to vote by their families, tribes, clans, and local and spiritual leaders. In some constituencies, particularly in Balochistan and NWFP, rival candidates and political parties have also had mutual agreements to restrain women from casting their votes. According to various reports:

i) In some areas in Bajau, Mohmand, Khyber, Orakzai and North Waziristan Agencies of FATA, not a single female vote was cast in the 1997 elections. In Jamrud, only 37 out of 6,600 registered women voted. This was largely because of resistance by male family members, announcements by mosques declaring their voting as un-Islamic, and threats by tribal councils.

ii) In one village of Punjab, women were granted the right to vote for the first time in 1998, almost 30 years after the introduction of universal adult franchise in the country.

iii) A SAARC observer team in the 1997 election noted that women were physically stopped from voting in Balochistan.

iv) In 1993, in a settled district of NWFP, candidates from PPP and ANP, as well as an independent candidate, signed an agreement with each other and village elders to disallow women from voting. Similar instances have been reported from Karachi (Sindh) and Sheikhupura (Punjab)

The Code of Conduct for General Elections, 1997, further forbids political parties, contesting candidates and their workers to propagate against women's participation. However, no action in this respect has been taken by the concerned authorities even when it has been brought to their attention by women's advocacy groups. In 1993, WAF reported the agreement between candidates in NWFP to the Chief Election Commissioner and demanded action against them, but nothing was done. In 1997, despite wide coverage by the media and reports by advocacy organisations, no attempt was made to charge those making violent threats against women in FATA. There are also reports that women are made or persuaded to vote in situations where the context between political parties or candidates is close. In the 1988 elections, where provincial elections were held after national elections, it was reported that PML supporters sent out their female family members in much larger numbers when they realised that the PPP had again a slight edge over them in provincial elections. In FATA, during the 1997 elections, a candidate who vociferously opposed women's registration and voting in one area where he had less support ensured that women voted in another area favourable to him. Reports from Balochistan also indicate in constituencies where political parties or candidates feel strong, there is a limited registration of women or they are not allowed to cast their vote. But where the opponent is considered strong, they actively register their women voters and send them to vote.

Whatever the motives behind making women vote, the practice results in breaking the taboos which exist in several areas against their voting and makes women familiar with the electoral process, a first step towards a more genuine exercise of their rights. Earlier, women have equal rights to participation in local government elections. However, the same factors listed above contribute to their lower levels of participation than men. As local government elections have been held infrequently in the last two decades, statistics on women's participation do not exist.

NGOs and advocacy groups have been encouraging women to participate in elections at all level, including the local level. There are no government programmes to encourage women to participate in local government elections. On 14 August 2000 the Military Government announced plans for conducting local government elections under revised rules and regulations aimed at giving more power to local governments.

In the rural areas there are three types of local governments: the Union Councils (village level) and the Tehsil Councils (sub-district level) and Zila (district) Councils. Union Councils have 21 members, out of which there are 12 General seats (8 men and 4 women); 6 seats for workers/peasants (4 men and 2 women) and one seat for minorities. The Union Nazim (President/Administrator) and Naib Union Nazim (Vice President/Deputy Administrator) are both ex -officio members of the Council. Thus of a total of eighteen directly elected seats, six are reserved for women. As in the initial version of plan announced by the Chief Executive on August 14, 2000, in the final plan total number of seats of Tehsil Council is not given. It depends on the strength of union councils in each tehsil. Naib Nazim of the union council will be member of Tehsil Council.

Reservation

Thirty three per cent of the general seats are reserved for women while twenty per cent each is allocated for peasant workers and minorities. Similarly the total number of seats of District Council is not given. It will depend upon the strength of Union Councils in each district. Union Council Nazim will be a member of District Council. There is no proper setup of training among government institutions nor in political parties. Recently Jamat-I-Islami (religious political party) started a training program for their women. At the NGO level and civil society organisations, several NGOs have worked out different strategies to increase women's participation in politics, but the number of NGOs directly working on the issue on a sustained basis is very limited.

To increase the level of women's participation and make it effective in local elections Aurat Foundation with collaboration with several other organisations and member of program networks run a campaign involving several public meetings, preparation and distribution of materials and intensive advocacy and lobbying. It resulted in Punjab increasing women representation to 12.7 per cent and 25.8 per cent in Balochistan.

For the first time in Pakistan's history people and NGOs were involved in Local Government Plan 2000 (devolution of power). Even grass-root level organisations took a leading role for women representation and again Aurat Foundation planned a huge campaign with civil society groups at the national level and tried to cover 7,000 union councils. In addition to the Aurat Foundation there are five or six other organisations working on training and political education like Pattan in Multan, Sungi in Hazara division and SAP-PK in some part of NWFP and Punjab and Sindh.

Under the Local Government Plan 2000, the Government plans to initiate training of councillors, including women councillors. They plan to involve civil society organisations that specialise in providing training. For the first time in Pakistan civil society organisations have initiated a collective campaign for women representation and training in local government. The initiative was started by the Aurat Foundation and later joined by Muthida Labour Federation, SAP-PK, SAVERA, PILER, Sungi Development Foundation, Khwendo Kor, HRMDC, SBRC, Pakistan NGO Federation along with four provincial coalitions and lot of other organisations. The campaign is called the Citizens Campaign for Women's Representation in Local Government. This campaign has great potential to improve the representation of women in local government.

The Government of Pakistan will hold Local Government elections from December 2000 to June 2001 for devolution of power. Under this plan elections will be held for local government from the level of the Union Council - the lowest tier of Local Government - to the district level. The Plan includes a radical component of reserving 33 per cent seats for women at all tiers of local governance, which will be filled through direct election by the entire electorate at the level of the Union Council and by indirect elections at the higher levels. This is the first time that both the percentage and the direct elections for women have included at any level of governance. This achievement has been the direct result of lobbying and advocacy by civil society organisations for a number of years.It is expected that as a result of this, at least 20,000-25,000 women will be elected as local councillors at the lowest tier of the Union Council alone, which will be a milestone in Pakistan's political development as for the first time such a high number of directly elected women will be participating in local governance.These women will require support at various stages of the political process, starting from their mobilisation as candidates, support in the electoral process, capacity building for effective participation and representation and developing their political strength in the post election scenario as a powerful pressure group that impacts at the grassroots level.

Women as Candidates

The first stage will be to mobilise women to stand as candidates for the reserved seats at the union Council level and ensure that there is local support for them. At the same time there will be a need to build an environment in the constituency, which is not hostile but actually supportive for women to play their role as candidates and representatives of the people. This will need to be combined with some political orientation for the candidates for them to participate in the electoral process with some knowledge.In collaboration with all its networks and with all the major civil society networks, Aurat Foundation (AF) will coordinate a citizen's campaign to ensure that women stand for elections in all the Union Council elections to be held from December 2000 to June 2001. Elections to the higher tiers, which will be held from July to August 2001, will be the second phase of this Project, for which a project proposal will be presented later.

The general objectives will be to:

i) Mobilise women candidates in 7,000 Union Councils across the country.
ii) Create public acceptability about the role of women as public representatives.
iii) Create an enabling environment at the local level for prospective candidates.
iv) Undertake orientation for women candidates about Local Government and the electoral process.

The short-term objectives will be to:

i) Set up the institutional framework to undertake the Campaign at the national, provincial and district levels.
ii) Conduct one national and four provincial level orientation

meetings for representatives of activist organisations.

iii) Conduct 106 orientation meetings for members of the District Coordination Committees that will coordinate the Campaign in all the districts.

iv) Conduct meetings at the divisional level for selected DCC members who will undertake the political orientation of the women candidates.

v) Hold meetings at the Union Council level to promote acceptability of women as public representatives.

vi) Identify women candidates in every Union Council and link them with their local support.

vii) Provide orientation to about 70,000 women candidates on Local Government and electoral processes.

viii) Prepare inputs for the electronic media through major current affairs programs, talk projecting the importance of women's representation and participation in Local Government elections as candidates and as voters.

ix) Project the same objectives through the print media in every major daily and the popular magazines right down to the district editions.

x) Prepare and disseminate posters, leaflets, pamphlets, stickers and cassettes of songs for voters and candidate education.

The Provincial Steering Committees (PSCs) will be formed on the same pattern, involving the major provincial or regional support organisations. They will also from the subcommittees for their functioning. They will set up the following committees:

i) Campaign Management Committee, headed by the Provincial Coordinators.

ii) Finance Management Committee

iii) Political Orientation Committee

iv) Monitoring Committee

v) Media Committee.

The PSCs will also hold planning and review meetings each electoral phase. The PSCs will play a more active role in the orientation of candidates, in field monitoring and promotion through the media because they will be closer to the electoral process. The National Steering Committee and the PSCs will be provided a secretariat, which will be set up at the regional offices of the Aurat Foundation. The secretariat will be run by the National and Provincial Coordinators of the Campaign, who will be appointed by the NSC and will act as the secretaries of the respective Steering Committees.The National Steering Committee (NSC) will be formed with representative of three to four major national support organisations and representatives of labour federation and the media. The NSC will be responsible for managing the Campaign and disbursing the funds. The NSC will elect an organisation from among them to receive the funds for the Campaign from the funding agencies.The NSC will appoint the Provincial Steering Committees (PSCs) and, with their consultation, the District Coordination Committees. The NSC will function through the formation of the following subcommittees:

i) Campaign Management Committee, headed by the Coordinator of the Campaign
ii) Finance Management Committee, headed by a Finance Manager
iii) Formation of DCCs Committee
iv) Media Committee

Role of NSC

The NSC will manage the Campaign with the assistance of the PSCs, through setting up the District Coordination Committee (DCCs), assigning them responsibilities and monitoring the Campaign through setting up Control Rooms to map out the mobilisation of candidates and the building up a supportive environment through some field visits. They will also stay closely in tough with the Election Commission, the Ministries of Women's Development and Local Government, to keep watch and report on attempts to hamper and harass the candidates and voters. They will provide support and intervene where problems arise within the DCCs or at the Union Council level.

The NSC will hold a meeting to appoint the National and Provincial Coordinators and the organisation through which the funds will be channelled. The subcommittees will also be appointed. There will later be a planning meeting before each phase and a review meeting after each electoral stage. Representatives of major support organisations, NGO networks and labour federations in the NSC, in consultation with the PSCs, will form the DCCs, comprising of activists of local level organisations and media professionals. Responsibilities will be taken by the major networks of Aurat Foundation, like the Network of Citizens Action Committees for Women's Rights in 50 districts and the Network of the Political Education Program in 54 districts, (with some overlap), the member organisations of the provincial NGO coalitions like the Sindh NGO Federation, the Balochistan NGO Federation, the Sarhad NGO Ittehad, the Punjab NGO Coordination Committee, and the labour federations and some other professionals organisations, etc., to be part of the DCCS.

The responsibilities of the DCCs will be to:

i) Coordinate the Campaign at the district level.
ii) Share and assign responsibilities to all possible support structures to cover as many of the Union Councils in the district as possible.
iii) Organise support-building meetings in the Union Councils.
iv) Identify women willing to stand for elections in all the Union Councils.
v) Set up a Control Room at the DCC headquarters to map the Union Councils and identify local support and resistance in each Union Council.
vi) Involve the local media in the Campaign.
vii) Facilitate provision of ID cards and voter registration especially to female candidates.
viii) Report to the Provincial and National Steering Committees on a regular basis.

As soon as the Steering Committees are formed and the secretariats are set up, a two day orientation will be held at the national and provincial levels for activists from the key national and provincial origination. Orientation for DCC activists about the Campaign will be held at the district level. Thee will be another orientation at the divisional level for selected members of the DCCs and especially women activists for conducting the orientation for the candidates.

As the women candidates announce their intention to stand and a minimum sufficient number is identified, the DCCs will undertake a simple orientation program for them. The program will be done phase-wise to synchronise with the election phases. For this the support organisations will do workshops of the DCC members who will be involved in the orientation program.Local Government in Pakistan exists under the supervision of the various provincial governments, who merely delegate some of their functions and responsibilities to local governments by the promulgation of ordinances. The local government ordinance of 1979, with its amendments is in operation in the Punjab, Sindh, and the NWFP, while in Balochistan local government are under the 1980 ordinance. These ordinances specify functions of local governments.

The Basic Democracies system was seen as a substitute for universal suffrage and it served as an electoral college to elect the President and the assemblies. However, with the fall of the Ayub Khan regime with which it was closely associated, Basic Democracies fell into disfavour. Besides, the first general elections of 1970 and the separation of East Pakistan from Pakistan resulted in the formation of a new system of government in the country. Ironically though, the proposed elections to be held under the People's Local Government Ordinance of 1975, promulgated by Pakistan's first democratically elected government, to elect town and municipal committees were never held.If the first martial law government was the pioneer in devising an extensive system of local governments, it was the second martial law regime of General Zia that implemented the principle of elected local governments, which were revived in 1979 under the provincial local government ordinances, which, with amendments, are still in operation in Pakistan.

Elections for local councillors have been held on a nonparty basis in 1979, 1983, 1987, and 1991. Now third martial law government has introduced a new setup for local government.The period since 1985 has seen four general elections in Pakistan where the people were asked to choose members of the provincial and national assemblies. In the absence of elected assemblies local governments were the only popularly elected bodies and thus played important political and developmental role.The common behaviour of people and government towards local government institutions has always been rather casual. The constitution of Pakistan does not recognise local government as the third tier of government. Without constitutional protection most of the time they perform their duties as non-elected institutions. Second problem in local government institutions is inadequate representation of marginalised sections of society.

Local Governments

The total number of seats reserved for women in all local governments is approximately 46,620. These figures are collected in light of the existing no of Union Councils, which might be enhanced during delimitation process in accordance with the Census figures of 1998. According to a rough estimate after the delimitation process across the country the number of reserved seats for women might increase to 70,000 keeping in view the increase in the number of Union Councils. The situation of women in Local Government institutions is always worst in Pakistan. In every election, even when they are selected as a councillor, women representative depend on people from influential and majority groups. If they want to contest general election on general seats they have to contest as independent candidates because most political parties and other set ups discourage them and try to exclude them from the whole process. Majority groups wish to have only females elected who do not become a problem for them and can be easily used for their vote bank. Consequently appropriate and active females have to make a deal with majority group in election to become a candidate.

After becoming a councillor they have to please the chairperson and other elected male councillors, otherwise they do not get development projects. Because most women councillors do not have their own funds and are reliant on their male colleagues, they cannot pressurise them or even oppose the projects of male councillors. This severely restricts their ability to undertake projects or meet the needs of their constituencies. Although Balochistan is a backward province, during the last local government's elections women's representation was fairly reasonable. The number of female councillors was about 17 per cent.

Keeping in view the backwardness of the area, its conservative social set up and restrictions on the mobility of females, this ratio of female representation was quite satisfactory. The comparison between local bodies elections of 1991 and 1999 in Balochistan revealed that the female participation had increased during the last elections. In 1991 elections, 847 seats were reserved for women, out of which 87 remained vacant. However, in 1999 elections the situation was a bit different.

1,871 seats were reserved for women. 1,530 seats were filled in the first stage of polls.

During bye elections all the remaining seats were filled. It was encouraging that in some of the general seats females contested polls against male candidates. Their contesting election on general seats was a positive sign. For the first time in the history of the country such a large number of women were elected on reserved seats in Balochistan.

In Punjab the situation was different. Elections of Union Councils, one of the important components of local bodies, could not be conducted despite the fact that the Punjab Government gave undertaking before the Lahore High Court for early holding of the said polls. If these elections were held in the 3,043 union councils across the province, it would have resulted in election of at least 10,000 women. In elections of remaining local bodies 1,348 women got elected on reserved seats. The ratio of females was less compared to Balochistan.

As majority of the lady councillors got elected on reserved seats through indirect elections therefore they had inferior status compared to their male counterparts who were elected through direct polls. Although, there was no legal difference between the councillors elected on reserved seats and those elected on general seats, social attitudes, prevailing political scenario etc., made the councillors elected on reserved seats including women and minorities, inferior in status.

Lahore Corporation

One such attitude was experienced in a meeting of Lahore Metropolitan Corporation, when a female councillor was subjected to heckling by a male councillor during her speech. Other female councillors protested against that attitude and according to news reports, they even tried to give him a thrashing. This attitude is not only confined to local councils.

Such incidents also happen in other tiers of elected bodies including the parliament and provincial assemblies. In the suspended National Assembly, the Leader of the Opposition was a female. The stories and rumours spread regarding her personal and marital life were also a portrayal of this traditional mentality. In the presence of such attitudes, social values and dogmas, the philosophy of "reserved seats" often turns into a misnomer and such seats appear to lack any utility.

The women elected on these seats have to face the hostile attitude of their male counterparts, resulting in the shattering of their confidence.

As the women councillors lack any constituency from where they are elected therefore they have to make more efforts for establishing their credibility for which they need resources, time as well as support of people. For making all these efforts they have to overcome their domestic responsibilities and also to generate monetary resources for meeting the expenses.

Pakistan : Prime Minister Benazir Bhutto

The Setting

Gender Bias

It was in 1988 on 2nd December that Ms. Benazir Bhutto became the first women Prime Minister of her country and first also in the Muslim World. Her Pakistan People's Party which was founded by her father, the late Zulfikar Ali Bhutto, secured the largest number of seats in the National Assembly though not an absolute majority. An alliance of the opposition parties made Benazir target of their criticism. They cabled a no confidence motion in National Assembly (Parliament) against her government in November, 1989, she had then been in the saddle barely for eleven months. They manipulated 107 votes in the first chamber which had 234 members. The no-confidence motion was defeated and Benazir's government was saved at that time (Boston Globe, No. V. 2, 1989) Benazir was apprehensive of being arrested if she had been defeated by the no-confidence motion. She alleged that opposition leaders had a plan to arrest her and the top 100 leaders of her party. (Arab News, Nov. 1989, 3). The opposition used the Islamic card to oust Benazir from her ruling position because they argued that according to Islamic traditions a woman cannot be the Head of the state or the government. General Ziaul Haq had utilized the Islamic slogan for eleven years of his rule. In the 1989 polls Islamic Democratic Alliance which was full of rifts and factions, united only for the ouster of Benazir by using the Islamic card (Ahmad Rashid, June 1989; Choudhary Mahfuzal, 1990, 668).

In the earliest years of the formation of Pakistan, when General Ayub Khan was Chief Martial Law Administrator, he himself contested Miss. Fatima Jinnah, the sister of the late Quaide Azam Mr. M.A. Jinnah, for Presidency. General Ayub Khan successfully obtained a decree from the Ulema (religious scholars) that a woman could not be the Head of the State under Islamic law. Ayub defected Miss Fatima Jinnah (Munir Mohammed, 1979, 90-91). An English daily, *The Nation* of Lahore expressed fears that the Ulemas were bent upon frustrating Benazir's efforts to become the next Prime Minister. The daily held that she was the daughter of Z.A. Bhutto and was the most charismatic leader of the possible move by the religious scholars, to declare that woman could not become the executive head of the Islamic Republic of Pakistan.

Positive gender discrimination was followed during Zia's regime. His ordinance allowed upperhand to the males as against the females. The onerous evidence required by a women to prove a crime against her, encouraged men to use the Ordinance to force women into submission by charging them with adultry. Dr. Rashida Patel of the All Pakistani Womens Association held that Zina (the Ordinance) had adversely affected the status of women especially for those who were convicted and sent to the prison. Many jail reform commissions were appointed. They gave several recommendations to improve the condition of women in jails. But the situation remained abysmally desperate. The convicted women were raped and subjected to different kinds of physical torture. Because of the conservative character of the Pakistan society, these were not even reported and taken notice of. Trafficking in children and incidents of rapes increased, since Zia's Ordinance gave additional leverage to men. The bias in Pakistan's unequal society had continued even against males of some sects of Islam like the Ahmadiyas. This sect of about 20,000 (twenty thousand) people were declared un-Islamic. They were prevented from practicing their religion and to hold their annual gatherings scheduled to be held in Rabwah. The spiritual base of this sect was in Jhang district in Punjab. The sect was decreed outside the fold of Islam by an Act of Parliament in 1974. They were persecuted under that Act of Parliament in 1974. They were persecuted by the radical Muslims (Chand Attar, 135).

The image of the Pakistan People's Party in the eyes of the common man was that of a party which stood for Islamic ideals and the principles of Deen, which the founding fathers of Pakistan had reiterated. Pakistan Peoples Party stood for Islamic ideals of freedom, equality, fraternity and social justice. It was totally different from Mullah's Islam. The ideologies of anti-imperialism and socialist revolution had inspired the educated youth all over the Third World. In Pakistan this section of the population saw the Pakistan Peoples Party, as a socialist party. The leaders repeated the "Moist" slogans of revolution, because Pakistan was a friend of People's China and was against Soviet Union. People's China proved to be faithful to Pakistan during the 1965 war with India. Zulfikar Ali Bhutto held that Islamic socialism, joined together the historical egalitarian traditions of Pakistani people with the present day aspiration of the whole humanity. This party became a force to reckon with between 1967 and 1970.

Islam and Islamization

In the name of Islam and its purity the rulers of Pakistan competed with each other in rejecting, oppressing and persecuting even intellectuals of great calibre.

The pride of Pakistani Science Professor Abdus Selem who was an Ahmadiyya (or Ahmadi) was placed outside the pale of Islam by Pakistan's laws. Muhammad Zafarullah Khan was chosen by Jinnah for the post of Pakistan's first Foreign Minister. He was perhaps the most distinguished one in that post. He was chased out of the government just because he was an Ahmadiyya. It was the anti-Ahmadiyya riots in 1953, which had created the conditions for the army to make its entry into dictatorial position.

The Ahmadiyyas believed in Mirza Ghulam Ahmad Qadiam (1835-1908) of the Punjab, whom they considered a prophet. This was in conflict with the main line Islamic faith in the impossibility of any prophet appearing after Muhammad. (Das Gupta, Punyapriya, 1994, 7).

Ahmadiyyas were persecuted by every Pakistani regime. Zulfikar Ali Bhutto strengthened his "Islamic Socialism" by enacting a constitutional amendment which branded the Ahmadiyyas non-Muslims. Zia-ul-Haq banned the use of Muslim terminology by the Ahmadiyyas also their converting people to their faith.

Under the so-called democracy of Benazir, persecution of the Ahmadiyyas continued with unabated fanaticism. "Towards the end of 1989, the entire population of the Ahmadiyyas headquarter town of Rabwah was charged with violation of the law, forbidding members of the sect to perform Muslim rites including the declaration of the basic Islamic faith, about the unity of God and the apostle ship of Muhammad. The passports held by Ahmadiyyas mention them as "non-Muslims". They have no say in the election of the Prime Minister or the President who must be a "Muslim".

It was through the slogans of Islamization that the Pakistani politicians had been trying to manipulate the masses for getting into power positions.

But Iftikhar Gilamai who was one of the senior members of Benazir's Pakistan People's Party (PPP) summing up the situation in 1992 observed "We have decided to settle once for all the question whether the mullas are supreme in this country or the people and their representative" (Noorani, A.P. December 4, 1992, 44).

As early as in August 1947, in the Constituent Assembly, Jinnah the founder of Pakistan himself had observed, throwing off the two Nation theory.

"We are starting with this fundamental principle that we are all citizens of one state..... I think that we should kept that in front of us as an ideal, and you will find that in course of time Hindus and Muslims would cease to be Hindus and Muslims, not in the religious sense because that is the personal faith of each individuals, but in the political sense as citizens of the state". (Noorani, December 4, 1992, 44). Having won Pakistan Jinnah considered two Nation theory obsolete. The differences between the Hindus and Muslims were minimised.

The ironical situation in favour of Islamization was created mostly by the Jamaat-e-Islam founded by Maulana Abul Ala Maudooni. It was this Jamaat which had bitterly opposed the formation of Pakistan but once it was established they became vaguard of the movement for Islamization. They agitated for declaring Pakistan an Islamic State.

Dr. Javed Iqbal – the son of the poet philosopher Mohammed Iqbal condemned the politicians. He was addressing the people in Lahore on Iqbal Day, on April 21, 1992, where he roundedly criticized the politicians vehemently (Noorani, 1992, 44). A section of the audience shouted at him and he had to leave the podium.

Gen Zia created the Federal *Shariat* court in 1979 by an amendment to the Bhutto constitution of 1973 and got it confirmed by the National Assembly in 1985. He got this confirmation in lieu of his promise to life Martial Law. Federal *shariat* court was Zia's quaint creature. Chapter 3A of the constitution contained Articles 203 a to 203 J, which concerned the courts. It was empowered either of its own motion or on the petition of the citizen or the government to examine and decide whether any law is "repugnant" to the injustices of Islam. Appeal against its ruling lay to the Shariat Appellate Bench of the Supreme Court.

The judges of the Shariat Court enjoyed less security of tenure than did a civil servant. They held office during the pleasure of the President. The Shariat Court was called to give judgement of 'rajm', i.e., punishment of stoning to death. The Chief Justice who ruled, that it was not Islamic, was removed from office. The courts performance record had been dismal. In 1989 it ruled that the provision of the Land Reform Act 1972, imposing limits on holdings were un-Islamic. It struck down banking interest and applied its ruling retrospectively to past commitments. One of these commitment was regarding the Employees Provident Fund. It struck at democracy.

President Ishaq reproached Benazir for not getting enacted the Shariat bill for Islamization of the country. Nawaz Sharif got it enacted by weakening it. The English print media especially the *Nation, Frontier Post* and *The Muslim*, criticized the Shariat Bill.

Military

Within the Troika consisting of the President, Prime Minister and Army the Military had always played the most important role in the politics of Pakistan. It was a strong force and was ever ready to intervene in politics at the first opportune moment. Benazir had to confront not only the army but also more powerful authority of the president in a parliamentary political setting. Her Pakistan People's Party was not in absolute majority in the National Parliament. The opposition leaders did not leave any stone unturned for proving her government.

Prime Minister, Benazir dismissed General Hamid Gul, the Chief of the Inter Service Intelligence Directorate because he had served under General Ziaul Haq. It was during Zia's regime that the Eighth amendment to the Pakistani constitution granted more powers to the President. With enhanced authority the President could appoint the joint Chief of Staff. Gulam Ishaq Khan on one occasion told General Aslam Mirza Beg that "the Army Chief ensured the continuing existence of democracy in Pakistan. (*Eastern Economic Review*, March 15, 1990, 18-20). Though President Ishaq Khan dismissed Benazir's government, earlier he had turned down the opposition's demand for fresh parliamentary elections (*Arab News,* March 13, 1990, 1). The Eighth amendment was made by military dictator General Zia who himself had come to power by illegitimate means. Benazir suspected a quasi military intervention behind being ousted from power (*New York Times*, Aug 8, 1990). (Sirohi Seema 1990, 18).

Manipulation under Doctrine of Accountability

Under the doctrine of accountability Benazir and her husband were charged with corruption. References against them were subjected to judicial procedure. The doctrine of quasi-judicial accountability was created even before Pakistan as a sovereign state came into existence. Several laws enforcing this type of accountability were means to disqualify inconvenient politicians for a limited period. Gen Zia used this doctrine diabolically against Zulfikar Ali Bhutto and others. As soon as Pakistan assumed statehood, public and Representative Officers bill called PRODA was passed by the Constituent Assembly. Under this law the Governor General was empowered to appoint tribunals to try legislators and ministers if they were found guilty of corruption. They could be disqualified for a period of not exceeding ten years. The power to punish and determine whether the accused person was to be disqualified was given to the Governor General. He had the discretionary power in these matters. The tribunals could only accredit their opinion about the proof or otherwise or the allegation. (Chand Attar, 1991, 58). (Kaushik, S.N., 129-30). Some important politicians were disqualified under this doctrine of accountability. The Elective Bodies Disqualification Order (EBDO) was promulgated in August 1959 it pave the way for Ayub's Basic Democracy experiment. Through this he sought to make it seem that the military rule was actually a civilian rule. In 1977, the Holders of Representation (Prevention of Misconduct) Act and Parliamentary and Provincial Assemblies (Disqualification of Membership) Act were passed by Zulfikar Ali Bhutto's government. The intention was to put pressure on opposition politics of the Pakistan National Alliance. After seizing power Zia promulgated two ordinances— P.O. 16 and 17 of 1977. These gave him more powers and he could move against Zulfikar Ali Bhutto's (misconduct). Many politicians who were afraid of Zia's power, sided with him.

The Premiership

The satire about the continuous presence of military rule in Pakistan was very ably depicted in V.A. Dulla's review of a book (*Waiting for Allah*, Pakistan's struggle for Democracy) by Christina

Lamb, "We apologies for the temporary democratic interruption. Normal Martial Law will be resumed shortly". These words were a graffiti on a Karachi wall in August 1990—The military rulers seemed to talk to each other about democratic rule in the country "We are just letting the children play for a while". Benazir was sworn as Prime Minister on December 2, 1988 and dismissed by President Ghulam Ishaq Khan on August 6, 1990—just after twenty months.

President Ishaq Khan was actually in consultation with the military when he decided to nominate Benazir as the Prime Minister. An important element in this decision was the pressure of U.S.A., which was exerted through the army. The latter was apprehensive of another break away by the province of Sind, where discontent was brewing. It was the most volatile of all the provinces in Pakistan. Benazir was a premier whose hands were bound by unwritten conditions imposed by the political system of Pakistan. There was to be no interference by her with the army and there was no question of lowering the defence budget. Shahabzada Yakub Khan was to continue as External Affairs Minister as before. Benazir could not get along with the President who was seemingly holding a brief for the army.

The military rulers subverted the political process in the name of state construction. Liaquat Ali Khan was assassinated in October 1951, Prime Minister Zulfikar Ali Bhutto was ousted from power in 1977 and was tried for criminal acts and hanged. All the three Prime Minister Junejo, Benazir and Nawaz Sharif worked under the shadow of the army. They were all dismissed before their full term lasted.

Zulfikar Ali Bhutto took over as President and Chief Martial Law Administrator on December 20, 1971 and Ghulam Ishaq Khan was then a bureaucrat under him. Though a popular leader Bhutto did not pay attention to building up his popular base. The party was neglected and loyal party workers were made to fell alienated. Zulfikar Ali paid more attention to the army. He freely invited the army officials for consultations on matters political even at the time when the opposition was campaigning against him on the ground that they felt that March 1977 elections were rigged.

Even Benazir had to come to an understanding with the army and the U.S.A. Instead of building up democratic institutions she later on took up quarrels with the army like her father. Army in

Pakistan had come to know that it could survive without any popular support. (Jalal Ayesha). Before entering into second period of Premiership, Benazir's action in supporting the Eighth Amendment and President's autocratic powers, during Prime Minister Shah Nawaz's ouster moves, deep cited her contradictory stand on democracy. To explain this action of hers, one had to find the political isolation in which she had landed, after her ouster from power. She desired to be in the hub of politics. She tried to bring the All Party Committee (APC) to support her demand. She could end her political isolation only by this.

Under her first Prime Ministership she had alienated many of her colleagues in Movement for Restoration of Democracy (MRD). Those like the People Democratic Party, the National People's Party the Pakistan National Party and such others had not been satisfied with her during the MRD campaign. They fell out in the provinces. The Awami National Party and the MQM had sided with the MRD during the anti-Zia period leading to 1988 elections. They also left Benazir during her Prime Ministership. Benazir's government had moved against the Jamhuri Watan Party which got infuriated against her.

For Benazir in 1993 elections the priorities were withdrawal of cases against her and the release of her husband Mr. Zardari. She patched up with Nawaz Sharif against the President. They Hyat rape scandal weakened President's position. Farhat Hayat was related to Army Chief of Staff General Farukh Khan. For him the gang rape incident was a matter of personal honour. Victims father had first complaint to the President and appealed for justice. But the President ignored it and the media took up the question. This was the opportunity for Benazir for patching up with Sharif and the Army promoted that compromise. (*Frontline*. February 1-14, 1992, 33-42).

Constitution and Democracy

Since the inception of Pakistan state there were many issues which endangered its unity and territorial integrity. These were ideology, distribution of powers and function between the centre and the units, the basis of representation in the federal parliament, special powers of the Head of the State and foreign policy. Pakistan had to pass through murders of Prime Ministers, Presidents and other politicians. There were coups and counter coups. The Presidency the army, the bureaucracy and the aristocracy connived to maintain a non-democratic authoritarian political system. The basis of dictatorship was strengthened by the captains of business, finance and industry. Several constitutions were presented and promulgated but the authoritarian head of the state twisted them to remain in power. East Pakistan with 54 per cent of Pakistan's population returned the same number of deputies to the parliament as did West Pakistan with a 46 per cent of the population.

The constitution gave extraordinary power to the President. After its promulgation it lasted only for two and half years, when the government decided to hold the first general elections in February, 1959. With the active help of the army, a palace coup was staged setting at nought the provisions of the constitution. The Army intervened and its chief ruled as the ex-officio President. This practice was maintained till the Zulfikar Ali Bhutto's Interregnum.

The army chief imposed the constitution of his own discretion. It was called Martial Law in Mufti. It lasted for six year after which, there were mass protests and rebellions. The army put up its chief, General Yahya Khan as another Chief Martial Law Administrator (CMLA). He landed Pakistan into a civil war and led it to surrender to India in 1971 Indo-Pak war. He was also responsible for the dismemberment of Pakistan.

Zulfikar Ali Bhutto was people's choice in the election of 1970. The democratically elected Assembly unanimously passed a permanent constitution. But General Zia again subverted the democratic set up. Hamza Alvi had observed that "a remarkable fact about the political situation in Pakistan has been the ability of the army to have direct dealing with foreign powers (notably with the U.S.A)". He holds that their variety of affiliation and interests have resulted in powerfully entrenched positions within the army on behalf of the various interests. The cost of bureaucracy is parallel, for many acquired extensive business interests; some had become millionaires (Hamza Alvi, July, August 1972, 49).

Pakistan could not witness any general elections since her birth till 1970. Till 1965, the Head of the State Ayub Khan was an unelected ruler. The Constituent Assembly of Pakistan was formed even before the state of Pakistan came into existence. The members were those who were elected in provincial assemblies in 1945-46. The same members again elected the second Constituent Assembly. In any country the extreme forces of right or left could be balanced only by the middle classes. But Pakistan did not have any middle class worth the name. The general elections did not take place till 1970 and this delayed the developmental process of Pakistan.

Gen. Ayub Khan promulgated and preached what he called the Basic Democracy. He imposed limitations on the District and Divisional Councils. All this restricted popular participation. The Councils did not possess any independent power under the Basic Democracy. There were no division of powers between the administrative departments and the councils.

The Central Government was in the form of a hierarchical bureaucracy. Basis Democracy created indirect representation. It established a National Assembly in the Centre and Assemblies in the provinces. The 1962 constitution for the Republic of Pakistan was known as the Basic Democracy, with very little democratic element in it. The Basic Democracy did not produce leadership in the country.

In course of time Zia came to consider Zulfikar Ali Bhutto as number one political enemy. Bhutto was arrested, prosecuted and finally hanged. As mentioned earlier the electoral process became a tool for Zia the CMLA.

After a non-party general elections in February 1985, the Junejo government was constituted. It was an irony that the same Junejo formed a party--the Pakistan Muslim League (PML). When Junejo became showing his independence, Zia felt uneasy and dismissed the government. But he declared elections in 1988 as scheduled. Again he planned strictly for a non-party government, so that it could play a second fiddle to him (Sreedhar, Kaniyalit John, Pande Savita).

Democracy did not totally die down because the Pakistan judiciary tried to assert itself as the final arbiter in disputes regarding political power. On September 27, 1988, the Lahore High Court declared the dismissal of Junejo Government, by the erstwhile, President, on May 29, 1988 as unconstitutional. It was a historic judgement. The Supreme Court confirmed this decision when the government of Pakistan went into appeal before it against the decision of Lahore High Court.

Zia's regime had set itself for unmitigated rule of the army. He reduced the civil bureaucracy into the position of a junior partner and diminished the powers of the judiciary. In partner it was a rule by Martial Law Ordinances, especially the notorious Provincial Constitutional Order of March 24, 1981. According to which no action of the military regime could be challenged in any Civil Court. Zia's pretense to "Islamise" the Pakistani Society affected the status of women religious minorities besides creating grotesque distortions in the judicial and political framework.

On Oct. 2, 1988 the Supreme Court of Pakistan delivered another historic judgement. It held that the elections to be held on November 16, 1988 had to be on the basis of political parties and not on non- party basis. The President Ghulam Ishaq Khan and his Advisers accepted the verdict.

Since, February 1981, 'Movement for the Restoration of Democracy ' was born as one more effort to save Pakistan from authoritarian rule of the Military Generals. The opposition parties came together with Pakistan People's Party as the dominate constituent group.

It was a loose gathering known as Movement for the Restoration of Democracy. In Pakistan (MRDP), the parties which remained outside the MRDP were the religious and the rightist parties like the Jamaat-e-Islam and certain Muslims League groups.

After Zia, there were dramatic changes in the political situation in and outside Pakistan, which were favourable for democracy in Pakistan. President Ishaq Khan decided to hold elections on party-lines. The Soviet-American cold war had vanished. The Gulf War had stopped. The Afgan issue had gradually disappeared.

The Chief Justice of Pakistan, Dr. Nasim Hasan Shah's book *Judgements on the Constitution; Rule of Law and Martial Law in Pakistan*, highlighted the difficulties faced by the Pakistani judges in upholding the rule of law. In one of his visits to India he held that Pakistani courts were better than the Indian courts in matters of maintaining the democratic structure in their countries. He cited the Pakistan Supreme Court verdict of 26 May, 1993, which restored the National Assembly, dissolved by President Ghulam Ishaq Khan a month earlier. Dr. Shah hinted at a similar situation in India when the assemblies in four Bharatiya Janta Party ruled states, were dissolved but were not restored through the court verdict. Ultimately fresh elections were ordered. (*The Hindustan Times*, Patna, Friday, 11 February, 1994) During a tenure of over twenty-five years as a judge of the Supreme Court he delivered number of judgements of great importance. Once he was even served a notice of "contempt" from the Martial Law authorities during Yahya Khan regime.

A judge of the Supreme Court since 1977 Dr. Shah ruled on the question of the validity of the Martial Law proclaimed by General Ziaul-Haq in 1988 and by President Ghulam Ishaq Khan in April

1993. The Assembly in the Second instance was restored by the Supreme Court in May 1993.

It was only with Benazir that succession of democratic governments were ushered in Pakistan. Before that it never had an elected government. After the assassination of its first Prime Minister Liaquat Ali Khan, it came to be ruled by succession of Generals. The only bride interval was provided by Zulfikar Ali Bhutto who got elected. But he also started as the Chief Martial Law Administrator. Zia died in an air crash on 17th August, 1988, Ghulam Ishaq Khan took over as President by virtue of being the chairman of the Senate of Pakistan as stipulated in Article 49 of Pakistan's Constitution, it was for the first time in a decade the offices of President and Chief of Army Staff were separated. He did not last long in the government.

The inherent defects in the power structure of Pakistan, made it possible for General Zia, to usurp power and rule for eleven years. Perhaps he would have continued to impose his undermocratic rule on Pakistan if he had not died in an air crash. According to most observers which include scholars like Emma Duncan an Christian Lamb, it was the combination of the army and the bureaucracy which ruled the country. It seemed next to impossible to dislodge them from their power positions. They could ignore and subvert any new policies which any elected government would initiate.

Ethnicity and Violence

Punjabis who were the major ethnic group in Pakistan were in majority in the defence forces. They formed a solid group in it. They pulled the strings of the government, who so ever would have been in the government.

Pakistan had three other provinces Sindh, Baluchistan and North West Frontier. They had distinct cultural and linguistic identities, different from each other (See Sharan Sarojini and Vivekananda Franklin, 1991, 75). Benazir's province Sindh had been in a state of armed insurrection against Punjabi Army domination. Sindh had remained volatile on the question of Mohajir settlement on its land and their (Mohajir's) demand for a homeland by curbing out a province from Sindh. Sindh could be next to East Pakistan, which could have walked out of the country, if it did not get justice. The social structure of Sindh was highly feudal. Large areas of land were owned by a small section of landlords or as they were called Waderas. Bhuttos and Zardaris belonged to this feudal section. Sindhi society had bonded labour known as Haris. They did the cultivating work. The bonded labours had been forced to take to looting and murders, since last eight hundred years because of starvation situations created by the economic system in those areas. Sindhi people today were under the deep influence of the Sufis, who were considered to be rebels of Islam. These sufis spoke in simple local languages about Love and god. They did not enter into high talks about the intricacies of Islamic theology. Sindhi people felt an affinity with each other because of the common influence of the holymen and the shrines of great souls in Sindh.

Among the cities of Sindh, one finds Karachi to be the predominate port of Pakistan. In Karachi the biggest city of Sindh, more than nine million people resided according to 1991 figures (Dulla, V. A. 1991, 81).

Large tracts of land area had been under the control of drug media. A constant internecine war had been going on between the rival factions.

There had been a dial-a-Kalashnikov service. On the outskirts of Karachi there was an illegal settlement of more than a million inhabitants. The regular features of the community here was violence in its temper. Curfew seemed to be normal affair. The ethnic group of Mohajirs who left India for Pakistan after or before Partition were yet not assimilated in the Pakistani society, which was dominated by Punjabis and Sindhis. The capital of Sindh *viz.* Hyderabad withnessed furious ethnic clashes between Mohajirs and Sindhis. Kidnappings of wealthy industrialist became an industry especialised for ransoms.

Baluchistan, another province of Pakistan occupied almost half the territory of the nation. It was persuaded by the defence forces to join the new country of Pakistan. It was still ruled by its tribal laws. The North West Frontier Province was one more province of Pakistan which often went out of control of the Government. It had been haven for drug running and arms smuggling. It provided the routes for transportation of weapons by U.S.A. to the Afghan rebels, during Soviet occupation of Afghanistan.

Corruption

General Zia's rule in Pakistan could be perpetuated till his death in the air crash, because of Soviet intervention in Afghanistan. Millions and millions of dollars poured into Pakistan from U.S.A. and other countries for Afghan refugees. That became a source of gigantic proportion of corruption. The Pakistani Army got the opportunity to swallow much of it.

On the economic front, the opportunities for development were wasted due to corruption. Pakistan was the second largest exporter of cotton, third in the export of rice. Its per capita income of $390 (Three hundred ninety U.S. Dollars) was one of the highest in the Third world, through income distribution was disgusting. Twenty-two families controlled more than two-thirds of the nation's wealth. They owned 66 per cent of the industries, 97 per cent of the insurance and 80 per cent of the banking. The black money was estimated to be double the whole money. The investors called Pakistan "SKIMOCRACY", where Palm greasing from Minister down to chaprasi was an essential part of the government practice, (Dulla, V.A., 81) which was acquiesced in by the people.

Leader and the Style

Tough Fighter

Benazir was only twenty-five when she alone had to bear the responsibility of keeping in touch with the people, when her father Zulfikar Ali Bhutto was awarded death sentence by Pakistan's Courts. She had been placed under detention at Karachi for four months even before the death sentence was handed over to her father in March. She was released before the execution took place. Her activities were curbed by the Martial Law. Benazir had gained experience in the campaign management of elections which were postponed the year before. She had been fresh from Oxford and Harvard where she had her education. She found herself landing in the midst of Pakistani politics after 1977 July coup. She was active in the election campaign and had established a good rapport with the people. The workers and members of the Pakistan Peoples Party and the supporters of Zulfikar Ali Bhutto found in her a leader who was very close to the founder of PPP. When President Zia lifted the ban on political activities on 28 August, 1978, it fell upon Benazir to be the spokesman of the party on behalf of her father. She visited Larkana on Eid festival, continuing the tradition of her father. She met peoples, toured Frontier province and many other places. She found people's response spontaneous.

She was hailed as the "daughter of Pakistan". To be more at home with the people and establish rapport with them like her father, she wore a cap resembling that of her father. The Sword as the symbol of the Pakistan Peoples Party was utilized to make the masses feel that it meant "Sword of Ali" which promised victory. (Schoffeld Victoria Cassell 1979, 66).

Benazir was very popular with a section of the people because they were engulfed with sympathy wave for a daughter, whose father has to be hanged and mother was under house arrest. It was alleged that she herself was humiliated and tortured by the police, jail authorities and the army personnel on several occasions and along with her mother she was secluded from the outside world. The Pakistan Peoples Party members had been so much certain about Benazir's victory, in any election in Pakistan, that they would say that even the servants of Bhutto family would win, if they contested in the polls. Inspite of the fact that Zulfikar Ali was condemned to death. Benazir and her party still retained the support of a section of the masses. It was only Indira Gandhi among Asian Leaders who could retain her popularity with people even when she fell from power.

Benazir had to fight against heavy odds. After Zulfikar Ali Bhutto received the death sentence, Begum Nusrat Bhutto was going to visit her husband for the first time. She was ordered to subject herself to body search she refused. Benazir once took two new plates for her father to replace those which were impregnated with grime. She was refused entry into the prison premises. (Schoffeld Victoria Cassell, 1979, 66).

The humiliations and tortures undergone by Benazir made her a though fighter. Her will to come out of the political hurricane became stronger. Benazir began her tours again when the prosecution started its submission. But the authorities were furious and arrested her five hundred kilo metres away from Karachi on 4th October. The detention order served on her on the plane itself. She refused to board the plane alone. She demanded the company of Yasmin Niazi—the daughter of Zulfikar's dentist. Benazir was forcibly dragged across the tarmac of the airport. Her clothes were torn and her feet were injured. All this happened in front of the horrified onlookers. Benazir was dumped in Punjab. (Schoffeld Victoria, 1978, 138).

If one goes through the happenings in Benazir's early political life, one finds her maintaining wits and courage in the face of crisis. There were many dramatic moments and situations. She wrote in her autobiography "Zia was about to kill my father... My mind raced. We had to her the word out to send the last call to the international community... I wrote a new one (message)"... "I think they are calling us for our last meeting." I scribbled furiously to a friend on the outside, hoping she would alert the party leaders who in turn would inform the diplomatic corps and mobilise people Benazir, 6).

Benazir was ill when she was allowed to visit her father for the last time. As soon as it dawned on her that it was the final meeting she said to her mother, "But we will be brave and not cry". Benazir and her mother requested the jailor to allow them to embrace Zulfikar Ali Bhutto. The request was turned down. The bars of the cell came in between Zulfikar behind and Nusrat and Benazir outside. They could only hold Zulfikar's hands by extending their hands across a wooden table placed in front of the cell. (Schoffeld Victoria, 1978, 223-36).

Image Projection

Benazir attempted to portray herself as a progressive socialist and a democrat. She criticized the right as an evil. She stressed the need for socialism as a panecea for all the ills of Pakistan.

"A mixed economy, informed with an egalitarian spirit, is the inevitable need. That is all. But the autocratic rulers supported by feudal elements have called genuine democrats leftists. That is how the PPP was dubbed left in 1968-69. That is how they are doing it now... some of us, including me, are socialists, though we are prepared to give capitalism all the reasonable chance it should expect. But the existence of right—and evil from every progressive viewpoint is there alright ... We will fight this evil force of the Pakistan right. First of all we should call it by its proper name; facism... The second political reality, the alienation of the people... The assumption is, if the Indians were to mount an attack from the east the people especially in Sindh, the NWFP and Baluchistan (and also the common folk in Punjab under the influence of PPP) will not actively resist. The Indians can then have a Walk-over or some equivalent of it. Similarly, it is claimed, if the Russians were to do any real mischief mongering from the north, much the same would happen... Our position is clear". (Pakistan: The Gathering storm 33). In her writings, Benazir dealt with political, social and economic conditions of Pakistan during military regimes. She had plans for her party to resist the military rulers, who were responsible for all the decay in the Pakistan system. The task for the Movement for Restoration of Democracy (MRD) was clear. They were not to allow Gen. Zia to split the people. To carry out this negative programme of action the member of MRD had to (a) expose the misdeeds of the Generals, (b) to build up an organisation which could work with people so that they did not give chance to Zia, to win in the proposed referendum, (c) to involve the people by making available to them all informations about the issue of referendum, (d) to notify a number of successive successors at every level and in the knowledge of as many people as possible, and (e) to spread the message of MRD (especially of PPP) through all means without inviting the direct wrath of military authorities. The places where contacts with people could be established were mosque or assemblages any where. The message could be spread through chits or mouth (Benazir, 1988, 36-38).

About the military regimes in Pakistan Benazir thought it was running a system of exploitation. The economy of Pakistan was by nature exploitative. The power of the landlords over their tenants was absolute. All tenants were liable to be evicted from their lands even from those lands they had tilled for generations, at the whims of landlords. Three-fourths of Pakistanis were engaged in agriculture, the maximum exploitation took place here. International Finance men with the power of final say, decreed that there had to be free imports into Pakistan and that the protection to local industries needed reduction.

Consequently, the foreign capitalists began to take on a larger role in exploiting the common man – the consumer. The cities and villages were hard hit by unemployment. The people were forced to forget their country and emigrate to the gulf countries in search of jobs. The major categories of exploiters were traders, bureaucracy and soldiers. These ran the economy of the nation in such a manner that the chasm between the poor and rich had deepend (Benazir, 1988, 42).

Benazir found the Army at the heart of bureaucratic corruption. The Martial Law opened the gates for corruption. Their policy of denationalisation of institutions without setting any conditions or criteria gave opportunities to the prosperous military men to negotiate with the buyers of industrial units at their own price. No one could do anything without giving bribe to the officials. Oppression of poor, increased tax burden, the loot by the rich, depressed domestic industries, economy of servitude iniquitious social order and Islamic window-dressing were the features of Pakistani social/political/economic system (Benazir, 1988, 44-69).

As a Democrat

During Benazir regime the media was set free and it could report human rights violations in Pakistan. "Probably not a day passed that some newspaper did not report a case. Whether this was right or not is another point, but the freedom the media enjoyed during Benazir's rule was more than ever before and this helped to create an awareness among the people". (Chand Attar, 94).

Benazir made efforts to project her image as a democrat. She claimed to be a mass leader but she lacked the knowledge and methods of communicating with the masses. In a meeting held in Islamabad on November 13, 1990, the workers of the Pakistan Muslim League reacted against Benazir's maiden speech in the National Assembly, as the leader of opposition. The alleged that she did not understand the needs and aspirations of the Pakistani masses. Her speech was foreign to the masses and she had very little understanding about her country's people and their hopes. Her ideals were not inspired by the philosophers or the writers of Pakistan.

Ghazanfar Hussain Jafri who presided over the meeting of the Pakistan Muslim League workers, remarked before the news men, that Benazir drew on foreign inspirations in her speech and rarely quoted from Quran and Sunnah. Jafri told newsmen that she acted so well that all those present, specially the diplomats felt that they were being entertained to a Shakespearean theatre. She seemed at best to be a leader of the western elite and not the Pakistani masses.

During the election campaign, the Islamic Jamboori Ittehad of Nawaz Sharif had attempted to project Benazir as an agent of India's Research and Analysis Wing (RAW). India had always remained an important issue with the politicians in Pakistan. Those who aspired for victory in elections, aroused and manipulated the masses on the basis of their anti-India rhetoric. Benazir in her turn had also harped on the Kashmir and the Babri Masjid issues. She criticized Prime Minister Nawaz Sharif for his callousness in not referring to the explosive issues of Kashmir and Babri Masjid, at the Summit of SAARC at Male in November (21-23) 1990.

When Benazir assumed power as the Prime Minister second time after defeating Nawaz Sharif, she took up harder line against

India. She did not miss any opportunity on any national–international forum to raise the issues of human rights violations in Kashmir and rest of India. She fell in the traditional line of her father and other Pakistani politicians, who attempted to divert the attention of the Pakistani masses from their deteriorating condition. Before she wielded the power of a Prime Minister she outlined the foreign policy objectives to be followed by Pakistan. In the book *Gathering Storm* she said that Pakistan should be friend to both India and Russia. "The People should throw the Generals out". "Let us not enable them to hold the country hostage to their power in hijacker fashion". Who may turn out to be jokers as Yahoo proved to be in East Pakistan.

In August 92, India did not heed to the friendly gesture of Nawaz Sharif, the former Prime Minister of Pakistan, for a dialogue on Kashmir. When Benazir came to power the Indian Prime Minister P. V. Narshimha Rao took the initiative for talk about Kashmir, while congratulating her on assuming Prime Ministership of her country in October 1993. Because of the momentous changes in world politics Benazir agreed. India's successful handling of the Hazratbal crisis and the U.S.A. pressure upon both the countries induced them to talk. But with Benazir "anti-India" had been a must. She had to compete with other leaders in showing to her people that she contributed to the idea that being anti-India, was an aspect of Pakistan nationalism.

Human Right was another issue for Benazir to keep alive the Kashmir issue. But she could not go beyond a point. India had ample evidence against Pakistan for her intervention in Indian affairs and encouragement and assistance to the forces of subversion in India.

Feudal Background

Christopher Thomas, the correspondent of the *London Times* in Pakistan, said about elections in Pakistan in 1991, that "the green flag of the Muslim League flies over the mud huts of Visvian Village. The 200 poor and illiterate adults who live here, will cast their votes on election day in accordance with the landlord's instructions. This is the way of politics in feudal Pakistan. Now political issues and ideologies are at stake. The Zamindar has been buying votes and loyalty for years and nobody will disobey him in flat featureless Punjab, where more than half the population lives and politics is a simple transaction of votes for favours". (Attar Chand, 1991, Preface). The dispatch of the above correspondent reported that the landlord-cum-politicians gave as much as Rs. 15000/- (rupees fifteen thousand) to peasant families in need of dowry to pay in their daughter's marriage. The politicians in Pakistan were mostly feudal landlords, tribal and clan leaders or wealthy industrialists. Nawaz Sharif the interregnum between Benazir's two Prime Ministership periods, was one of the wealthiest persons in Pakistan. In fact in Pakistan it was the rich families only who played the game of politics. Local people had to now before the whims of these politicians. The family feuds were carried on through politics. It became a process for settling old personal scores. Once in power the political leaders distributed rewards and punishments. Reward consisted of jobs, money and positions and punishment consisted of legal harassment and public enquiries. Corruption in this way came to be known as "Shifarish" and became institutionalized.

Benazir belonged to an aristocratic family of Sindh. Bhutto family descended from one of the largest land-owing families in Pakistan. The Bhutto family owned virtually the whole province of Sindh. As time passed, the area of land under Bhuttos diminished, yet large tracts of land around the village of Larkana, 350 miles from Karachi were under their possession. Larkana bordered near the ruins of Mohenjodaro (Mound of Dead). Bhutto family was proud of their ancient lineage like Mohenjodaro which could boast of an ancient Indus Valley civilization, dating back more than 2000 years. B.C. (Schoffeld Victoria Cassel, 1979, 140).

Benazir says in her autobiography that they had Hindu ancestry ".......as children we were told that we were either descendents from the Rajputs, the Hindu Warrior class in India which was converted to Islam at the time of Muslim invasion or from the conquering Arabs, who entered India through our home province of Sindh giving it the name "The Gateway to Islam". (Benazir, *The Daughter of the East*, 26).

Sir Shah Nawaz Khan Bhutto was the grandfather of Benazir. He was the former Prime Minister of the Junagadh State before the partition of India. He had been vestowed with knight-hood by the British for his services to Bombay Presidency. Benazir's grand mother was Lady Khurshid. (Benazir, *The Daughter of the East, 29)*.

Benazir's mother "came from the new class of urban industrialists whose views were more cosmopolitan than those of the land owning class, while the Bhutto women still lived in Purdah ....my mother" says Benazir "and her sisters went around Karachi without veils and drove their own cars. Daughters of an Iranian businessman they had gone to the college and after the birth of Pakistan even served as officers in the National Guard, a paramilitary force of women" (Benazir, *The Daughter of the East*, 30).

Zulfikar Ali Bhutto was twenty-four when Benazir was born. Zulfikar Ali Bhotto was sent to the United Natons by the President Iskander Mirza, when Benazir was only four years old. Her father's subsequent government postings as Commerce Minister under Ayub Khan, then as Minister of Energy, Foreign Minister and leader of Pakistan's delegation to the United Nations off and on, for seven years, kept Benazir's both parents away from home much of the time (Benazir, *The Daughter of the East*, 29).

Benazir was thus exposed to the outer world and high circle of diplomats, statesman and officers since her adolescence. Moreover she was trained by her loneliness to become self reliant "My mother usually travelled with his (father)" leaving the children viz. Benazir and her younger brothers Mir, Shah and Sister Sanam at home with the household staff. "Look after the other children" my parents would charge me "you are the eldest" ...... "I was eight when I left nominally in charge of the house, when my parents wore away" (Benazir, *The Daughter of the East*, 30).

As mentioned elsewhere, Benazir had a good exposure and belonged to such parents who were liberal in views. Her father used to tell her that he wanted one thing from her, that she should do well in studies. As the children grew older, Zulfikar Ali Bhutto hired tutors to instruct them in Maths and English in the afternoons, after school. He kept track of their school reports by phone from whereever he was, outside Pakistan. "Luckily I was a good student" Benazir says "for he had great plans for me to be the first woman on the Bhutto family to study, abroad". (Benazir, *The Daughter of the East*, 30).

"At three, I was sent to Lady Jennings nursery school" wrote Benazir. Then she was sent to one of the top schools in Karachi at five. The top school was the Convent of Jesus and Mary. Medium of instruction in the school was English. Bhuttos spoke the native languages of Sindh or Persian or the national language Urdu at home. Persian was the language of Benazir's mother and Sindhi of her father.

Benazir graduated from Oxford University in U.K. and before that obtained a degree from the Harvard University in U.S.A. Among all the women Prime Minister of South Asia, Benazir was provided with greater educational opportunities, because of her family's outlook and high positions her father occupied. Benazir proved to be a writer as seen in her autobiography "the Daughter of the East" about which she considers "not an indepth study of Pakistan, but a glance into the transformation of a society from democracy, to dictatorship. Let it also be a call for freedom" (Editors Note 1-2).

Another book written by Benazir has been the *Gathering Storm* published by Vikas Publishing House Pvt. Ltd., New Delhi, 1983.

Impact

Weakening of the Party

The Pakistan People's Party was on the verge of split in 1993, because of the circumstances out of control of Benazir. She had to ease out her mother Nusrat from the chairmanship of the ruling Pakistan People's Party. Benazir was elected chairperson of the Party by the Central Executive Committee (CEC). She told newsmen in early December 1993, that the defacto arrangements about the party had to be formalized. "I respect Begum Sahiba (Nusrat) because she is my mother and the widow of my leader (Zulfikar Ali Bhutto)". Some saw Benazir's husband Asif Zarkari's hand behind the removal of Nusrat from the Chairmanship of the Pakistan Peoples Party. Others were simply afraid of the claims of Benazir's recalcitrant brother Mir Murtuza, for the party leadership. Nusrat insisted that she was appointed chairperson of the party for whole life by her husband. It was her husband who had founded the Pakistan People's Party in 1967. Benazir had been the defacto chairperson until now. But Nusrat disobeyed, the party's directive and in utter disregard for party-discipline campaigned for her son Mir Murtaza. Mir referred to Benazir as Mrs. Zardari and predicted split in the party. An influential daily of Pakisan Dawn pointed that for the old guards of the PPP who felt alienated Mir Murtaza might seem like a hero".

The headlines from Pakistan newspapers shreiked "Blood spills over ZAB birthday cake, Blookd spills at Bhutto's birthday party". On January 5, 1994, there was a police firing resulting into one death at Larkana in Sindh. It was the birth anniversary of the Martyr-leader. (*Frontline*, January 28, 1994, 25).

Mir Murtaza was the only surviving son of Zulfikar Ali Bhutto. He was leading a crowd of few hundred in a march to the grave of his father, when the police firing took place. He was under a court injunction that prevented him to go near his father's grave for paying homage. He was placed under the Court's injunction just after Zia hanged Zulfikar Ali Bhutto.

Some reports spoke about a dispute in the family over property. But others did not think it was that simple. The question was that of which first egg or the chicken. There was no doubt the Zulfikar Ali fathered the Pakistan People's Party, but the close association between the Bhutto family and the party dimmed the distinction between them. The Pakistan People's Party, made its debut on the political scene of Pakistan as a popular movement. Later on the Bhutto family began to consider it as their freedom. Zulfikar was the first popularly elected leader in the truncated Pakistan. He managed to sustain his enthusiasm for his ideologies *viz.* liberty and social justice. His widow Nusrat now claimed that her only leader was Zulfikar Ali Bhutto whose guidance she could follow:

Actually, it was Benazir who could covert Zulfikar's legacy (the PPP) into an asset. It was during Zia's regime that Nusrat and Benazir worked together. But when Benazir stepped into the second contest for Prime Ministership, Nusrat began accusing her and campaigned for her son Mir Murtaza. According to Nusrat, Benazir had included in her cabinet Zia's "yes men". Benazir had to play the game of real politics. She know that in Pakistan's politics Military always had the upper hand. She was determined to see that her position as Prime Minister was not endangered. She had to keep some of Zia's men in her cabinet. She had to see that to alienate Mir Murtaza was a must for her survival in politics. She seemed ruthless when she saw to it that Murtaza was tried for all charges of terrorism and treason. She cited the example of her husband Asif Zardari, who had to struggle hard for being acquitted in about twelve cases (*Frontline*, January 28, 1994, 25-28).

Nationalism Based on Anti-Indianism

The masses of Pakistan had been manipulated by all the leaders of their nation to believe that India was their natural and permanent enemy. This was strengthened and confirmed by Benazir during her two regimes. The Indian masses have also been fed on the idea that the subscribers to the two Nation Theory were enemy number one. The Kashmir issue has been made a permanent issue between Pakistan and India. Pakistanis were confirmed in their suspicion about India's evil intention when India helped East Pakistan to secede from Pakistan and became a Sovereign State.

After Zia, Islamabad's policy towards India continued with its India bogey stance. During the two tenures of Benazir, the basic assumptions of Pakistan's foreign policy could not change. The mutual suspicion between India and Pakistan was a product of history. The Pakistanis had been fed upon the idea that there cannot be any peace between these two nations. While addressing the U.N. Assembly in December 1971, Zulfikar Ali Bhutto vowed to wage a war of thousand years against "Hindu India". He also used unparliamentary language like "Indian dogs". He was personally present at Lahore Airport to receive the JKL hijackers of an Indian Airlines Fodder Friendship plane. Bhutto exhorted them to blowup the plane, which they did.

Benazir stepped into the shoes of her father and continued vigorously the Anti-Indian rhetoric. She tried hard to raise issues like Kashmir and the human rights of the infiltrators and the terrorists sent by ISI into India to destabilize the country.

India remained the most important and constant and controlling factor in Benazir's foreign policy. It was keeping in the tradition of her predecessors.

Pakistan's nuclear policy was also a part of its efforts to match India in nuclear field. India had exploded an underground nuclear device in Pokharan. Islamabad could not afford to lag behind. It had to develop its own nuclear capacity so that it could counter India's nuclear capacity.

For the rulers of Pakistan 'anti-Indianism' stood for Pakistani nationalism. The demand for Pakistani nation had come more vigorously from those who were still called Muhajirs— the refugees. They were emigrants from India. They alleged discrimination from all the regimes in Pakistan including Benazir's. They had been demanding their own province. (Sharan Sarojini and Vivekananda Franklin, 1991).

8

The Assessment

Pakistan's population was officially estimated at 131.6 million in January 1996, comprising 47.5% women and 52.5% men. The population growth rate remains as high as 2.8% per annum. Based on a 1993 survey, 46.1% of the population is under 15 years of age and 4.1% over 65. According to the 1981 census, 72% of the population live in rural areas. A 90% of the households are headed by men and most female-headed households belong to the poor strata of the society. The population density is 106 persons per square km. The total fertility rate was 5.4% in 1990-91.

The main ethnic groups in Pakistan are the Punjabis of Punjab, the Sindhis of Sindh, the Baluchs of Baluchistan and the Pathans of the North-West Frontier Province. The Punjabis are the principal ethnic group comprising two-thirds of the population. There are also a number of small tribal groups in remote areas. Pakistan is an Islamic country and 97% of the population follows Islam. The important religious minorities are Christians, Hindus and Parsis.

The sex ratio in Pakistan is such that there are 110.6 men per 100 women. This phenomenon is attributable to male-favoured sex ratio at birth and higher female mortality. Further, in urban areas this sex ratio is 115.3 men to 100 women, whereas in rural areas it is 108.7 men to 100 women. Such a difference could be attributed to a large male out-migration from rural to urban areas.

In Pakistan, educational attainment shows poor results. Particularly the educational status of Pakistani women is among the lowest in the world. According to the 1981 census, the literacy rate for the population of 10 years and above is

26.2%. However, there are distinct gender and rural/urban differentials concealed in the literacy rate. Women have a literacy rate of 16%, as against 35% for men. Similarly, the literacy rate for the urban population only is 47.1%, whereas the literacy rate for the rural population is 17.3%. Moreover, this rural/urban differential is more pronounced in the case of women than men.

The literacy rate for urban men (55.3%) is more than twice the rate for rural men (26.2%). However, the literacy rate for urban women (37.3%) is more than five times the rate for rural women (7.3%).

In Pakistan's economy women play an active role. But their contribution has been grossly underreported in various censuses and surveys. Consequently, official labour force statistics show a very minimal participation of women. For example, the 1991-92 Labour Force Survey revealed that only about 16% of women aged 10 years and over were in the labour force and in comparison, the men's participation rate was 84%.

On the contrary, the 1980 agricultural census showed that women's participation rate in agriculture was 73% and that women accounted for 25% of all full-time and 75% of all part-time workers in agricultural households. Also, the 1990-1991 Pakistan Integrated Household Survey indicated that the female labour force participation rate was 45% in rural areas and 17% the urban areas. Thus it is clear that if women's contribution to economic production is assessed accurately, a conservative estimate of women's labour force participation would be between 30% and 40%.

Development of Agriculture

According to the 1991-92 Labour Force Survey, agricultural and allied industries absorb the largest proportion of employed persons, both women and men, particularly in the rural areas. However, the proportion of the persons engaged in the agricultural sector is higher among rural women (79.4%) as compared to rural men (60.8%). The Human Development Index (HDI) rank of Pakistan is 119 th of 146 countries, indicating low life expectancy at birth, low educational attainment and low income. It demonstrates that Pakistan is faced with a difficult task in human resource development. The

Gender-Related Development Index (GDI) rank of Pakistan is 120th of 146 countries. This illustrates that the human development gap is further aggravated by substantial gender disparities. The difference between HDI rank and GDI rank is -1, indicating that the country performs relatively worse on gender equality than on general achievements alone.

Agriculture occupies a strategic place in Pakistani economy. It directly supports three-quarters of the population, employs half the labour force and accounts for one-quarter of Gross Domestic Product. Pakistani women play a major role in agricultural production, livestock raising and cottage industries. Women often devote more time to these tasks than men do. They participate in all operations related to crop production such as sowing, transplanting, weeding and harvesting, as well as in post-harvest operations such as threshing, winnowing, drying, grinding, husking and storage.

Women in the Farms

Rural Women in Pakistan carry out these tasks in addition to their normal domestic chores of cooking, taking care of children, elderly and disabled, fetching water and fuel, cleaning and maintaining the house as well as some of its construction. Obviously, these women work longer than men do. Surveys have revealed that a woman works 12 to 15 hours a day on various economic activities and household chores.

Women from an average farm family remain extremely busy during the two farming seasons in sowing and harvesting. In some ethnic groups, especially in the southern regions of Pakistan, a husband may marry more than one woman to supply additional farm labour. In Barani (rainfed) agriculture, where crop production is not sufficient to meet subsistence needs of the households, men have traditionally sought employment in the non-farm sector. As a result, women have to take over a substantial burden of the work in agricultural production. Moreover, dramatic growth rates in cotton production have generated tremendous demand for female labour. Such production-labour interactions have led to the increasing feminization of agriculture.

Punjab Province accounts for the bulk of agricultural output in the country. However, Baluchistan and North-West Frontier Province are poor and backward. Endowed with fertile lands, Sindh Province produces 30% rice, 25% of the rice cotton, 23% of the sugarcane and 18% of the wheat in the country. In Pakistan, women participate extensively in the production of major crops, but the intensity of their labour depends on both the crop in question and the specific activities related to that crop. Women's participation is particularly high in cotton, rice, pulses and vegetables. Rice and cotton cultivation in Sindh jointly account for more than one-third of women's annual agricultural activities. Similarly, women's participation is the highest in cotton production in Punjab. Picking cotton is exclusively a women's task. Their participation is the lowest in sugarcane production.

In the rainfed areas of Punjab, women contribute to almost all of 22 identified crop tasks with the major contribution to seed preparation, collection and application of farmyard manure, husking maize and storage. Men's involvement is higher in the early stages of cultivation such as field preparation. Men also monopolize mechanical work. For example, they carry out mechanical threshing (with animal or fuel-powered machines), while hand-threshing is a women's domain of task. Driving tractors and watering the fields are also men's job. Food processing and storage is an area where women's participation is considerably higher than men's.

A survey conducted in five districts of NWFP reveals that 82% of women participate in agro-based activities. They spend 45% of their time and are responsible for 25% of the production of major crops. They produce 30% of the total food. One study in rice and cotton producing villages in Pakistan showed that in agricultural activities women spent 39.34% and 50.42% of their time in rice and cotton growing areas respectively. Even invisible activities take almost as much more time as visible ones. Invisible activities include carrying meals, drinks, etc. from the house to men working in the field; kitchen gardening (in cotton areas); cleaning and drying farm produce for storage; and making clay storage bins. Actually, women provide 29% of the labour input in rice and 24% in cotton production.

Forest and woodland amounted to only 4.4% of the land area in 1993. Many of wooded areas are severely depleted as a result of overexploitation. Forestry production declined from

1.07 mill. cubic metres in 1990/91 to 377,000 cu.m. in 1995/ 96.

Rural Women

Rural women in Pakistan use forests as a source of items essential for survival of their households. Fetching water and collecting fuelwood for cooking and fodder for domestic animals come in the daily routine work of rural Pakistani women. Grazing animals is a very important component of the daily work life of rural women. Marine fisheries in Pakistan engage some 90,000 people. They operate mainly from Karachi and the cost of Sindh. The export of fish and fishery products, particularly shrimp, is an important source of foreign currency. Fisheries is an area of interest to women. It has been found that traditionally, women were involved in fishing business as entrepreneurs. But presently with the expansion of fishing business into an industry, women no longer manage the business as they did in the past. Rather they are involved in peeling shrimps, weaving nets, making fish baskets, etc. as labourers.

In Pakistan, livestock is an important component of farming systems. It accounts for 26.4% of all the value of agricultural production. Livestock is raised for draft power, milk and meat. Poultry, sheep and goats are very important to rural women for they are often the only source of income fully under their control.

Women make a considerable contribution to livestock production and this contribution is more visible than their work in crop production. A rural woman in Pakistan works 15.50 hours a day, spending 5.50 hours in caring for livestock, but provide only 50 minutes for the care of her own children. Women involved in caring and rearing of livestock and poultry, carry out wide range of tasks such as making feed concentrates, feeding, collecting fodder, grazing, cleaning animals and their sheds, making dung cakes, collecting manure for organic fertilizer, as well as milking, processing and marketing of animal products (making ghee, selling eggs, etc.)

In Pakistan, women are responsible for 60% to 80% of the feeding and milking of cattle. Women in Sindh and Punjab spend from one-fifth to a quarter of their daily working hours in livestock-related activities. Dairy production is very important for women in most provinces except Baluchistan where the climate is not favourable to dairy cattle raising. With the exception of a few large cities, all fresh milk consumed in Pakistan is based on small domestic production run and managed by women.

Women are playing a crucial role in rural poultry farming. Over 90% of the rural families keep an average of 12 adult birds per family and hatch chicks under a brood hen. The women apply their own methods of rearing, brooding, breeding, and management based on the experience handed down from the elder family members.

Land, forests and pastures have been degraded by prolonged misuse. The rich soils of the Indus basin are experiencing water logging and salinity, wind and water erosion and rapidly spreading desertification. Forests are near extinction. Rangelands are being denuded. Such ecological resource depletion has profound impact on women's basic roles of obtaining fuel, fodder and water. Shrinking of mangrove stands caused by scarcity of fresh water after the barrages were built, has made coastal women walk longer for the collection of fuelwood for the household and fodder for the livestock.

The women of Baba and Bhit islands say that it often takes them nearly half a day to gather fuelwood. They sometimes have to bring back the young branches. Growing desertification caused by changed farming practices in fragile ecosystems has made women walk for miles in search of water.

Women in Sindh walk up to 10 miles to fetch water. Moreover, as soils degrade due to deforestation, salinity or waterlogging, and food and income decline, women are found to become marginalized. They are left with the responsibility of taking care of degraded land holdings when men migrate from the villages.Women cotton pickers in Pakistan suffer from blisters and skin rashes caused by the chemicals sprayed to protect cotton plants from pests.

Role in Conservation

Women of Pakistan play an important role in environmental conservation. They take care of farmyard manure collection and its application, which has important consequences in soil fertility management. Women posses knowledge of herbs for medicine for both general and reproductive health, food and fodder. They also know the location of pastures and water sources, etc.

Women generate income through various non-farm activities. Cottage industry is one of the major areas of involvement of rural Pakistani women. Weaving cloth and rugs, and sewing constitute important components of rural women's non-routine tasks.

Rural women in Sindh are skillful in producing Rilee (hand-made bed sheets) and Sindhi Topees (caps), etc. of export quality. Women also generate cash income through the sale of livestock products. Though to a lesser extent, rural women also work on others' holdings outside their homes. They account for 16.1% of the total agricultural labour and 10.2% of non-agricultural labour. Nonetheless, there is significant variation by agro-ecological zones in opportunities for wage employment. The demand for female labour which is seasonal and limited to specific tasks, is mainly concentrated in the southern cotton belt and irrigated regions.

Nearly 34% of the population lives below the poverty line in Pakistan. When it comes to rural areas, this proportion becomes one-third to one-half and women disproportionately share the burden of poverty, which has a twofold impact. On one hand, the women's workload for family survival increases and on the other, their share in food and nutrition intake decreases further. A 70% of rural women does not have an adequate calorie intake in their diet, and 90% of pregnant women suffer from anemia. In addition to being poor and malnourished, the mass of rural women in Pakistan suffers from too many pregnancies. Women share only 20.8% of total earned income in the country.

The divergence between economic growth and human development is greater in Pakistan than in most other countries and the country treats it women very poorly, with some of the lowest achievement on indicators of gender development.

In Pakistan women considerably contribute to the food security. Women's overall involvement in crop and livestock production has a direct bearing on household food security. They dominate food processing thereby contributing to diversity in diet, supplying important vitamins and minerals and reducing food losses. For example, Sindhi women indigenously practice drying vegetables and preparing different kinds of pickles. Moreover, women prepare food for their households and thus are responsible for ensuring nutrition and healthy lives in the family.

Women as wage earners provide cash income to purchase food for the families. In the poorest families women's earnings are critical to the subsistence of the households and considerable number of working women are the principal income earners in low income families.

In order to support effective and equitable agricultural and rural development, policy makers and planners in Pakistan need to:

— reform land policy to ensure gender equity as well as class equality (in view of 40% of the arable land owned by large land-owners);
— resolve both conceptual and methodological problems and collect sex-disaggregated data so as to generate a proper estimate of women's economic participation;
— improve all data bases on women which are currently very inadequate;
— improve policy and planning processes to be participatory as well as gender-sensitive;
— make the extension system more equitable to cover female farmers and food crops grown by them instead of merely focussing on male farmers and commercial crops; and
— support policy shifts to encourage rural agro-based small-scale industries, which have employment-generating potential for the vast majority of rural women.

Priorities

Agricultural and rural development programmes in Pakistan need to include the following areas of intervention in order to address both women's and men's priorities:

— recognize women's pivotal contribution to the rural economy and include them in farming systems improvement programmes;
— conduct basic surveys to identify the varying problems of rural women in different agro-ecological and socio-economic conditions so that appropriate intervention needs could be identified;

- launch massive basic and functional literacy programmes for women so that they are able to learn and apply improved agricultural technologies;
- train female agriculture extension workers in order to approach women farmers more easily;
- provide rural women the knowledge of animal diseases, vaccination and treatment of simple ailments;
- train rural women in preserving and processing of various fruits, vegetables and livestock products;
- assist women in marketing their products though the establishment of cooperatives;
- improve the skills and efficiency of rural women through appropriate technology and range of extension service;
- develop integrated credit programme that considers all aspects of enterprise inputs;
- focus on lessening the workload of already overworked rural women before introducing any improved agricultural technologies which require additional time and energy to learn and ultimately use; lessen socio-cultural constraints to women's access to education, training, employment, etc. by using mass media programmes;
- introduce rain-fed farming/agro forestry practices to rural women in order to develop livestock and poultry.

Role in Socio-economic Development

Rural women contribute to socio-economic development in three major ways: through the community and nation, at the household level and through the future generation. At the national and community level, rural women are a source of labour—their own as well as through reproduction, new additions to the labour force. They are also producers of marketed and non-marketed output, much of which is not accounted for in conventional national accounts, and source of savings and accumulation; they are often better savers than men. They are the vital link between the present and the future, between production and consumption, between savings and investment and between poverty alleviation and environmentally sustainable growth.

Poor rural women should not be treated merely as the "target" groups of social welfare programmes; rather their principal role as agents of economic development should be recognised and enhanced. To elaborate on the economic role of rural women, they are the major food producers in developing countries and generate a large part of the family's cash income. The improvement in household food security and nutrition and in food distribution between households, has, in many cases, proved contingent on women's access to income and their role in household decisions on expenditure. In general, women have a stronger voice in household decision making when they contribute cash income, as in many landless households, than when they do not earn any income.

Resource-poor families are even more dependent than others for subsistence on women's labour in the food sector and/or on their earnings from waged labour and off- farm enterprises. While women's incomes are significantly and positively associated with children's nutritional status, especially in the poorer segments of the population, there is evidence that mothers' excessive labour burdens can have negative implications for child nutrition, as they are able to give less time to proper food preparation.A preoccupation with the cash economy and methodological and attitudinal bias against the value of women's work make them statistically marginalised, though their contribution may be highly significant. The unpaid home and farm activities of women make a vital contribution to the economy of poor rural households in developing countries. The poorer the household and the country, the more hours women work and the greater are their contributions to the economy and to family welfare; however, rural women's non-marketed domestic activities such as cooking, childcare, water and fuelwood collection, food storage and processing and other household tasks are left out of official statistics that measure economic and agricultural output. Improving women's productivity, income and quality of life therefore implies a multidimensional contribution to overall growth and development. As producers, women can contribute to alleviating rural poverty, to overall growth and to capital accumulation.

Increasing the income of women consumers will result in an increase in demand for goods and services and contribute to the growth of other sectors, which will in turn raise demand for the products and services of the poor. The rural poor suffer from a significant gap between their potential and actual productivity, and the productivity gap of poor rural women is much wider than that of poor rural men. Rural women will gain proportionally more if investment allocations and development efforts are shifted in their favour; they can go from a situation of being triply disadvantaged to one in which their contribution will have a multiplier effect, in the household, in the community, nationally and most important of all, in the future generation. The status of poor rural women has to be assessed, economically, socially and culturally.

Regional Differences

Leaving aside regional differences, the common thread is that socio-economic and political power is unequally distributed between the sexes. It is necessary to place women's participation within the context of the family and social economy so that rural development projects can be accurately designed to respond to the needs of the target population.

Women's non-market work subsidises the community's market work and their contribution is visible at all levels, in household chores, children and family subsistence, but has been treated as invisible and unaccountable. The challenge is to change the attitudes of society and individuals and introduce simple accounting procedures to give full recognition and support to women's role and work, creating a basis for investment and growth. It also means a recognition, at the micro-level, of the link between non-marketed domestic work and income-generating activities.

Specific methodological problems which marginalise rural women's work include: data collection during short, pre-determined periods, which does not account for women's seasonal work; a narrow definition of economically productive work, which is biased against women; an arbitrary division between marketable produce and produce bound for home consumption, which renders many female activities marginal; gender-differ-entiated perception of male and female work, influencing data collection; and fragmentation of women's work in terms of time and tasks performed, which influence women's own perception of their activities. Field work has demonstrated that the problem of women's statistical invisibility will not be resolved easily by using female enumerators and respondents. Methodological evolution must go hand in hand with changes in attitude.

Rural poverty, the status of women, family well-being and national development are closely interlinked. The promotion of family well-being and national development depend on the vital link between women's productive and reproductive role to be given greater recognition and support. The starting point of reference is the household, followed by the community and the nation. The definition of "household" need not be the traditional one which implies a husband, father or brother as the head, but a social one which includes households headed by women.

The indicators used to measure the status of women represent economic and social factors which affect their productive and reproductive roles. Social and economic factors need to be realigned, so that they have a positive impact on women's productive and reproductive roles and these roles become more balanced. A more equitable sharing of decision making, responsibilities and resources is called for in the household to reduce the burden of women's reproductive role and enhance the efficiency and return of their productive work.

Women's reproductive and productive roles are influenced by cultural and social biases, access to health care—maternal and child health and family planning included—and to sanitation as well as to water and fuel. Household decision making regarding the allocation of resources and sharing of household chores and responsibilities, including childcare, are vital to a more balanced role. Childcare facilities and access to education and training enhance women's economic role. Other factors reflecting their status include access to income and employment, which is affected by labour market conditions and the female/male wage ratio, access to financial services, land and other farm assets, and markets and marketing services. Of equal importance is women's access to inputs, appropriate technology and extension services.

Status in Society

Women's status in a society can be evaluated either by measuring separate indicators or by an integrated index.An index of women's status has been developed which combines women's health, education, role in the labour force, contraceptive usage and female/male wage ratio. If relevant data had been available for a larger number of countries other indicators could have been included, to reflect such important factors as women's participation in decision making, ownership of assets including land, access to skill development and training, access to financial services, markets and so forth.Information is still scanty on these aspects of women's standing in society. Following the methodology developed here, the index of women's status has been calculated for 114 developing countries and the countries have been ranked accordingly. The index takes values between zero and one. The closer the value is to one, the higher the measured status of women in that country. Does it really make sense to attempt to devise a quantitative measure of the status of women? The answer is yes, because qualitative assessment, while illuminating, does not allow comparative analysis between different situations.

Quantitative indicators related to the well-being of women and their status in society are useful in designing appropriate intervention programmes. However, the content of such programmes cannot be determined without an indepth knowledge of the status of women, in order to decide on the most suitable strategy. The female/male wage ratio gives only a rough guide to the situation in the labour market, since reliable data are difficult to come by. It is in any case a poor indicator of the overall relative earning status of women since a large part of women's work is unpaid family labour and receives no value in economic analysis. Therefore, in a sense, even this limited information on the female/male wage ratio overstates the earning status of women. Participation in the labour force, or lack of it, can be viewed as a measure of the under-recognition of the value of women's labour. For these 114 developing countries the female labour force participation rate was estimated at only about 30 per cent in 1965 and 1988; clearly most of the women in the labour force have remained invisible, not covered by formal surveys and censuses. The female labour force participation rate has not changed significantly for any region except sub-Saharan Africa where it has gone down from 37 per cent to 29 per cent. It will be misleading to read this as real decline in women's labour force participation since it is due to women's moving out of, or not entering the formal labour market. For example, this decline in sub-Saharan Africa can be attributed to women being pushed out of the formal labour market due to cutbacks in public expenditures, due to structural adjustment programmes and also due to an increase in households headed by women which inhibits their participation in the formal labour market. Latin America and the Caribbean are the only regions where the majority of women are employed in the non-agricultural field.

Women's domestic conditions can be measured by the percentage of households headed by women and average hours spent in household work and in collecting water. However, because of problems of definition, measurement and data availability, these indicators have not been included in the calculation of the index of women's status. Data on the number of hours women work in the home or in collecting water were available for only a few countries. Also, the treatment of women's status as heads of households raises difficult questions about the concept of "head of household" and the distinction between households headed by women *de facto* and those headed by women *de jure*. Perhaps the most intractable problem relates to differences in the definition used by various agencies in collecting data in the field, which makes figures from different sources incompatible.

A majority of developing countries have signed the Convention on the Elimination of All Forms of Discri-mination Against Women adopted by the UN's General Assembly in 1979 and many have been formally guaranteed equal political rights in national constitutions, progress in eliminating discriminatory aspects of civil and family law, labour legislation, and agricultural and financial sector regulations have been slow and uneven.

Legal Rights

Women's explicit legal rights have improved substantially in Latin America over the past decade. In Asia and the Near East, progress in establishing women's formal legal rights have similarly failed to be adequately reflected in practice. Of particular importance to rural women is the development of legal measures and administrative regu-lations to improve their secure access to land. A second area of concern is the review of civil codes that treat women as legal minors, requiring, for example, their husbands' signature to open bank accounts or to obtain credit. Equally important for rural women, especially in Asia and Latin America, is new labour legislation supporting their equitable access to rural labour markets, mandating equal pay for equal work, and improving working conditions while enforcing legal standards. A fourth priority is to improve rural women's access to informal sector markets by eliminating discriminatory licensing and price control measures. As heads of households, men not only control most household resources but are normally the direct recipients of project resources targeted at households. These principles hold even when men are not the primary source of household income and when women manage important household resources and conduct various household enterprises on a relatively autonomous basis.

In most societies there is still male control of land, major livestock resources, a large share of subsistence output and the bulk of "household income". Women are in general dependent on men for final decisions with respect to virtually everything that affects their lives and are therefore more vulnerable to poverty.

Many developing countries have legally affirmed women's basic right to own land, actual female control of land is practically non-existent. Administrative, economic, and cultural constraints combine to deny most rural women both ownership and effective control. Where land titles have been distributed, they are nearly always allocated to male heads of households. In Islamic law, women's land ownership rights are explicit, but they do not always control *de facto* land use. Under both the civil and the customary laws of Bangladesh adult women have the right to own property, either purchased with their own earnings or received as a gift.

Muslim and Christian women may inherit property, but Hindu women can take only a limited lifetime interest in inherited property. In India, women's right of inheritance is given by religious laws which are different between religions. Where the civil code exists alongside other systems of law, it is usually overhidden by these systems of religious law, as well as by custom. Steps have been taken to reform the personal Hindu laws to expand women's rights of access to land.

Subsequently, under the commune and production brigade and team system, women retained their right of access to land but were discriminated against in the form of lower work points and were considered as a labour reserve, to be used mainly when men were not available. Women were also deprived of the control of their income; the wife's earnings were automatically added to that of the husband and handed over to him as the head of household.

Rural women are highly involved in the care of livestock. They often have traditional ownership rights to small ruminants and poultry and at times to cattle and larger livestock as well. Rural women's rights to livestock products allow them to improve family nutrition and to earn small personal incomes. Cattle and draught animals are normally controlled by men, even when women may formally own a few cattle. Just as land improvement projects may erode rural women's access to land rights, their livestock rights and access to income from livestock products may be threatened by livestock projects, most of the projects which improve livestock breeding, health, and use of animal traction are directed at men. Commercialised processing of dairy products by private enterprises or parastatal organisations, and the introduction of quality regulations, have also been organised in a manner that eroded rural women's income from traditional milk-processing activities in Latin America and increasingly in Africa and the Near East.

Rural women's traditional functions and rights in the livestock sector must be studied and enhanced by aid agencies and women must be accorded access to improved resources and training, in new production methods if they are to gain rather than lose, from project interventions.Women can be trained as village vaccinators and paravets especially for the type of livestock they own for. Women who head their own households, as well as married women, should have full access to credit for purchases of livestock and poultry, construction of pens and animals and inputs of feed or medical supplies. IFAD's experience shows that emphasis on developing the small ruminants owned by women creates additional income which they can control. Special efforts should be made to promote the cooperative use of animal traction resources within families.

Women's access to draught power may also be improved by facilitating cattle and oxen ownership by small groups of women who may decide to hire male labour for ploughing their own fields, or to rent out the animals to others. Such arrangements are particularly important where male out-migration is significant. Women's individual or collective ownership of oxen, donkeys or camels should also be promoted in order to improve women's ability to transport and market food and fodder crops, fuelwood and water. Since few poor women have access to modern inputs which would enhance productivity, their incomes are primarily allocated to pressing consumption needs; also appropriate inputs and technologies are seldom available in rural areas. Rural women's activities in animal husbandry, food processing, crop storage and marketing are similarly bereft of modern technology. Development projects are major sources of access to improved inputs, technology, training, and credit for a wide range of farm and off-farm enterprises. Many studies have demonstrated that when men receive resources and training, the benefits rarely "trickle down" to women.Women's own enterprises are improved only if women themselves gain access to new inputs, in order to break the vicious circle of low productivity. Such access, however, must result in improved incomes that women can control and use to purchase the inputs they require.

Women farmers face multiple constraints in obtaining access to improved seeds, new crop varieties, knowledge about improved cropping systems and other forms of technology. Since they are poor and most of their productive activities are not market oriented, project designers, credit officials and extension staff too often assume that women can afford neither to purchase modern inputs, nor to reimburse credit. Women's lack of legal rights to the land they cultivate also often circumscribes their membership to farmers' organisations and hence their access to inputs, services and credit, while women's crops, livestock activities, and especially crop processing and storage have received relatively little attention in agricultural research and technology development programmes.

Governments should be encouraged to protect women's interests under conditions of technological change. Many ideas are lost over time because they are not recorded and systematically passed on to the new generation of women.The search for appropriate technology for women should lead to packages, judiciously combining traditional and modern ideas. Simplicity in use is desirable in technology for poor rural women, but all techniques should be amenable to upgrading to avoid confining women to the low-level technology trap. New technologies should always be assessed from this perspective before they are introduced. Women farmers also frequently have to pursue additional employment as a source of cash income and IFAD's sub- regional pilot project to develop and disseminate appropriate food processing equipment for rural women in sub-Saharan Africa aims to introduce them to new technology. This grant partially finances a pilot project tc promote technical improvements in locally-produced food processing equipment which is adapted to women's needs and traditional work habits.

The project is being implemented through the United Nations Industrial Development Organisation (UNIDO) in cooperation with national and regional institutions in Burkina Faso and Mali. Links are being established with current IFAD projects to test and replicate the results of the pilot projects. The development and diffusion of technology appropriate to women's major tasks require increased research funds to be allocated to women farmers' traditional crops, small livestock and poultry, food processing and off- farm production. Problems are not limited to these areas alone.

New crop varieties are rarely tested or demonstrated on women's fields, so that agricultural researchers have learned little about women's specific problems with new varieties. This should change; research should be conducted on women's farms and research institutes and extension services should encourage the allocation of land to women's groups for demonstration farms on which new crop varieties and new cultivation techniques can be tested. Women often respond differently from men to new crop varieties because of their concern with problems related to processing and/or storage characteristics.

Women are often also limited in their ability to phase the process of cultivation of certain high-yielding varieties in the recommended manner. The overwhelming emphasis given in agronomic research to high yields often results in serious neglect of processing and storage and seasonal labour problems. As a result, appropriate technical messages to improve women's productivity are lacking. Also, technologies have to be developed to help generate women's off-farm employment. The IFAD has designed projects stressing time and labour-saving technologies for women, while seeking to ensure that these are environmentally sound. An example is IFAD's Artisanal Fisheries Project in the Aby Lagoon in Cote d'Ivoire. Here, assistance is given to women who not only do some subsistence farming (mainly growing cassava) but also earn cash income through smoking fish. Through the use of improved ovens, the project seeks to halve the time needed to smoke fish and also to conserve wood—the ovens run on coconut fibre. At first, due to a lack of proper awareness, the fish-smoking ovens were not adopted.

Women extension agents were appointed to strengthen the extension effort and promote the new techniques, which were then increasingly accepted by women. On the whole, Africa's female farmers have failed to benefit adequately from the introduction of new technologies. Lack of coordination in the variety of imported equipment can result in increased production costs, difficulties in maintenance and inefficiencies in equipment use. Also, a new technology may be inappropriate or may be disseminated in an unsuitable fashion, or may not take into account the limited purchasing power of women and their health and safety.

Women's full role in production-related activities needs to be brought into the mainstream of extension and training. This is a vital step in the process of commercialisation of women's activities. Both extension and training have to be geared to the total needs of women as producers, and this can be achieved only if programmes are designed to be gender-responsive. Evidence from different regions indicates that women farmers are rarely reached by extension services.

The basic constraints on women's access to extension in agriculture and livestock are: a relative lack of technical messages to improve the productivity of their agricultural activities, due to inadequate agronomic research traditional foodcrops; the very limited number of women extension agents trained in agricultural subjects: and, perhaps most important, a general perception that women are primarily homemakers rather than decision-making farmers, a perception that rationalises focusing extension services on male "farmers" who are expected to direct the work of female "family labour".

Women were the main recipients of agricultural technical messages under IFAD's National Extension Project, and they have shown themselves to be very receptive to agricultural innovation. The reorganisation of agricultural extension under this project brought agricultural assistance and advice to many women for the first time. The project has been successful in extending new technologies such as row planting, intercropping of maize with beans, fodder cultivation and improved pest and disease control in potatoes. Many women farmers started applying fertiliser for the first time, introduced zero-grazing, maintained better quality plants, and were reporting substantially higher coffee pruning, disease and pest control and weeding. The use of traditional village work groups to spread technical assistance has greatly improved women's access to the extension service as Kenyan women frequently form such groups for agricultural work, cottage industries and other joint enterprises.

Another important factor in the transfer of new technology to women farmers has been the improved link between research and extension. The agricultural extension services in nearly all developing countries are over-whelmingly male-dominated. The United Nations Environment Programme (UNEP) reports that less than one per cent of government employed "agricultural advisers" in Asia and the Near East are women, less than 3 per cent in Africa, and only 8.5 per cent in Latin America.

Agricultural training for women has been minimal or non-existent. Recently agricultural and livestock courses have been introduced and attention has been paid to off-farm income-generating activities, but many programmes are still very heavily oriented toward home economics. Women rural agents are often employed in ministries of social affairs or in community development rather than in the ministry of agriculture. In some countries women extension agents trained primarily as home economists are being retrained in agricultural subjects. Retraining is widely recommended as a means of making female extension agents knowledge and work more relevant to the major productive activities of women farmers, but in many cases even the best women extensionists and home economists find that their access to appropriate retraining, especially degree-conferring programmes that would facilitate career advancement, is extremely limited. Another important approach lies in retraining male agents to work with women farmers, particularly in the context of women's groups.

Agricultural extension supervisors and additional women technical specialists, particularly those dealing with women's crops and livestock, are needed to retrain and supervise existing male extension staff.

Providing appropriate extension to women is an acquired skill that can be practised by men as well as women where local customs permit. The shortcomings of existing training programmes have to be identified and, where necessary, new training programmes that are gender disaggregated should be developed to take into account socio-cultural differences among the trainees. Formal and informal training mechanisms may then be used to modify the existing roles of men and women. It may be desirable to implement, at the regional level, organised gender-specific training programmes for trainers, technicians and all personnel involved in agriculture/livestock and rural development projects.

The formation of women's groups may help to reduce the cost of training and extension services. More important, perhaps, is the creation of broader-based women's organisations in order to focus on their self-perception and identity. All too often, the language used by administrative officials in communication and training is alien to the target group, particularly if they are women among whom illiteracy is high. Joint efforts between trained personnel and others, including effectiveness of training for production and budgeting, family planning. The potential benefits beneficiaries, may improve the training and reduce costs.

Women should include farm processing technology, planning accounting and auditing and implicit cost is justified by of such training, although there will sometimes be a need to provide grants for developing institutions for training and education. One of the primary objectives of gender-based research, extension and training should be a reduction in women's workload, both for domestic and marketed production and increase in their productivity.

Women farmers and small traders who market their own produce commonly face barriers related to state licensing requirements, quality or sanitary regulations that put them at a disadvantage in competition with large-scale producers, and they may even suffer police harassment on roadways and in urban and rural markets. Women traders are also constrained by insufficient working capital, and poor storage and transport facilities. Furthermore, information on market prices in various parts of the country is often unavailable to women producers and small-scale women traders; this reduces their bargaining power with wholesale traders and subjects them to unfair competition.

Women also face other gender-specific constraints on their marketing activities. For example, patriarchal ideologies motivating men to attempting to control all household income may force women to hide their marketing activities; their access to more lucrative markets is thereby reduced.

Traditions of women's seclusion can make them dependent on men or children to market their output. Reliance on children restricts women to selling in markets nearby, whereas reliance on husbands may reduce their ability to control the income obtained. Projects have often paid insufficient attention to marketing issues and problems when attempting to improve crop, livestock and non-farm production. Market failure can easily lead to project failure if producers cannot realise an adequate income from market-oriented production.

Projects can aid part-time women traders and small- scale women farmers by providing credit for working capital and for crop storage to allow producers to avoid selling at low seasonal prices, by-helping to organise producer marketing groups and small-scale traders' cooperatives, by improving storage in local and regional markets and by providing information on marketing conditions and regional prices through radio broadcasts. Project marketing components should take particular care not to displace traditional women traders and should attempt to assure an adequate representation of women producers and traders.

Rural women's limited incomes, lack of collateral and social and economic-subordination drastically constrain their access to almost all forms of credit from financial institutions and government agencies. Women have comprised only seven to 11 per cent of the beneficiaries of these credit programmes in both rural and urban areas. Commercial banks will not make loans to poor rural women because they are unable to meet the banks' stringent collateral requirements.

NGOs and international financial institutions such as IFAD have taken the lead in demonstrating that poor rural women can be reached through group lending and savings programmes. The repayment records of these women have often been superior to those of their male counterparts. Recent experience in the provision of credit to rural women via small group lending schemes, NGO-sponsored micro- enterprise credit projects, savings and loan clubs has demonstrated that poor rural women can make productive use of credit in a wide range of agricultural and non-farm micro-enterprises that they fit into or around their agricultural and domestic work.

The presence or absence of such links between women and credit has to be understood within the framework of their role and responsibilities in the social and economic systems. Social and household responsibilities claim an inordinately women's time, leaving them little opportunity to establish an interactive relationship with financial institutions and thereby strengthen their productive role. The situation is further aggravated by a lack of basic information on credit availability and procedures, as well as trained staff to deal with women's issues.

Inadequate training means women are unable to utilise credit effectively. They also lack the type of collateral required by financial institutions, and their illiteracy acts as a constraint to their entry into profitable economic opportunities and makes it hard for them to deal with the procedural formalities. For many women, previous experiences with regard to formal credit have been negative since institutions have not been fully responsive to their needs, in terms of the size, purpose and timing of loans; this makes them hesitant to avail themselves of the new opportunities offered by development projects. Rural women's natural aversion to risk, poor institu-tional motivation and a lack of coherent government policies regarding credit for women, are other limiting factors. Two basic problems underlie the widespread perception that poor rural women are not appropriate targets for most credit programmes. The first relates to rural women's role as family labourers in many farming systems and the second to women's heavy involvement in the production of goods and services that are directly consumed within the family. When a major share of women's agricultural labour is performed as family labour on fields controlled by males, most project designers and credit administrators assume that it is only the male "farmer" who makes the cropping and input decisions and that only the "head of the household"—assumed to be male—should be the direct recipient of credit and the person responsible for its repayment.

Major rural credit programmes need to target rural women's multiple activities and make credit available to married women as well as to women who head their own households. A second problem in providing credit to rural women stems from women's primary involvement in the subsistence sector. Rural women's heavy responsibility for providing goods and services for family consumption not only limits the time they can devote to market-oriented activities, it also makes them appear as poor credit risks to financial institutions and other credit providers, including project designers and managers.

However, raising the productivity of women's subsistence activities by new technology is essential to improving household food security and family welfare. The core of the problem in providing credit to purchase inputs for subsistence production is the inability of credit managers to imagine how loans for subsistence activities can be repaid. Credit officers normally assume that the activities for which loans are given must themselves produce an adequate financial return to sustain repayment.

A more realistic understanding of the functioning of poor rural household economies and particularly of rural women's dual participation in both subsistence and market-oriented activities is the key to breaking through the credit barrier. The use of productivity-enhancing inputs can increase the size of this marketable surplus. Women should therefore be seen not solely in terms of their subsistence activities, but rather as overall producers of goods and services. Poor women's earnings from such employment are, however, usually much lower than the imputed net return to labour that could be obtained from cultivating. Their own foodcrops, if yield were raised by using fertilisers, improved verified or other improved technology. Income to repay these loans may be generated either from an enhanced ability to generate a marketable surplus from subsistence- oriented production or from women's traditional off-farm income-generating activities.

The capacity of the financial intermediaries to reach the rural poor in general has to be strengthened and their personnel and procedures must be reoriented to be more sensitive to the needs of poor rural women. The staff of financial intermediaries should be trained to have a clear understanding of the economic role of women, both through marketed and non-marketed production and through their social and family responsibilities. The latter will help them to appreciate the fact that, in order for to have more time for production activities and for dealing with financial institutions, appropriate provision may have to be made for loans to support social responsibilities and household consumption during the loan period. Loans for social responsibilities could be organised on a community basis, with group repayment, while individual loans could be guaranteed by women's groups mobilised for the purpose. For women to be viable recipients of credit, they must be given assistance to enter the market and gain bargaining power. Women's technical and market situation should be carefully analysed to ensure that their activities are financially profitable and that they have control over their production and income and how the household production system is organised.

However, appropriate crop and livestock insurance may be devised to support women's credit-based activities. It will help if the interest rate remains stable during the life of the loan, if all loans include a grace period, preferably flexible, and if the amortisation of past loans includes repayment in kind where appropriate. Women's enterprises are critically import and consideration should be given to establish supervised credit schemes for them. This will help to encourage the demand for credit by rural women where such demand may otherwise lag.

In particular, supervised credit combined with extension and training can reduce both production and transaction costs and make the products of women's enterprises competitive, also in export markets. Financial institutions' approach to credit rural women has to be flexible in order encourage them to save and to respond to the wide range of credit demand that may arise from potential clients' diverse socio-economic needs.

Women are known to be good savers and in many countries informal savings associations are very active. The task is to establish a link between these informal efforts and formal credit delivery institutions. Equally important is the cost of credit delivery. Such costs must not be unduly inflate and passed on to the recipient of credit. It is therefore necessary to carry out a comparative analysis of the non-formal credit system—moneylenders, shopkeepers, NGOs etc.—in the areas which women often resort to. IFAD has demonstrated the effectiveness of reaching poor farmers with credit by linking village-based savings and loan groups with larger governmental credit programmes or with the banking sector.

For poor rural women in particular, banks' normal constraints on lending to women can be overcome by providing group guarantees to replace individual collateral and by providing an alternative mechanism for screening individual members' loan applications. Commercial or government banks often require institutional support and training to undertake this new form of lending to the poor, but once appropriate administrative mechanisms are in place credit programmes with links to formal financial institutions have good prospects for sustainability and replicability.

Rural women gain experience in dealing with financial institutions and those whose credit record is good may be able to obtain future loans on a retail basis by grassroots institutions: it is unrealistic to expect formal financial institutions to cover all potential female credit recipients in rural areas.

Creating and strengthening links between banks and government-sponsored seasonal credit programmes and village-based savings and credit groups is an extremely important means of increasing the availability of credit to poor rural women. Group liability for individual credit may need to be strengthened, with some form of disaster insurance provided from project funds and/or supplemented with group savings.

Whether rural women are best reached through women's groups or through groups open to both men and women will depend largely on the degree of social segregation characterising the local culture and on the history and openness of existing groups in accepting poor men and women.

Women's groups may have the advantage of focusing credit and inputs linked to credit on the particular activities that characterise the women's economy. Potential women beneficiaries are probably the best source of information on this issue. They should be involved in discussions of all matters related to planning credit programmes.

An increasing number of women in developing countries are seeking to sell their labour. However, agriculture-based employment offers women only limited opportunities to earn adequate income. Quite often agricultural technologies adopted by commercial farms do not generate new farm employment opportunities. While opportunities for seasonal waged employment exist, their scale is not sufficient to absorb the large number of women seeking work.

Many rural women are marginalised into migrant labour work, floating between rural and urban and peri- urban areas as petty traders, street vendors, construction workers, domestic servants, and the like. Their working conditions need to be safeguarded and they should be accorded minimum wage protection under the existing law. Since the food security of poorer households is usually dependent on women's earnings, low-paying jobs and lack of regular employment for women often mean inadequate food security and poor family nutrition.

Support for rural women should focus on generating off- and on-farm regular employment and on improving waged incomes. Improving the technical skills of women through better education and training also improves their access to better paid jobs. Poor rural women engage in micro-enterprises covering a wide range of activities, including food and beverage processing, producing and selling handicraft goods, and petty trading. Micro-enterprises in informal sectors offer opportunities for entrepreneurial rural women, though official surveys and census data pick-up of these activities.

Many off-farm activities are becoming the exclusive domain of women entrepreneurs as men are out because of limited market and earning unities. However, these women receive little support from outside; their bargaining power is low and, particularly when they are they may have to depend on diaries to obtain inputs and market their products. The dynamics of off-farm activities are such that the benefits of labour intensity, local materials and local markets turn out to be constraints to product diversification and market expansion.

Other constraints on women involved in such micro-enterprises include interference by men, women's raiding of cash to meet domestic expenditure, fragmentation of profits, lack of infrastructure, appropriate inputs and technical services along the entire production and marketing chain, lack of appropriate managerial skills, competition with formal enterprises, and, most importantly, lack of access to credit and financial services. Considerable scope exists for expanding informal micro-enterprises. Such activities should be seen as linking agricultural and non-agricultural rural activities. Women's involvement in micro-enterprises has to be fitted into their domestic role, and in particular into their role as food providers.

Micro-enterprises should be compatible with, and linked at all stages to, the agricultural cycle. Such micro- enterprises have to be developed within an environment in which past initiatives, male or female-managed, have not necessarily performed well. This has not always been the fault of the enterprises themselves—it may be due to weaknesses in the support infrastructures and the capacity of the target population to deal with the complexity of such initiatives, especially where rural women are involved. Particular attention has to be paid to the value added of rural micro-enterprises in order to make them competitive with other household-based marketed and non-marketed production, and also to justify the allocation of resources to them as opposed to other sub-sectors.

Poor rural women should be encouraged to venture into micro-enterprise activities since they represent a more efficient allocation of individual family and national resources, land, labour and capital, than exists at present.

National governments, donors and NGOs must work together to strengthen rural women's participation in micro-enterprises. The return for the existing activities must be improved and new opportunities created. Rural women must be given access to technology which they can easily absorb. Also steps have to be taken to salvage traditional technologies and improve upon them.

Appropriate technology for rural micro-enterprises managed by women should contribute, in particular, to increased employment and income-earning opportunities, faster production, manpower savings, less expensive raw materials, increased efficiency, reduced fuel costs, better product quality, consistent production flows, and optimum marketing conditions. Extension agents will also have to be trained to respond to the needs of poor rural women seeking to develop off-farm income-generating activities.

Rural women's health is often seriously compromised by overwork, undernutrition, and repeated child-bearing. Among several indicators of women's poor health status in developing countries, perhaps the most dynamic is the rate of maternal mortality which is, at an average of four maternal deaths per 1,000 live births, over four times the average for industrial countries.

The World Bank's estimate of maternal mortality in low-income developing countries, excluding India and China, is six per 1,000 births, but countrywide averages go as high as 20 per 1,000 births in Ethiopia, where data are available only for births taking place in health facilities. Lack of adequate curative and public health facilities in rural areas seriously increases women's vulnerability to prolonged illness and early death. The availability and quality of health services are but one aspect of the myriad factors affecting rural women's health status.

Rural women's ability to control family or individual incomes therefore has an important bearing on their access to health services and on their ability to influence the type of services provided. The same is true of public health services and infrastructure related to health.

Rural women's ability to contribute to the construction and maintenance of village water supplies, for example, will affect their availability, particularly in the current period of government expenditure reductions. Donors have often been active in this area, but have tended to neglect to involve women in planning and maintaining water points.

The education of the population in general and their sensitisation to women's needs and role in society may also help to eliminate cultural practices and taboos which may be harmful. These include female circumcision, young age at marriage, intra-family food distribution and nutritional taboos against eggs, milk and meat during pregnancy, as well as voluntary nutritional deprivation with the aim of having a small baby. The general health and well-being of women, their nutritional status and maternal mortality are affected by economic factors as well as social and cultural factors. A dearth of health facilities and services, and heavy burdens on rural women, combine with social factors such as early marriages, repeated pregnancies and a traditionally low status in society to give a bleak outlook for rural women's health. These socio-economic factors have a strong impact on the health and nutritional status of women and they must be considered in any attempt to alleviate the situation.

Women's lower literacy limits their access to remunerative waged employment to decision-making positions in peasant organisations: and development projects, to certain types of modern technology, and to institutional resources require formal application procedures such as bank credit and government training programmes. Where rural women's access to economic and opportunities and their ability to participate in community decision- making processes are particularly affected by illiteracy, and especially in cases where women express a clear demand for literacy training, projects should aim to provide those literacy skills most essential to improving women's access to economic and social resources. Rural women's access to formal education has been growing, though slowly, in most countries, but here again structural adjustment has brought reductions in fiscal expenditure which threaten educational services at all levels.Project designers must recognise that rural women have a rich traditional, knowledge of the production, processing, storage, and nutritional characteristics of a wide range of crops and wild plants, in methods of soil conservation and enrichment, and in issues related to livestock rearing. Agricultural and livestock research institutions have much to learn from rural women, although little has been done to investigate and build upon their knowledge and insights.

Participatory methods of project planning and management can help to open two-way communication between women farmers and livestock producers, and extension and research staff, so that more effective methods of cultivation, and management of the environment in general, can be developed and popularised.

IFAD-financed projects focus primarily on raising the economic productivity, incomes and general welfare of poor rural women. It may be necessary to provide support for rural women's training and education, particularly as these relate to economic productivity, and the fund would first and foremost seek to mobilise the resources and expertise of external cofinanciers such as UNICEF whose mandate is closer to these areas of legitimate concern.

Under the community development programme, poor rural women are benefiting from literacy classes and training in health, nutrition and hygiene. External resources have also been mobilised by IFAD to finance rural women's education and training under the Belgium Survival Fund (BSF) for the Third World (a Fund established in 1985 by an act of the

Parliament of Belgium), in which IFAD collaborates with WHO, UNICEF and UNDP in assisting the most vulnerable segments of the rural population in the five countries of the Horn of Africa. When no external cofinancing is available, and these components covering training and education may still be essential to the production and income objectives of IFAD's project, the Fund carries out discussions with the recipient government to obtain domestic financing to the maximum extent possible. Literacy, numeracy and training in agricultural and horticultural techniques, as well as in savings and management of household finances, are being provided. In addition, this support is being provided for training teachers of primary and secondary schools and for more than 2,000 scholarships for girls to attend school.

Membership of rural organisations also allows people to represent their interests to government authorities, project management and employers. Rural women's access to these organisations is, however, often severely limited. While there may not be any law which prohibits women from becoming members, they may still be excluded because membership is based on land ownership or a head-of- household extension. Even when a few women manage to participate in rural organisations because of their status as heads of households, or because government or project administrators require a minimal level of female participation, they usually form only a small minority of the membership.

Other factors, such as women's domestic labour responsibilities during the customary meeting time, or husbands' opposition, can reduce women's ability to defend their particular interests. Donor-financed projects have sometimes attempted to improve women's representation in beneficiary committees by requiring a certain level of female participation. Too often, however, these efforts are limited to stipulating that two or three women be appointed as members or women's representatives. Where customs of male and female segregation inhibit simultaneous interaction, or where women are expected to defer to men in public, separate women's organisations should be formed and accorded equal access to decision-making processes that affect the allocation of resources.The formation of such groups also facilitates communication with the target population so that their needs can be better identified and their support and feedback enlisted. The group approach to extension, training, credit and marketing is featured in almost all IFAD's projects targeting women. For extension, it has been related to an attempt to better link agronomic research with farmers' needs through a two-way communication process facilitated by retrained extension workers.

The Bay Region Agricultural Development Project in Somalia is expected to conduct agronomic trials on farmers' fields and to reach women contact farmers and groups. Under the Farmers' Groups and Community Support Project in Kenya the number of women extension workers will be increased from 20 per cent to 40 per cent of the total and women farmers will be organised into groups to facilitate the dissemination of technology and improve credit delivery to poor rural women.Mechanisms must be in place to gather gender-specific information at the household level and analyse it carefully. Women are particularly vulnerable to gender-specific impoverishment, therefore it is important to analyse the intra-household processes characteristic of a poor population.

No systematic information is available on household production systems and sub-systems run by men and by women. It is often not appreciated that the household production system consists of subsystems such as food and cash crop production, livestock production, processing and small-scale manufacturing which need to be separately analysed, with the links between them understood and reflected in support activities.One practical way of determining women's access to resources is to study the nature of the tasks that men and women normally perform and the length and arduousness of their respective labour days. The tension is better understood if looked at in terms of the male sector, the female sector and the joint sector within the household economy. With hard data one can test the hypothesis that the male sector is formal, organised and closely integrated with the market, while the female sector is informal and less well organised, and linked only tenuously to the market. It is important for planning and project design to know who makes decisions within the household and who is in control of the farming cycle. A second issue affecting women's welfare in households headed by males is the extent to which household income is pooled and women have influence over the allocation of subsistence and monetary incomes. Indirect indicators may provide much of the necessary information. For example, the relative level of men's versus women's and children's nutritional and health status as well as gender differences in the consumption of clothing, education, and consumer goods can provide information on women's influence over the use of household income and on the relative level of women's poverty.

Bibliography

Balchin, C., Women, law and Society , Shirkatgah, Lahore, Pakistan, 1996.

Gazdar, H., "Poverty in Pakistan: A Review", in Shahrukh Rafi Khan (eds), 50 Years of Pakistan's Economy, Oxford University Press, Pakistan, 1999.

Government of Pakistan, "Report of the Commission of Inquiry for Women" , Pakistan, 1997.

Hakim, A., etal., Pakistan Fertility and Family Planning Survey 1996-1997, Islamabad, akistaN, 1998.

Human Rights Commission of Pakistan, "State of Human Rights in 1998", Lahore, Pakistan, 1999.

Human Rights Commission of Pakistan, " State of human Rights in 1998",Lahore, Pakistan, 1999.

Human Rights Watch (HRW), Double Jeopardy : Police Abuse of Women in Pakistan, USA 1992.

Jalal, Ayesha, "The Convenience of Subservience: Women and the State of Pakistan", in Women, Islam and the State, (ed.) Deniz Kandiyoti, Philadelphia : Temple University Press, 1991.

Kazi, S., "Gender Inequalities and Development in Pakistan", in Shahrukh Rafi Khan (eds) 50 Years of Pakistan's Economy, Oxford, University Press, Pakistan, 1999.

Klein , H. G. and R. Nestvogel, " Women in Pkistan ", Vanguard, Pakistan, 1992.

Mehdi, Rubya, "The Offence of Rape in the Islamic Law of Pakistan", Women Living Under Muslim Laws, Dossier 18, BP 23, 34790 Grabels, France, July 1997.

Ministry of Health, "National Health Policy", Islamabad, Pakistan, 1997.

Saeed, A., "Structural Issues in Women's Development in Pakistan", United Nations International Children's Emergency Fund, Islamabad, pakistan, 1990.

Sathar, Z. and S. Desai, "Work Patterns in Rural akistan: Intersections Between Gender, Family, and Class",Working Paper No. 90, Research Division, 1996.

Sathar, Z. and S. Kazi, "Women's Autonomy, Livelihood and Fertility", Pakistan Institute of Development Economics, Pakistan, 1997.

The World Bank, "Women in Pakistan: An Economic and Social Strategy", Washington, D.C., USA, 1989.

Tinker, Anne G., "Improving women's Health in Pakistan", The World Bank, Washington, D.C., USA, 1998.

UNiCEF, "Children and Women in Pakistan" A Situation Analysis", Islamabad, 1998.

United Nations Development Programme, " A Profile of Poverty in Pakistan", Islambad, akistan, 1999.

Zaheer, H., "Women in Education in Pakistan", Ministry of Women's Development, 1998.

Index